Philosophy and the City

Philosophy and the City

Classic to Contemporary Writings

Edited by
Sharon M. Meagher

STATE UNIVERSITY OF NEW YORK PRESS

Front and back cover photos courtesy of Susan Scranton Dawson, "Stack I" © 2007 by permission of the artist; Susan Scranton Dawson, "Downtown Spring I" © 2007 by permission of the artist. For information on the artist, contact Laura Craig Gallery, 307 Linden Street, Scranton, PA 18503. 570-963-7995.

Published by
State University of New York Press, Albany

For information, contact State University of New York Press, Albany, NY
www.sunypress.edu

Production by Diane Ganeles
Marketing by Fran Keneston

Library of Congress Cataloging-in-Publication Data

Philosophy and the city : classic to contemporary writings / edited by
Sharon M. Meagher.
    p. cm.
Includes bibliographical references and index.
ISBN 978-0-7914-7307-8 (hardcover : alk. paper)
ISBN 978-0-7914-7308-5 (pbk. : alk. paper)
    1. Cities and towns—Philosophy.   2. Urbanization—Philosophy.
3. Sociology, Urban—Philosophy.   I. Meagher, Sharon M.

HT113.P46 2008
307.7601—dc22   2007013090

10 9 8 7 6 5 4 3 2 1

*This book is dedicated to
David Fine*

Contents

Preface

Philosophy and the City is an edited anthology that contains philosophical essays and excerpts from classic to contemporary works in philosophy relevant to the city. Readings focus on the European and American traditions in philosophy and relate primarily to modern, Western cities, but include a range of diverse perspectives that integrates issues of gender, race, and class. Although it is my sincere hope that many different types of readers may find this book of interest and assistance, the text is intended for use in undergraduate philosophy classes where instructors want to provide historical and thematic context for the history of social and political philosophy and/or aim to show how philosophy speaks to contemporary social and political issues. The book is designed primarily for undergraduate philosophy and political theory courses and secondarily for graduate-level courses in urban studies where background in urban philosophy would provide background context for current work.

I have found that the readings can be effective for a number of undergraduate courses, ranging from introductory philosophy courses to advanced surveys of social and political theory. Adult learners responded particularly well to these readings in our required introduction to philosophy course because they had an easier time comprehending how and why philosophy matters when the readings were linked to contemporary urban problems that they cared about. Because urban philosophical writings span both the entire period of Western philosophy as well as a range of philosophical subfields, the text can work effectively to introduce students to both the history of Western European traditions through primary texts and an understanding of the breadth of what counts as philosophical inquiry.

The text also works well in general surveys of social and political philosophy because such courses usually work best if organized around a common theme. The increased emphasis on civic engagement, citizenship, and sustainability issues has engendered a renewed focus on the city. The rise of globalization and the decline of the nation-state have made cities more important and central in both our economic and political lives.

Despite the fact that this text works well in a variety of existing courses, I hope that more colleagues will consider developing a course specifically on the city. From the nineteenth century until only very recently, voices from social science have dominated urban planning discourse. While the social sciences have contributed much to the analysis of urban problems, philosophy can and should take a more explicit role again. Absent explicit philosophical analysis, we lack both a discourse of urban ideals as well as a way to examine critically existing value assumptions. A philosophy course that specifically targets urban philosophy can contribute to urban studies and civic education programs and help revitalize an understanding of public philosophy.

My course aims at getting students to think differently about the cities where they are studying and the urban neighborhoods where they live. I have found that by linking urban theory to issues of sustainability that students are more motivated to connect to local urban issues. Moreover, they are more likely to see the relevance and value of urban theory. In the course I reintroduce students to the city in ways that increase their meaningful participation in it.

In a survey of students who completed a course using these readings, 89 percent of the respondents claimed that it was "very true" that "after taking this course, I have a better understanding of the relevance of philosophy to city issues and/or public policy"; the remaining 11 percent responded "somewhat true." All of the students responded that it was "very true" or "somewhat true" that they have a better understanding of the history of political philosophy (the majority responding "very true"), and all responded that they "have a better understanding of what it means to be a citizen." These results indicate that a philosophy course based on these readings can be extremely effective in responding to the demands that philosophy instructors increasingly face, namely, to make philosophy relevant to students' everyday lives and concerns, and to renew the role of the humanities in civic education.

My own interest in this project developed from my work doing urban community organizing and development work in Scranton, Pennsylvania, where I also work as a philosophy professor. My students and colleagues started asking questions about whether and how my work in philosophy was connected to my city work. I decided to develop a course that would allow students to explore those questions with me. This reader is the result of having tested various readings with my students and developed an effective, flexible course based on these readings.

Given space, time, and copyright limitations, it is impossible to collect everything that all philosophers have written about cities in one book; my selection principle has been one of finding texts that present a representative sampling of philosophical positions regarding cities from ancient Greek to contemporary times. This book focuses specifically on philosophy's contributions to urban discourse. These choices were made after extensive reading and research on the history of Western philosophy and the city. Although I included a few pivotal texts that are readily available in the public domain, I omitted others (like Cicero and Plutarch) who are not as frequently included in surveys of Western philosophy but can be easily included through internet links. I chose readings that the average undergraduate reader finds accessible, although some readings are more challenging than others. The text contains more readings than some instructors could comfortably cover in a semester in order to provide greater choice and flexibility.

The text is organized so that instructors can adopt it for a variety of courses and teaching styles. The major readings are printed in chronological order, and some instructors may find it very useful to work through the text in just that way. Another major option is to organize a course based on some or all of the topics by which the second half of the text is organized. When I teach the course, I generally adopt a hybrid of both approaches, taking the students through two quick tours of the history of philosophy, first by focusing on the question "what is a city?" and then by focusing on the question "what is citizenship?" Having laid that historical foundation, we then explore the remaining questions and readings by examining the issues and studying the essays I recommend in each section.

Philosophers generally have focused on broader questions and issues concerning cities, questions that focus on urban ideals and values. These issues underpin more contemporary debates about more specific urban problems like racial violence and urban poverty, problems that are addressed in other more social scientifically oriented anthologies on cities. As such, this text might be fruitfully combined with such texts for instructors interested in examining the full dimension of contemporary urban problems.

But I invite each instructor and general reader to devise his or her own tour through philosophy and the city; the brief introduction that follows provides some highlights of possible paths that one can take. In addition, I am completing a monograph (currently under contract with State University of New York Press) that instructors may find useful in guiding their own reflections on the history of philosophy and the city. The monograph also might fruitfully be combined with this text for advanced undergraduate or graduate courses.

I also have developed a Web site (www.philosophyandthecity.org) to provide supplementary materials for the text as well as a blog where instructors and students can communicate with one another. We are witnessing a return of philosophers to the city, and I hope that all of us will join in dialogue with one another as we take that journey; the Web site will provide one forum by which to do so.

OUTSTANDING FEATURES OF THE TEXT

- Only text that anthologizes philosophical writings on the city from Ancient Greek to contemporary times

- Incorporates a wide range of philosophical perspectives, from classic historical texts to contemporary ones in the analytic, American Pragmatist, and continental traditions

- Encompasses full scope of urban issues, from the sociopolitical to the built environment

- Includes case studies that explicitly connect philosophical writings to critical urban issues, demonstrating how philosophy matters to the city and how the city matters to philosophy

- Highlights diversity issues concerning race, gender, and class

- Includes both American and global issues

- Brief introductions to each reading

- Questions for review and discussion following every reading

- Has a Web site, www.philosophyandthecity.org, which includes supplementary teaching materials, more exercises for discussion and assignments, Web links to additional resources, and a discussion forum blog

Acknowledgments

This book is dedicated to David Fine, my tireless undergraduate research and teaching assistant who is now on his way to a great career as an academic. David worked with me for more than two years on this project; his enthusiasm, brilliant ideas, wonderful collegiality, and diligent research and feedback helped carry this book to its completion. I could not have done it without him.

This work has been supported by the generosity of the National Endowment of the Humanities that provided grants that enabled me to participate in two summer institutes on the humanities and cities. I am grateful for the support I have received at my home institution, the University of Scranton. The provost and academic vice-president, Harold W. Baillie, the associate provost, E. Springs Steele, and the dean of the college of the arts and sciences, Joseph Dreisbach, all provided me with sabbatical and research release support as well as a budget for permissions costs and student research assistance. I also thank my colleagues in the philosophy department who supported my course on which this book is based and who spread themselves thin so that I could take a sabbatical leave to finish editing and writing.

I also would like to thank my friends and colleagues in philosophy who encouraged and supported my forays outside of philosophy and even academe into city life and public policy, and convinced me that it was worth making the trip back to share what I had learned about both philosophy and the city. Particular thanks in this regard to Ellen Feder, Linda Alcoff, Margaret McLaren, Kelly Oliver, Sean O'Connell, Ellen Armour, Mary Rawlinson, Eva Kittay, Dick Howard, Noëlle McAfee, and Tina Chanter.

I also want to thank those contemporary philosophers whose work has been included in this text for their generosity in granting copyright permissions and their overall enthusiasm for the project. In particular, I would like to thank James Conlon, William Gavin, Robert Gooding-Williams, Elizabeth Grosz, Andrew Light, Eduardo Mendieta, Gail Weiss, and Cornel West who lent personal assistance in securing permission to their work.

This book has been many years in the making. I am very grateful to Tristan Palmer who initially encouraged this project, State University of New York Press editor Jane Bunker who brought it to fruition, and my many students at the University of Scranton who read various drafts.

COPYRIGHT ACKNOWLEDGMENTS

The following texts are in the public domain and did not require permissions (listed in alphabetical order by author):

Addams, Jane. "The Subjective Necessity for Social Settlements" in *Philanthropy and Social Progress: Seven Essays, Delivered Before the School of Applied Ethics at Plymouth, Massachusetts During the Session of 1892*. New York: Thomas Y. Crowell, 1893, pp. 1–26 (excerpts).

Aristotle. *Politics*, Book 1, ch. 1; Book III, ch. 3, 4, 6. Trans. B. Jowett.

Engels, Friedrich. "The Great Towns" in *Conditions of the Working Class in 1844* (excerpt).

Hobbes. *De Cive*, ch. V, sec. 7–12; ch. VI, sec. 1, 9, 15, 18–20, ch. X, sec. 1. Source: London, printed by J.C. for R. Royston, at the Angel in Ivie-Lane, 1651.

Machiavelli. *The Prince*, ch. 5, *Discourses*, Book I, ch. 1

More, St. Thomas. *Utopia*, Book II (excerpts). Source: 1901. New York: Ideal Commonwealths. P. F. Collier & Son. The Colonial Press.

Pericles' funeral oration (as quoted in Thucydides' *History*); trans. B. Jowett.

Plato. *Crito*, 49e5–54e and *Republic, Book II*, 368e1–374. Trans. B. Jowett (and updated by Sharon Meagher).

The editor gratefully acknowledges the receipt of permissions for the following works (listed in alphabetical order by author):

Augustine, Saint, Bishop of Hippo. POLITICAL WRITINGS/AUGUSTINE, translated by Douglas Kries & Michael W. Tkacz; edited by Ernest L. Fortin, Roland Gunn, and Douglas Kries; introduction by Ernest L. Fortin. Copyright © 1994 by Hackett Publishing Company. Reprinted by permission of Hackett Publishing Company, Inc. All rights reserved.

Benjamin, Walter. Reprinted by permission of the publisher from THE ARCADES PROJECT by Walter Benjamin, translated by Howard Eiland and Kevin McLaughlin, pp. 23–24, 31, 88, 126, Cambridge, Mass.: The

Belknap Press of Harvard University Press. Copyright © 1999 by the President and Fellows of Harvard College.

Bickford, Susan, "Constructing Inequality: City Spaces and the Architecture of Citizenship" *Political Theory*, ed. Mary G. Dietz (28/3), excerpts from pp. 355–370. Copyright © 2000 by Sage Publications. Reprinted by permission of Sage Publications.

Conlon, James, "Cities and the Place of Philosophy," *Philosophy in the Contemporary World*, vol. 6, no. 3–4 (Fall–Winter, 1999), excerpts: p. 44, beginning 5 lines from top with "I want to . . ." to p. 46, second column, end of second full paragraph; p. 47 first column, beginning with new section "Philosophy and the City" to end on p. 49. Permission granted by the author.

Dewey, John. Excerpts from "Philosophy and Civilization," pp. 4–10 in *The Collected Works of John Dewey: The Later Works, 1925–1953, vol. 3: Essays, Reviews, Miscellany, and "Impressions of the Soviet Union"* © by the Board of Trustees, Southern Illinois University, produced by permission of the publisher.

Foucault, Michel. DISCIPLINE AND PUNISH by Michel Foucault. English Translation copyright © 1977 by Alan Sheridan (New York: Pantheon). Originally published in French as *Surveiller et Punir* copyright © 1975 by Editions Gallimard. Reprinted by permission of Georges Borchardt, Inc., for Editions Gallimard.

Gavin, William J. "The Urban and the Aesthetic," *Religious Humanism*, 1971, vol. 5, pp. 171–172. Reprinted by permission of the HUUmanists Association and the author.

Ginsberg, Robert. "Aesthetics in Hiroshima: The Architecture of Remembrance," in *Philosophy and Architecture*, ed. Michael H. Mitias. Amsterdam: Rodopi, 1994 excerpts pp. 221–224, 227–234.

Gooding-Williams, Robert. Copyright © 1993 by Routledge, Inc. "Look a Negro!" (excerpt) by Robert Gooding-Williams in *Reading Rodney King/Reading Urban Uprising*. Edited by Robert Gooding Williams. Reproduced by permission of Routledge/Taylor & Francis Group, LLC.

Grange, Joseph. Selections from ch. 12 "The Philosopher and the City," in his THE CITY: AN URBAN COSMOLOGY. Albany, NY: State University of New York Press, 1994. Permission granted by State University of New York Press.

Grosz, E. A., "Bodies-Cities," in *Sexuality and Space*, edited by Beatriz Colomina Princeton: Princeton Architectural Press, 1992. pp. 241–254.

Excerpt: SECTION II, pp. 244–249. Reprinted by permission of Elizabeth Grosz.

Francis, Lee. "We, the People: Young American Indians Reclaiming their Identity," excerpts. From the book *Genocide of the Mind: New Native American Writing* edited by Marijo Moore. Copyright © 2003. Appears by permission of the publisher, Thunder's Mouth press/Nation Books, A Division of Avalon Publishing Group, Inc.

Habermas, Jürgen. "The Public Sphere," translated by Shierry Weber Nicholsen, in *Jürgen Habermas On Society and Politics: A Reader,* ed. Steven Seidman (Boston: Beacon Press, 1989), excerpts pp. 231–232, 236; Originally published as "Öffentlichkeit" in Jürgen Habermas, *Kultur und Kritik,* © 1973 by Surkamp Verlag, Frankfurt am Main. Reproduced with permission of Suhrkamp Verlag.

Hayek, Friedrich. Excerpts from "Housing and Town Planning," in *The Constitution of Liberty,* Friedrich Hayek. Chicago: University of Chicago Press, 1960. Copyright © 1960 by the University of Chicago Press. Reproduced by permission of Taylor & Francis Books UK and the University of Chicago Press.

Heidegger, Martin. Pages 143–148 from POETRY, LANGUAGE, THOUGHT by MARTIN HEIDEGGER. Translations and Introduction by Albert Hofstadter. Copyright © 1971 by Martin Heidegger. Reprinted by permission of HarperCollins Publishers.

hooks, bell. "Homeplace: A Site of Resistance," chapter 5 in *Yearning: race, gender, and cultural politics,* (Boston: South End Press, 1990), pp. 41–49. Permission granted by South End Press and Between the Lines Publishing.

HRH The Prince of Wales, "Tall Buildings," Invensys Conference, QE2 Centre, London, December 11, 2001, excerpts. http://www.prince ofwales.gov.uk/speechesandarticles. Reproduced by kind permission of Clarence House, London.

Jefferson, Thomas. "Manufactures," in NOTES ON THE STATE OF VIRGINIA, ed. William Peden, University of North Carolina Press (Institute of Early American History and Culture), 1955, pp. 164–165. Permission granted by the University of North Carolina Press.

Kemmis, Daniel. Excerpts from THE GOOD CITY AND THE GOOD LIFE by Daniel Kemmis. Copyright © 1995 by Daniel Kemmis. Reprinted by permission of Houghton Mifflin Company. All rights reserved.

Lefebvre, Henri. Ch. 6 "Philosophy of the City and Planning Ideology," pp. 97–99 in Lefebvre, Henri, WRITINGS ON CITIES/HENRI LEFEBVRE; selected, translated and introduced by Eleonore Kofman and Elizabeth Lebas. Oxford: Blackwell Publishing, 1996. English translation, Introduction and editorial arrangement © 1996 by Eleonore Kofman and Elizabeth Lebas.

Light, Andrew. "Elegy for a Garden: Thoughts on an Urban Environmental Ethic" Philosophical Writings 14 (2000), 41–47 (excerpts).

Mendieta, Eduardo. Excerpt from Mendieta, E. "Invisible Cities: A phenomenology of globalization from below." (2001) City 5:1, pp. 7–26; excerpts from pp. 14–17. Reprinted with permission of Taylor and Francis, London. For information about the journal City, please see: http://www.tandf.co.uk/journals.

Mugerauer, Robert, "A Homecoming: Design on Behalf of Place" (excerpts) from his Interpretations on Behalf of Place: Environmental Displacements and Alternative Responses. Albany, NY: State University of New York Press, 1994. Permission granted by State University of New York Press.

Mumford, Lewis. "Retrospect and Prospect" from THE CITY IN HISTORY: ITS ORIGIN, ITS TRANSFORMATION, AND ITS PROSPECTS, copyright © 1961 and renewed 1989 by Lewis Mumford, reprinted by permission of Harcourt, Inc. The City in History by Lewis Mumford, published by Secker & Warburg. Reprinted by permission of The Random House Group Ltd.

Pratt, Geraldine, "Domestic Workers, Gentrification and Diversity in Vancouver" [my title] excerpt from her "Grids of Difference: Place and Identify Formation" in CITIES OF DIFFERENCE, ed. Ruth Fincher and Jane M. Jacobs. New York: The Guilford Press, 1998. Copyright © 1998 The Guilford Press.

Rousseau, Jean-Jacques. Reprinted with the permission of The Free Press, a Division of Simon & Schuster Adult Publishing Group, from POLITICS AND THE ARTS: Letter to M. d'Alembert on the Theater by Jean-Jacques Rousseau, translated by Allan D. Bloom. Copyright © 1960 by The Free Press. Copyright © renewed 1988 by The Free Press. All rights reserved.

Simmel, Georg. Selections from "The Metropolis and Mental Life." Translated by Edward Shils, in Georg Simmel: On Individuality and Social Form. Edited by Donald N. Levine. Chicago: University of Chicago Press, 1971.

Heritage of Sociology Series. Copyright © 1971 by the University of Chicago. All rights reserved.

Weber, Max. Selections from ch. XVI of MAX WEBER ECONOMY
AND SOCIETY, vol. 2, ed. Guenther Roth and Claus Wittich. Berkeley:
University of California Press, 1978. Copyright © 1978 by the Regents
of the University of California © copyright 1968 by Bedminster Press
Incorporated, New York. Exclusive English rights granted to University
of California by the German holder of rights, J. C. B. Mohr (Paul
Siebeck), Tübingen.

Weiss, Gail. Excerpts from "Urban Flesh," in *Philosophy Today*, vol. 49,
SPEP Supplement 2005, ed. Peg Birmingham and Steven Crowell. Copy-
right © 2005 DePaul University. Reprinted by permission of DePaul
University.

West, Cornel. From *Race Matters* by Cornel West. Copyright © 1993,
2001 by Cornel West. Reprinted by permission of Beacon Press, Boston
and by the author.

Young, Iris M. JUSTICE AND THE POLITICS OF DIFFERENCE. ©
1990 Princeton University Press. Reprinted by permission of Princeton
University Press.

Every effort has been made to trace copyright holders and to obtain their
permission for the use of copyright material. The editor and the publisher apologize for any errors or omissions in the above list and would
be grateful if notified of any corrections that should be incorporated in
future reprints or editions of this book.

Introduction

- "I am a lover of learning, and trees and open country won't teach me anything, whereas men in the city do." (Socrates in Plato's *Phaedrus*, 230 d 3–4)

- "Philosophers have thought the city; they have brought to language and concept urban life." (Lefebvre 1996, 86)

When the urban riots erupted around the world in 1968, scholars turned their attention to cities and urban problems that had been long ignored. Urban studies programs blossomed and grew. Now many colleges and universities also house urban outreach centers that connect academics and community members. Such outreach programs are emblematic of a further academic recommitment to cities, to public scholarship, and to civic engagement initiatives.

Some contemporary political philosophers have turned to the city in their quest for a grounding of social ethics and political theory informed by the communitarian critique of liberalism (Young; Friedman 1993, 251–253; Meagher 1999). Others have expanded philosophies of place and environment to focus explicitly on the city, integrating aesthetic, sociopolitical, and ecological concerns (Light; Mugerauer; Norberg-Schulz). Current philosophical inquiries into human nature and identity tend to focus on the relationship between place and identity formation as well as issues of diversity (Conlon; Bickford; Mendieta; Weiss). Theorists of globalization are increasingly seeing the "global city" as the new locus of ethical as well as economic concern (Kemmis; Mendieta; Sassen 2000). Now there is also an increasing interest in renewing the vocation of philosophers as public intellectuals, and of returning to humanities education as the foundation for civic engagement (see, e.g., Spellmeyer 2003).

The renewed interest in the vocation of the philosopher is still met with a great deal of skepticism concerning the public relevance of philosophy, especially in regard to urban problems. There remains a pervasive belief that the problems of cities are so great as to be intractable, a view that "nothing can be done and that in any event it is not philosophy's business" (Fell 1997, 27). Ironically, even such anti-urban attitudes demonstrate the importance and influence of philosophy on our cities, because anti-urban attitudes are shaped by a stream of philosophical thought that rejects the city as the place where human nature and philosophy are best realized. In the United States, anti-urban attitudes are rooted in its legacy of anti-urban theory that extends at least as far back as Thomas Jefferson (White 1962). Following Rousseau and others, Jefferson rejected the philosophical view inaugurated by the ancient Greek philosophers Plato and Aristotle that the good life could be best realized in the city. At the very least, then, the study of urban philosophy can and should play a central role in higher education civic engagement programs by confronting and critically analyzing anti-urban theory. Furthermore, philosophical traditions that link themselves positively to cities provide us with normative ideals of city life as well as civic engagement.

Our lives as citizens, that is, as civically engaged persons, are shaped by our answers to many questions. What is a good city? What is citizenship? How do we nurture meaningful, coherent communities that respect and support diversity? What standards of beauty should inform our architecture and urban plans? What kinds of built environments best sustain engaged human lives? How do we best achieve justice in our cities? These questions and their answers are informed by philosophy, yet they often remain hidden as unexamined assumptions in most urban policy discussions.

It is therefore often difficult to see why philosophy matters, especially to the city. "[Bertrand] Russell once observed that if the drawbridge operators went out on strike the impact upon the city would be felt immediately; if the philosophers went on strike, who would know it?" (Fell 1997, 27). Philosophers today often are spoofed just as Aristophanes characterized Socrates in his play *The Clouds*, that is, as impractical persons with their heads in the clouds who are pretentiously silly if not dangerous to the city.

In fact, "Socrates brought philosophy down from the skies to assume an earthly habitation" (McKeon 1949, 156); his interest was in making abstract philosophical questioning relevant to the city. Did Athenians find philosophy to be irrelevant or did it cut too close to home? Socrates described himself as a gadfly whose task was to raise awareness. But as Plato's allegory of the cave illustrates, those imprisoned in the darkness of ignorance will always find exposure to the bright light of truth to be painful (*The Republic*, Book VII, 514–521). In short, far from being irrelevant, Socrates made the philosopher all too relevant to the city, and thus found himself in danger. The Athenians' fear of philosophy had deadly consequences for Socrates, who was tried and convicted for the corruption of the youth of Athens and sentenced to death. But the attempts to banish philosophy from the city also have had detrimental consequences for cities. So, some philosophers throughout the history of Western thought have persisted in doing philosophy in and for the city.

The readings collected here are by philosophers from ancient to contemporary times, all of whom have written something about cities, urban problems, or the task of the public philosopher. These works have never been gathered together before. Although I had originally compiled the text in chronological order for simplicity's sake, reading the texts in chronological order reveals much about the history of philosophy and its relationship not only to cities, but to public life generally.

Western philosophy as we know it was born in the city; Socrates was the midwife. As the rural village became the ancient Athenian *polis* (city-state), philosophers such as Socrates raised questions about the very nature of this new form of settlement and way of life, and in doing so, developed a new way of thinking and inquiry that he distinguished from both classic Greek teaching as well as sophistry. Socrates called his teaching "philosophy." Although Socrates might have escaped the city and avoided execution, Plato's dialogues suggest that Socrates' relationship to the city was firmly entrenched well before his trial. As noted in the quotation from the *Phaedrus* at the outset of this essay, Socrates resisted an invitation to do philosophy outside the city's walls, claiming that only the city can teach him. For Socrates, the unexamined life—a life without philosophy—was not worth living. And the life of philosophy was nurtured within the walls of the city.

This is a familiar story to those who have studied Western philosophy, especially political philosophy. Many surveys of political theory begin with a section on philosophy and the city that focuses on the ancient Greek philosophy of Socrates, Plato, and Aristotle. And then philosophy seems to disappear from the city, at least in the way that we traditionally present Western intellectual history.

In an attempt to tell a different story, twentieth-century French philosopher Henri Lefebvre argues that in "classical philosophy from Plato to Hegel, the city was much more than a secondary theme, an object among others. The links between philosophical thought and urban life appear clearly upon reflection, although they need to be made explicit" (Lefebvre 1996, 86). *Philosophy and the City* aims to help readers make those connections and reflect on them.

This book offers a corrective to the usual history of philosophy by demonstrating that philosophy and the city have remained in productive tension with one another since Athens. The wisdom of philosophy is meant to be shared with citizens. As Richard McKeon argues, "political wisdom must be shared by all who benefit by it" (158). And that wisdom must be understood within the context of the city. In *The Good City and the Good Life*, Daniel Kemmis argues that if humanities and culture are not just words or academic constructs, then "their meaning had to be sought in and brought to bear on the real life of the real city" (59). The purpose and focus of this book is to do just that: to seek an understanding of philosophy in and through an examination of the city and to show how and why philosophy matters to the city.

I have already suggested briefly how philosophy might matter to the city, but we would be remiss if we did not also note philosophy's debts to the city. The city has been, and continues to be, an important crystallization of human civilization and its discontents. As such, cities focus and concentrate all of the key philosophical questions to which philosophers perennially return (Conlon; Fell 1997, 26; Mendieta 2001, 204, 208). The answers to those philosophical questions have varied throughout history, and we see them writ large in our cities. Further, cities also provide an important *context* for philosophical inquiry, the background against which philosophical questions are raised and shaped.

When we return to Western European philosophy's historical roots, we see that for ancient Athenians the city provided the very possibility of philosophy. As both Plato and Aristotle noted, philosophical reflection requires a certain amount of leisure time and active engagement in the social and political life of the city. Socrates, Plato, and Aristotle all shared an understanding of philosophy as the fundamental inquiry into human self-understanding within the context of human community. The city historically provided philosophy with its task, because the city defined what it meant to be a human (Fell 1997, 26).

But philosophy appeared in a certain kind of city, one that freed some from the drudgery of the work of economic subsistence. The ancient Athenian philosopher's life depended on the work of a majority of ancient Athenians, namely women and slaves, who were not granted the opportunity, education, or time to engage in philosophical reflection. Issues of diversity and social justice have been at the heart of the relationship between philosophy and the city since the rise of both in ancient Greece.

Cities are particularly effective in unlocking key questions in philosophy, questions not only in political and social philosophy, but also in metaphysics and epistemology, as we explore the essential nature of both city and humans, as well as in questions concerning place and identity formation, aesthetics, philosophy of race and diversity, and environmental philosophy. And the history of philosophy of the city is instructive in helping us map out how those questions shift over time, both in terms of the relative importance we give to them as well as in our answers.

Of course, both philosophy and the city have changed over time. Part of the historical role of the philosopher has been to define just what a city is. We will leave it to the philosophers anthologized here to take us through some of the most important variants in the history of the Western city, from the polis to the ancient Roman republic, the medieval walled city to the colonial settlement, the industrial city to the contemporary global city. While cities have changed over time, we identify all of these forms *as* cities (Weber; Mumford). All cities are human settlements that provide a relatively complex way of satisfying human needs that relies on human interdependence and some degree of specialization. Moreover, cities are occupied with what Lawrence Haworth calls the "whole round of life" (1963, 13), that is, with all facets of human endeavor and interest. Philosophers have differed in whether they understand the city primarily in terms of "urbs," that is, the physical layout and space of the city, or "civitas," that is, the people and their way of life, or some combination of the two (Kagen 2000, 9–10). We will see that while some definitions and metaphors have persisted through time, others fade away as new concepts are introduced and new historical circumstances demand new interpretations.

Cities can be defined in economic, political, and sociological terms. But the first thinkers to really explore the nature and concept of the city were philosophers. Philosophers began with questions about the very essence or nature of the city. Those questions were metaphysical as well as political, for they were viewed as the key to understanding human being—our very essence or nature. Pericles was not properly a philosopher, but his funeral oration helps us better understand Athenian ideals. Historians note that Pericles' description of the Athens of his day was not accurate; but he succeeds in beginning to articulate the ideals of the city—its democratic values and its reward of active citizenship—that later Socrates, Plato, and Aristotle scrutinize and thematize philosophically. For all three, justice was the city's central ideal that required inquiry and reflection. In his *Republic*, Plato creates a city "in speech" in a dialogue between Socrates and other Athenian citizens, because the justice of the individual is properly understood within the context of justice "writ large," that is, in the city (Book II, 368e1–374).

For Aristotle, the city is defined by its common end or good, which he identifies as justice (*Politics*, Book I). Pericles specifically praises Athen's openness, its willingness to welcome noncitizens, an issue slighted by his philosophical successors in favor of an emphasis on the essence of the city and the common good. We see this, for example, in Aristotle's introduction of the metaphor of the organism for the city. Aristotle likens cities to a living organism, a body politic, in which the whole is greater than the sum of its parts. A body politic is more than a collection of individuals. The common purpose of the city is to create and promote *eudaimonia*, which is best translated as "human flourishing." We fully realize what it means to be a human being in the polis. Aristotle asks what ideals are embodied in city life, what characteristics actual cities must have if they are to actualize those ideals. Socrates, Plato, and Aristotle were playing the role of the philosopher as gadflies who hold cities accountable to the values that they promise but do not always deliver.

We now leap forward in our story to the time of the decline of another great ancient city, Rome. In his philosophy of the city, St. Augustine blends the classic ideals of ancient Greek philosophy with Christianity. Influenced by Plato's emphasis on the importance of truthful definitions, Augustine argues that Rome was not really a city at all, since it failed to meet the definitional ideals articulated by Cicero. Augustine claims Rome failed to meet Cicero's definition of a republic as an "affair of the people" because there lacked common agreement about what is right (*City of God*, chapter 21). Through reason, a city should create a harmony among its parts. Augustine further argued that the common good lost on earth could only be re-created in a heavenly city.

By the time of the Renaissance, in Machiavelli's Florence, earthly cities and their princes seemed more interested in survival than in the common good. Machiavelli develops an instrumental morality that differs from both Greek and Christian moralities. For Machiavelli, the only worthy end is survival (power), and any means that secure that end are justifiable. While the end goal for both the Greeks and for Augustine is the good life, something that can only be realized in the city, the only end for Machiavelli is power. Machiavelli's conception of political rule is to exploit the prince's skill (*virtu*) to take advantage of what fortune provided in order to gain power, glory, and security. If a city creates problems for the prince, then Machiavelli advises the prince to destroy it rather than let it destroy his success. But Machiavelli distinguishes between two types of cities, those used to living under the rule of a prince (in which case the above applies), and those who live in freedom under their own laws. For Machiavelli, cities are only as good as the people who build them and create their laws.

While Machiavelli seems to give up on any substantive ideals, St. Thomas More, a British thinker of the same time period, created his *Utopia*. More's work is influenced by multiple ancient Greek influences, from the Stoics to Plato and Aristotle. His ideal city is Stoic in its intolerance for laziness or idleness. It is Platonic in his creation of an imaginary ideal city and its emphasis on communal organization and centralized political control. And it is Aristotelian in its understanding of human nature. More depicts humans as naturally cooperative and social. He focuses so fully on the need for common goals and bonds that he eliminates diversity from his city entirely.

Machiavelli, on the other hand, introduces an understanding of human nature that is competitive and individualist—a view that dominates the modern Western worldview. The reception of his work marks a shift in philosophical thinking about cities. Machiavelli's individualism and *realpolitik* are adopted by Thomas Hobbes, who also focuses on questions of survival. And during Hobbes's time we witness the development of the nation-state as the more important political entity than the city.

Although a few city-states (like Rousseau's beloved Geneva) continued to exist for the next centuries, the groundwork was laid for a shift of philosophy away from cities. The rapid urbanization (and correlative urban problems) that emerged as a result of the Industrial Revolution in the nineteenth century became the study of social scientists more than philosophers. A few philosophically trained social scientists like Georg Simmel and Max Weber tried to return philosophy to the question, "what is a city?" and examine the changing nature of the city over time, but most philosophers did not pursue the inquiry. And the intellectual work done by figures such as Engels usually has been read as social science rather than philosophy (Meagher 2007).

In the twentieth century, philosophers who worked on urban questions largely focused on the rapid growth of cities and the rise of the "mass man," which they saw as a distinguishing characteristic of the modern city (see Mendieta 2001, 204). Some, like Mumford, returned to ancient Athenian concepts of community for the antidote to the increasing anonymity of big cities. Others theorized that the growth of negative urban traits was linked to the rise of capitalism and turned to Marx for analysis.

In more recent years, we have witnessed yet another shift in philosophy's relationship to the city. Although earlier philosophers focused on issues concerning the nature of the city and concepts of citizenship, more recent writings tend to focus on the built environment and on issues of diversity and economic justice. Philosophy has tended to retreat from the broader questions about the nature of the city and citizenship to focus on more particular questions raised within and by cities. Those philosophers who still pursue questions regarding the nature of cities and citizenship often draw on, or respond to, classical ideals, while some of the newer questions mark the breaking of new philosophical terrain. Philosophers are increasingly engaged in interdisciplinary discourses on the city that cross boundary lines with social scientists, architects, urban planners, and urban geographers.

This is an admittedly brief and oversimplified history of the relationship between philosophy and the city. The purpose of this book is to allow readers to complete and/or correct that history by taking their own historical tours of the readings in Part I. In that history, we note not only changes in the philosophical questions raised in and about the city, but also differences in understandings of the philosophers' task or the philosophers' role in the city and city life. The task of philosophy and the relation between philosophy and the city are themselves deeply philosophical questions.

Socrates introduced the role of the philosopher as gadfly, as critical examiner of the city and the philosophical foundations on which it is based. Socrates remains the model for many philosophers of the city who follow him. In Part II, which is organized around the foundational questions of the city that philosophers address, I provide an additional reading that illustrates a philosopher "at work" on the specific question or some aspect of it. Essays in Part I that address these issues are noted in the introduction to each section. These essays illustrate various ways in which the philosopher's task has been interpreted, reinterpreted, and practiced. Following Wittgenstein, some philosophers understand their role as a matter of looking and seeing, that is, as clarifying important concepts that are sometimes lost amid competing traditions or ideological noise (Fell 1997, 28). Others follow Dewey in focusing on the role of the philosopher as an interpreter of meaning. Dewey argues that the role of philosophy is to serve as a bridge between the new and the old by articulating the basic values of culture and reconstructing them into a more coherent and imaginative vision. Although some may not agree fully with Dewey's argument, most philosophers would agree that an important role—if not the most important one—is to help us imagine what *ought* to be. In that sense, the philosopher judges and prescribes (Haworth 1963, 11).

When we read the history of philosophy and the city, we notice that philosophers have engaged critically with both specific cities and specific urban issues. But the philosopher takes up these problems in ways that are often distinctive from more familiar contemporary social scientific approaches. Philosophers usually refuse the role of "expert" or technical problem solver. The task of the philosopher and his or her role in the city is complex. The readings in this text help situate social scientific accounts of urban issues within a larger philosophical and intellectual context. So, for example, the book presents a broader theoretical context by which one can begin to understand the social scientific analyses of issues like urban violence and poverty by raising important questions about justice, difference, and race. While contemporary philosophy of the city engages in dialogue with the social sciences, philosophy more explicitly and directly makes value claims and grounds those claims in critical arguments (see Haworth 1963, 11).

To help the reader better understand and examine how and why philosophical argument provides a foundation for other urban discourses, Part II also includes case studies that encourage readers to think about specific urban issues philosophically. In some instances, the cases invite the reader to examine critically the philosophical assumptions being made. In other cases, the reader is given the opportunity to put his own philosophical understandings of the city to work.

The two types of cases included in Part II illustrate respectively how "philosophy matters" and how and why the "city matters." The readings organized under the heading "city matters" are more properly case studies. These readings represent a diverse set of challenges that cities face to which readings in the first section of the book (Part I) might provide some insight. The "city matters" essays are therefore intended to be used as case studies in the usual sense of the term; they present readers with the opportunity to think more broadly and more deeply about how philosophy might apply to a wide range of city matters. In some instances, readers may find that the cases challenge us to see shortcomings in some philosophical arguments when they are put to the test.

Philosophy matters, cities matter, and it is time that we attended to both. I have provided readers with at least two possible roadmaps (starting in Part I or starting in Part II) by which to navigate these readings. Adventurous readers will discover unmapped routes. I hope that all readers will find whatever journey they take to be challenging, enlightening, and rewarding.

REFERENCES

This list includes only authors and/or texts not anthologized in this book.

Fell, Gilbert. 1997. "What Has Athens to Do with New York?" *Contemporary Philosophy*, vol. XIX, no. 4 and 5, pp. 26–29.

Friedman, Marilyn. 1993. *What Are Friends For?* Ithaca, NY: Cornell University Press.

Haworth, Lawrence. 1963. *The Good City.* Bloomington and London: Indiana University Press.

Kagen, Richard L. 2000. *Urban Images of the Hispanic World 1493–1793*. New Haven and London: Yale University Press.

Kemmis, Daniel. 1995. *The Good City and the Good Life*. New York and Boston: Houghton Mifflin.

Lefebvre, Henri. 1996. "Philosophy and the City," in *Writings on Cities*. Trans. Eleonore and Elizabeth Lebas Kofman. Oxford: Blackwell Publishers.

McKeon, Richard. 1949. "Philosophy and Freedom in the City of Man," *Ethics: An International Journal of Social, Political and Legal Philosophy*, vol. LIX, no. 3, pp. 155–161.

Meagher, Sharon M. 2007. "Philosophy in the Streets: Walking the City with Engels and de Certeau," *City*, vol. 11, no. 1 (April 2007), pp. 7–21.

Meagher, Sharon M. 1999. "Tensions in the City: Community and Difference," *Studies in Practical Philosophy*, vol. 1, no. 2 (fall), pp. 203–213.

Mendieta, Eduardo. 2001. "The City and the Philosopher: On the Urbanism of Phenomenology." *Philosophy and Geography* 4, no. 2, pp. 203–218.

Sassen, Saskia. 2000. *Cities in a World Economy*. Sociology for a New Century Series. Thousand Oaks, CA: Pine Forge Press.

Spellmeyer, Kurt. 2003. "Taking the Humanities Out of the Box." *Arts of Living: Reinventing the Humanities for the Twenty-first Century*. Albany: State University of New York Press, pp. 3–25.

White, Morton and Lucia White. 1962. *The Intellectual Versus the City: From Thomas Jefferson to Frank Lloyd Wright*. New York: A Mentor Book, New American Library. © Harvard University and MIT Press.

PART I

Readings from Philosophy:
Classic to Contemporary

Classic and Medieval Readings
(500 BCE–AD 1499)

Pericles

Pericles (495 BCE–425 BCE) was an ancient Athenian leader during the Golden Age between the Persian and Peloponnesian wars. After the opening battles of the Peloponnesian War, he gave a speech honoring those who had died in battle. We do not have the actual text of Pericles' speech, but rather ancient Greek historian Thucydides' account of it in his history of the Peloponnesian War. Pericles lays out the ideals of democratic Athens.

Pericles' funeral oration was used as an occasion to praise Athens as well as criticize its enemies. Pericles outlines what he sees as the key features for Athens's success: its democratic constitution, its openness to the world, its active citizenry. He argues that Athens had become a model for others, and indeed history has shown that philosophers continue to return to the ideals of ancient Athens in developing their own concepts of both the good city and the good citizen. Although neither Thucydides nor Pericles were philosophers, the conceptualization of the city and citizenship expressed in Pericles' speech laid a foundation from which Socrates, Plato, and Aristotle built their political philosophies. These issues are also raised in selections by Hobbes, More, Weber, Addams, Young, Kemmis, and Gooding-Williams.

PERICLES' FUNERAL ORATION (CIRCA 431 BCE) (FROM THUCYDIDES, *THE PELOPONNESIAN WAR*)

Most of those who have spoken here before me have commended the lawgiver who added this oration to our other funeral customs. It seemed to them a worthy thing that such an honor should be given at their burial to the dead who have fallen on the field of battle. But I should have preferred that, when men's deeds have been brave, they should be honored in deed only, and with such an honor as this public funeral, which you are now witnessing. Then the reputation of many would not have been imperiled on the eloquence or want of eloquence of one, and their virtues believed or not as he spoke well or ill. For it is difficult to say neither too little nor too much; and even moderation is apt not to give the impression of truthfulness. The friend of the dead who knows the facts is likely to think that the words of the speaker fall short of his knowledge and of his wishes; another who is not so well informed, when he hears of anything which surpasses his own powers, will be envious and will suspect exaggeration. Mankind are tolerant of the praises of others so long as each hearer thinks that he can do as well or nearly as well himself, but, when the speaker rises above him, jealousy is aroused and he begins to be

14

incredulous. However, since our ancestors have set the seal of their approval upon the practice, I must obey, and to the utmost of my power shall endeavor to satisfy the wishes and beliefs of all who hear me.

I will speak first of our ancestors, for it is right and seemly that now, when we are lamenting the dead, a tribute should be paid to their memory. There has never been a time when they did not inhabit this land, which by their valor they will have handed down from generation to generation, and we have received from them a free state. But if they were worthy of praise, still more were our fathers, who added to their inheritance, and after many a struggle transmitted to us their sons this great empire. And we ourselves assembled here today, who are still most of us in the vigor of life, have carried the work of improvement further, and have richly endowed our city with all things, so that she is sufficient for herself both in peace and war. Of the military exploits by which our various possessions were acquired, or of the energy with which we or our fathers drove back the tide of war, Hellenic or Barbarian, I will not speak; for the tale would be long and is familiar to you. But before I praise the dead, I should like to point out by what principles of action we rose to power, and under what institutions and through what manner of life our empire became great. For I conceive that such thoughts are not unsuited to the occasion, and that this numerous assembly of citizens and strangers may profitably listen to them.

Our form of government does not enter into rivalry with the institutions of others. Our government does not copy our neighbors', but is an example to them. It is true that we are called a democracy, for the administration is in the hands of the many and not of the few. But while there exists equal justice to all and alike in their private disputes, the claim of excellence is also recognized; and when a citizen is in any way distinguished, he is preferred to the public service, not as a matter of privilege, but as the reward of merit. Neither is poverty an obstacle, but a man may benefit his country whatever the obscurity of his condition. There is no exclusiveness in our public life, and in our private business we are not suspicious of one another, nor angry with our neighbor if he does what he likes; we do not put on sour looks at him which, though harmless, are not pleasant. While we are thus unconstrained in our private business, a spirit of reverence pervades our public acts; we are prevented from doing wrong by respect for the authorities and for the laws, having a particular regard to those which are ordained for the protection of the injured as well as those unwritten laws which bring upon the transgressor of them the reprobation of the general sentiment.

And we have not forgotten to provide for our weary spirits many relaxations from toil; we have regular games and sacrifices throughout the year; our homes are beautiful and elegant; and the delight which we daily feel in all these things helps to banish sorrow. Because of the greatness of our city the fruits of the whole earth flow in upon us; so that we enjoy the goods of other countries as freely as our own.

Our military training also is in many respects superior to that of our adversaries. Our city is thrown open to the world; we never expel a foreigner and prevent him from seeing or learning anything of which the secret if revealed to an enemy might profit him. We rely not upon management or trickery, but upon our own hearts and hands. And in the matter of education, whereas they from early youth are always undergoing laborious exercises which are to make them brave, we live at ease, and yet are equally ready to face the perils which they face. [. . .]

If then we prefer to meet danger with a light heart but without laborious training, and with a courage which is gained by habit and not enforced by law, are we not greatly the better for it? Since we do not anticipate the pain, although, when the hour comes, we can be as brave as those who never allow themselves to rest; thus our city is equally admirable in peace and in war.

For we are lovers of the beautiful in our tastes and our strength lies, in our opinion, not in deliberation and discussion, but that knowledge which is gained by discussion preparatory to action. For we have a peculiar power of thinking before we act, and of acting, too, whereas other men are courageous from ignorance but hesitate upon reflection. And they are surely to be esteemed the bravest spirits who, having the clearest sense both of the pains and pleasures of life, do not on that account shrink from danger. In doing good, again, we are unlike others; we make our friends by conferring, not by receiving favors. Now he who confers a favor is the firmer friend, because he would rather by kindness keep alive the memory of an obligation; but the recipient is colder in his feelings, because he knows that in requiting another's generosity he will not be winning gratitude but only paying a debt. We alone do good to our neighbors not upon a calculation of interest, but in the confidence of freedom and in a frank and fearless spirit.

To sum up: I say that Athens is an education to all Greeks, and that the individual Athenian in his own person seems to have the power of adapting himself to the most varied forms of action with the utmost versatility and grace. This is no passing and idle word, but truth and fact; and the assertion is verified by the position to which these qualities have raised the state. For in the hour of trial Athens alone among her contemporaries is superior to the report of her. No enemy who comes against her is indignant at the reverses which he sustains at the hands of such a city; no subject complains that his masters are unworthy of him. And we shall assuredly not be without witnesses; there are mighty monuments of our power which will make us the wonder of this and of succeeding ages; we shall not need the praises of Homer or of any other panegyrist whose poetry may please for the moment, although his representation of the facts will not bear the light of day. For we have compelled every land and every sea to open a path for our valor, and have everywhere planted eternal memorials of our friendship and of our enmity. Such is the city for whose sake these men nobly fought and died; they could not bear the thought that she might be taken from them; and every one of us who survive should gladly toil on her behalf.

I have dwelt upon the greatness of Athens because I want to show you that we are contending for a higher prize than those who enjoy none of these privileges, and to establish by manifest proof the merit of these men whom I am now commemorating. Their loftiest praise has been already spoken. For in magnifying the city I have magnified them, and men like them whose virtues made her glorious. And of how few Hellenes can it be said as of them, that their deeds when weighed in the balance have been found equal to their fame! Methinks that a death such as theirs has been the true measure of a man's worth; it may be the first revelation of his virtues, but is at any rate their final seal. For even those who come short in other ways may justly plead the valor with which they have fought for their country; they have blotted out the evil with the good, and have benefited the state more by their public services than they have injured her by their private actions. None of these men were enervated by wealth or hesitated to resign the pleasures of life; none of them put off the evil day in the hope, natural to poverty, that a man, though poor, may one day become rich. But, deeming that the punishment of their enemies was sweeter than any of these things, and that they could fall in no nobler cause, they determined at the hazard of their lives to be honorably avenged, and to leave the rest. They resigned to hope their unknown chance of happiness; but in the face of death they resolved to rely upon themselves alone. And when the moment came they were minded to resist and suffer, rather than to fly and save their lives; they ran away from the word of dishonor, but on the battlefield their feet stood fast, and in an instant, at the height of their fortune, they passed away from the scene, not of their fear, but of their glory.

Such was the end of these men; they were worthy of Athens, and the living need not desire to have a more heroic spirit, although they may pray for a less fatal issue. The value of such a spirit is not to be expressed in words. Any one can discourse to you for ever about the advantages of a Brave defense, which you know already. But instead of listening to him I would have you day by day fix your eyes upon the greatness of Athens, until you become filled with the love of her; and when you are impressed by the spectacle of her glory, reflect that this empire has been acquired by men who knew their duty and had the courage to do it, who in the hour of conflict had the fear of dishonor always present to them, and who, if ever they failed in an enterprise, would not allow their virtues to be lost to their country, but freely gave their lives to her as the fairest offering which they could present at her feast. The sacrifice which they collectively made was individually repaid to them; for they received again each one for himself a praise which grows not old, and the noblest of all tombs—I speak not of that in which their remains are laid, but of that in which their glory survives, and is proclaimed always and on every fitting occasion both in word and deed. For the whole earth is the tomb of famous men; not only are they commemorated by columns and inscriptions in their own country, but in foreign lands there dwells also an unwritten memorial of them, graven not on stone but in the hearts of men. Make them your examples, and, esteeming courage to be freedom and freedom to be happiness, do not weigh too nicely the perils of war. The unfortunate who has no hope of a change for the better has less reason to throw away his life than the prosperous who, if he survives, is always liable to a change for the worse, and to whom any accidental fall makes the most serious difference. To a man of spirit, cowardice and disaster coming together are far more bitter than death striking him unperceived at a time when he is full of courage and animated by the general hope.

Wherefore I do not now pity the parents of the dead who stand here; I would rather comfort them. You know that your dead have passed away amid manifold vicissitudes; and that they may be deemed fortunate who have gained their utmost honor, whether an honorable death like theirs, or an honorable sorrow like yours, and whose share of happiness has been so ordered that the term of their happiness is likewise the term of their life. I know how hard it is to make you feel this, when the good fortune of others will too often remind you of the gladness which once lightened your hearts. And sorrow is felt at the want of those blessings, not which a man never knew, but which were a part of his life before they were taken from him. Some of you are of an age at which they may hope to have other children, and they ought to bear their sorrow better; not only will the children who may hereafter be born make them forget their own lost ones, but the city will be doubly a gainer. She will not be left desolate, and she will be safer. For a man's counsel cannot have equal weight or worth, when he alone has no children to risk in the general danger. To those of you who have passed their prime, I say: "Congratulate yourselves that you have been happy during the greater part of your days; remember that your life of sorrow will not last long, and be comforted by the glory of those who are gone. For the love of honor alone is ever young, and not riches, as some say, but honor is the delight of men when they are old and useless."

To you who are the sons and brothers of the departed, I see that the struggle to emulate them will be an arduous one. For all men praise the dead, and, however preeminent your virtue may be, I do not say even to approach them, and avoid living their rivals and detractors, but when a man is out of the way, the honor and goodwill which he receives is unalloyed. And, if I am to speak of womanly virtues to those of you who will henceforth be widows, let me sum them up in one short admonition: To a woman not to show more weakness than is natural to her sex is a great glory, and not to be talked about for good or for evil among men.

I have paid the required tribute, in obedience to the law, making use of such fitting words as I had. The tribute of deeds has been paid in part; for the dead have them in deeds, and it remains only that their children should be maintained at the public charge until they are grown up: this is the solid prize with which, as with a garland, Athens crowns her sons living and dead, after a struggle like-theirs. For where the rewards of virtue are greatest, there the noblest citizens are enlisted in the service of the state. And now, when you have finished mourning your own dead, you may depart.

Questions for Review and Discussion

1. Why does Pericles begin his eulogy for fallen soldiers with praise of the city?

2. Discuss two examples that Pericles gives in support of his claim of Athens' greatness.

3. Name two ways in which Pericles claims that Athens serves as a model for the rest of the world.

4. In what sense is ancient Athens a good model for the good city today? In what ways does it fall short?

Plato

Plato (428 BCE–348 BCE) was Socrates' (470 BCE–390 BCE) most famous student. Plato's philosophical writings take the form of dialogue and usually feature Socrates as a central character. Since Socrates preferred speech to writing, we know Socrates primarily through the work of Plato. Plato's dialogues are artfully constructed philosophical works rather than mere reports of conversations he observed of his teacher. Nevertheless, Plato wrote some dialogues to help us understand what happened to Socrates and how he responded. The *Crito* focuses on one episode after Socrates is awaiting execution in prison. Like all of Plato's dialogues, the work focuses on a central question. In the *Crito*, that question is: should Socrates escape from the city and avoid execution? Pay attention to how Socrates answers that question; it reveals his understanding of the relationship between philosophy and the city. Compare Socrates' conception of the relationship between philosophy and the city with that of Dewey, Grange, Conlon, and Young.

The *Republic* is Plato's longest dialogue; it focuses on the question of justice. While the dialogue begins with a question about the justice of the individual, in the passage that begins our selection Socrates suggests shifting perspectives to look at justice "writ large" by examining the justice of the city. Socrates and his interlocutor Adeimantus commence to build a city in speech. What do they imagine? This reading might be compared with Aristotle, Machiavelli, Hobbes, More, Weber, and Mumford on the development and function of the city and with Engels on the division of labor.

CRITO (CIRCA 387 BCE)

49e5–54e

SOCRATES: . . . Ought a man to do what he admits to be right, or ought he to betray the right?

CRITO: He ought to do what he thinks right.

SOCRATES: But if this is true, what is the application? In leaving the prison against the will of the Athenians, do I wrong any? Or rather do I not wrong those whom I ought least to wrong? Do I not desert the principles which were acknowledged by us to be just—what do you say?

20

CRITO: I cannot tell, Socrates, for I do not know.

SOCRATES: Then consider the matter in this way: Imagine that I am about to play truant (you may call the proceeding by any name which you like), and the laws and the government come and interrogate me: "Tell us, Socrates," they say; "What are you about? Are you not going by an act of yours to overturn us—the laws, and the whole city, as far as in you lies? Do you imagine that a city can subsist and not be overthrown if its decisions of law have no power, but are set aside and trampled upon by individuals?" What will be our answer, Crito, to these and the like words? Any one, and especially a rhetorician, will have a good deal to say on behalf of the law which requires a sentence to be carried out. He will argue that this law should not be set aside; and shall we reply, "Yes; but the city has injured us and given an unjust sentence." Suppose I say that?

CRITO: Very good, Socrates.

SOCRATES: "And was that our agreement with you?" The law would answer; "or were you to abide by the sentence of the city?" And if I were to express my astonishment at their words, the law would probably add: "Answer, Socrates, instead of opening your eyes—you are in the habit of asking and answering questions. Tell us,—What complaint have you to make against us which justifies you in attempting to destroy us and the city? In the first place did we not bring you into existence? Your father married your mother by our aid and begat you. Say whether you have any objection to urge against those of us who regulate marriage?" None, I should reply. "Or against those of us who after birth regulate the nurture and education of children, in which you also were trained? Were not the laws, which have the charge of education, right in commanding your father to train you in music and gymnastic?" Right, I should reply. "Well then, since you were brought into the world and nurtured and educated by us, can you deny in the first place that you are our child and slave, as your fathers were before you? And if this is true you are not on equal terms with us; nor can you think that you have a right to do to us what we are doing to you. Would you have any right to strike or revile or do any other evil to your father or your master, if you had one, because you have been struck or reviled by him, or received some other evil at his hands?—you would not say this? And because we think right to destroy you, do you think that you have any right to destroy us in return, and your country as far as in you lies? Will you, O professor of true virtue, pretend that you are justified in this? Has a philosopher like you failed to discover that our country is more to be valued and higher and holier far than mother or father or any ancestor, and more to be regarded in the eyes of the gods and of men of understanding? Also to be soothed, and gently and reverently entreated when angry, even more than a father, and either to be persuaded, or if not persuaded, to be obeyed? And when we are punished by her, whether with imprisonment or stripes, the punishment is to be endured in silence; and if she lead us to wounds or death in battle, thither we follow as is right; neither may any one yield or retreat or leave his rank, but whether in battle or in a court of law, or in any other place, he must do what his city and his country order him; or he must change their view of what is just: and if he may do no violence to his father or mother, much less may he do violence to his country." What answer shall we make to this, Crito? Do the laws speak truly, or do they not?

CRITO: I think that they do.

SOCRATES: Then the laws will say: "Consider, Socrates, if we are speaking truly that in your present attempt you are going to do us an injury. For, having brought you into the world, and nurtured and educated you, and given you and every other citizen a share in every good which we had to give, we further proclaim to any Athenian by the liberty which we allow him, that if he does not like us when he has become of age and has seen the ways of the city, and made our acquaintance, he may go where he pleases and take his goods with him. None of us laws will forbid him or interfere with him. Any one who does not like us and the city, and who wants to emigrate to a colony or to any other city, may go where he likes, retaining his property. But he who has experience of the manner in which we order justice and administer the city, and still remains, has entered into an implied contract that he will do as we command him. And he who disobeys us is, as we maintain, thrice wrong: first, because in disobeying us he is disobeying his parents; secondly, because we are the authors of his education; thirdly, because he has made an agreement with us that he will duly obey our commands; and he neither obeys them nor convinces us that our commands are unjust; and we do not rudely impose them, but give him the alternative of obeying or convincing us;—that is what we offer, and he does neither.

"These are the sort of accusations to which, as we were saying, you, Socrates, will be exposed if you accomplish your intentions; you, above all other Athenians." Suppose now I ask, why I rather than anybody else? They will justly retort upon me that I above all other men have acknowledged the agreement. "There is clear proof," they will say, "Socrates, that we and the city were not displeasing to you. Of all Athenians you have been the most constant resident in the city, which, as you never leave, you may be supposed to love. For you never went out of the city either to see the games, except once when you went to the Isthmus, or to any other place unless when you were on military service; nor did you travel as other men do. Nor had you any curiosity to know other cities or their laws: your affections did not go beyond us and our city; we were your especial favorites, and you acquiesced in our government of you; and here in this city you begat your children, which is a proof of your satisfaction. Moreover, you might in the course of the trial, if you had liked, have fixed the penalty at banishment; the city which refuses to let you go now would have let you go then. But you pretended that you preferred death to exile, and that you were not unwilling to die. And now you have forgotten these fine sentiments, and pay no respect to us the laws, of whom you are the destroyer; and are doing what only a miserable slave would do, running away and turning your back upon the compacts and agreements which you made as a citizen. And first of all answer this very question: Are we right in saying that you agreed to be governed according to us in deed, and not in word only? Is that true or not?" How shall we answer, Crito? Must we not agree?

CRITO: We cannot help it, Socrates.

SOCRATES: Then will they not say: "You, Socrates, are breaking the covenants and agreements which you made with us at your leisure, not in any haste or under any compulsion or deception, but after you have had seventy years to think of them, during which time you were at liberty to leave the city, if we were not to your mind, or if our covenants appeared to you to be unfair. You had your choice, and might have gone either to Lacedaemon or Crete, both which cities are often praised by you for their good government, or to some other Hellenic or foreign city. Whereas you, above all other Athenians, seemed to be so fond of the city, or, in other words, of us her laws (and who would care about a city which has no laws?), that you never stirred out of her; the halt, the blind, the maimed, were not more stationary in her than you were. And now you run away and forsake your agreements. Not so, Socrates, if you will take our advice; do not make yourself ridiculous by escaping out of the city.

"For just consider, if you transgress and err in this sort of way, what good will you do either to yourself or to your friends? That your friends will be driven into exile and deprived of citizenship, or will lose their property, is tolerably certain; and you yourself, if you fly to one of the neighboring cities, as, for example, Thebes or Megara, both of which are well governed, will come to them as an enemy, Socrates, and their government will be against you, and all patriotic citizens will cast an evil eye upon you as a subverter of the laws, and you will confirm in the minds of the judges the justice of their own condemnation of you. For he who is a corrupter of the laws is more than likely to be a corrupter of the young and foolish portion of mankind. Will you then flee from well-ordered cities and virtuous men? And is existence worth having on these terms? Or will you go to them without shame, and talk to them, Socrates? And what will you say to them? What you say here about virtue and justice and institutions and laws being the best things among men? Would that be decent of you? Surely not. But if you go away from well-governed cities to Crito's friends in Thessaly, where there is great disorder and license, they will be charmed to hear the tale of your escape from prison, set off with ludicrous particulars of the manner in which you were wrapped in a goatskin or some other disguise, and metamorphosed as the manner is of runaways; but will there be no one to remind you that in your old age you were not ashamed to violate the most sacred laws from a miserable desire of a little more life? Perhaps not, if you keep them in a good temper; but if they are out of temper you will hear many degrading things; you will live, but how?—as the flatterer of all men, and the servant of all men; and doing what?—eating and drinking in Thessaly, having gone abroad in order that you may get a dinner. And where will be your fine sentiments about justice and virtue? Say that you wish to live for the sake of your children—you want to bring them up and educate them—will you take them into Thessaly and deprive them of Athenian citizenship? Is this the benefit which you will confer upon them? Or are you under the impression that they will be better cared for and educated here if you are still alive, although absent from them; for your friends will take care of them? Do you fancy that if you are an inhabitant of Thessaly they will take care of them, and if you are an inhabitant of the other world that they will not take care of them? Nay; but if they who call themselves friends are good for anything, they will—to be sure they will.

"Listen, then, Socrates, to us who have brought you up. Think not of life and children first, and of justice afterwards, but of justice first, that you may be justified before the princes of the world below. For neither will you nor any that belong to you be happier or holier or juster in this life, or happier in another, if you do as Crito bids. Now you depart in innocence, a sufferer and not a doer of evil; a victim, not of the laws, but of men. But if you go forth, returning evil for evil, and injury for injury, breaking the covenants and agreements which you have made with us, and wronging those whom you ought least of all to wrong, that is to say, yourself, your friends, your country, and us, we shall be angry with you while you live, and our brethren, the laws in the world below, will receive you as an enemy; for they will know that you have done your best to destroy us. Listen, then, to us and not to Crito."

This, dear Crito, is the voice which I seem to hear murmuring in my ears, like the sound of the flute in the ears of the mystic; that voice, I say, is humming in my ears, and prevents me from hearing any other. And I know that anything more which you may say will be vain. Yet speak, if you have anything to say.

CRITO: I have nothing to say, Socrates.

SOCRATES: Leave me then, Crito, to fulfill the will of God, and to follow whither he leads.

THE REPUBLIC (CIRCA 380–360 BCE)

368e1–374

SOCRATES: I will tell you, I replied; justice, which is the subject of our enquiry, is, as you know, sometimes spoken of as the virtue of an individual, and sometimes as the virtue of a city-state (polis).

ADEIMANTUS: True.

S: And is not a city larger than an individual?

A: It is.

S: Then in the larger the quantity of justice is likely to be larger and more easily discernible. I propose therefore that we enquire into the nature of justice and injustice, first as they appear in the city, and secondly in the individual, proceeding from the greater to the lesser and comparing them.

A: That is an excellent proposal.

S: And if we imagine the city in process of creation, we shall see the justice and injustice of the city in process of creation also.

A: I dare say.

S: When the city is completed there may be a hope that the object of our search will be more easily discovered.

A: Yes, far more easily.

S: But ought we to attempt to construct one? For to do so, as I am inclined to think, will be a very serious task. Reflect therefore.

A: I have reflected, and am anxious that you should proceed.

S: A city, I said, arises, as I conceive, out of the needs of mankind; no one is self-sufficing, but all of us have many wants. Can any other origin of a city be imagined?

A: There can be no other.

S: Then, as we have many wants, and many persons are needed to supply them, one takes a helper for one purpose and another for another; and when these partners and helpers are gathered together in one habitation the body of inhabitants is termed a city.

A: True

S: And they exchange with one another, and one gives, and another receives, under the idea that the exchange will be for their good.

A: Very true.

S: Then, I said, let us begin and create in idea a city; and yet the true creator is necessity, who is the mother of our invention.

A: Of course.

S: Now the first and greatest of necessities is food, which is the condition of life and existence.

A Certainly.

S: The second is a dwelling, and the third clothing and the like.

A: True.

S: And now let us see how our city will be able to supply this great demand: We may suppose that one man is a husbandman, another a builder, some one else a weaver—shall we add to them a shoemaker, or perhaps some other purveyor to our bodily wants?

A: Quite right.

S: The barest notion of a city must include four or five men.

A: Clearly.

S: And how will they proceed? Will each bring the result of his labors into a common stock?—the individual husbandman, for example, producing for four, and laboring four times as long and as much as he need in the provision of food with which he supplies others as well as himself; or will he have nothing to do with others and not be at the trouble of producing for them, but provide for himself alone a fourth of the food in a fourth of the time, and in the remaining three fourths of his time be employed in making a house or a coat or a pair of shoes, having no partnership with others, but supplying himself all his own wants?

A: He should aim at producing food only and not at producing everything.

S: Probably that would be the better way; and when I hear you say this, I am myself reminded that we are not all alike; there are diversities of natures among us which are adapted to different occupations.

A: Very true.

S: And will you have a work better done when the workman has many occupations, or when he has only one?

A: When he has only one.

S: Further, there can be no doubt that a work is spoilt when not done at the right time?

A: No doubt.

S: For business is not disposed to wait until the doer of the business is at leisure; but the doer must follow up what he is doing, and make the business his first object.

A: He must.

S: And if so, we must infer that all things are produced more plentifully and easily and of a better quality when one man does one thing which is natural to him and does it at the right time, and leaves other things.

A: Undoubtedly.

S: Then more than four citizens will be required; for the husbandman will not make his own plough or mattock, or other implements of agriculture, if they are to be good for anything. Neither will the builder make his tools—and he too needs many; and in like manner the weaver and shoemaker.

A: True.

S: Then carpenters, and smiths, and many other artisans, will be sharers in our little city, which is already beginning to grow?

A: True.

S: Yet even if we add cowherds, shepherds, and other herdsmen, in order that our husbandmen may have oxen to plough with, and builders as well as husbandmen may have draught cattle, and curriers and weavers fleeces and hides,—still our city will not be very large.

A: That is true; yet neither will it be a very small city which contains all these.

S: Then, again, there is the situation of the city—to find a place where nothing need be imported is well nigh impossible.

A: Impossible.

S: Then there must be another class of citizens who will bring the required supplies from another city?

A: There must.

S: But if the trader goes empty-handed, having nothing which they require who would supply his need, he will come back empty-handed.

A: That is certain.

S: And therefore what they produce at home must be not only enough for themselves, but such both in quantity and quality as to accommodate those from whom their wants are supplied.

A: Very true.

S: Then more husbandmen and more artisans will be required?

A: They will.

S: Not to mention the importers and exporters, who are called merchants?

A: Yes.

S: Then we shall want merchants?

A: We shall.

S: And if merchandise is to be carried over the sea, skillful sailors will also be needed, and in considerable numbers?

A: Yes, in considerable numbers.

S: Then, again, within the city, how will they exchange their productions? To secure such an exchange was, as you will remember, one of our principal objects when we formed them into a society and constituted a city.

A: Clearly they will buy and sell.

S: Then they will need a market-place, and a money-token for purposes of exchange.

A: Certainly.

S: Suppose now that a husbandman, or an artisan, brings some production to market, and he comes at a time when there is no one to exchange with him,—is he to leave his calling and sit idle in the market-place?

A: Not at all; he will find people there who, seeing the want, undertake the office of salesmen. In well-ordered cities they are commonly those who are the weakest in bodily strength, and therefore of little use for any other purpose; their duty is to be in the market, and to give money in exchange for goods to those who desire to sell and to take money from those who desire to buy.

S: This want, then, creates a class of retail-traders in our city. Is not "retailer" the term which is applied to those who sit in the market-place engaged in buying and selling, while those who wander from one city to another are called merchants?

A: Yes.

S: And there is another class of servants, who are intellectually hardly on the level of companionship; still they have plenty of bodily strength for labor, which accordingly they sell, and are called, if I do not mistake, hirelings, hire being the name which is given to the price of their labor.

A: True.

S: Then hirelings will help to make up our population?

A: Yes.

S: And now, Adeimantus, is our city matured and perfected?

A: I think so.

S: Where, then, is justice, and where is injustice, and in what part of the City did they spring up?

A: Probably in the dealings of these citizens with one another. I cannot imagine that they are more likely to be found any where else.

S: I dare say that you are right in your suggestion, I said; we had better think the matter out, and not shrink from the enquiry.

Let us then consider, first of all, what will be their way of life, now that we have thus established them. Will they not produce corn, and wine, and clothes, and shoes, and build houses for themselves? And when they are housed, they will work, in summer, commonly, stripped and barefoot, but in winter substantially clothed and shod. They will feed on barley-meal and flour of wheat, baking and kneading them, making noble cakes and loaves; these they will serve up on a mat of reeds or on clean leaves, themselves reclining the while upon beds strewn with yew or myrtle. And they and their children will feast, drinking of the wine which they have made, wearing garlands on their heads, and hymning the praises of the gods, in happy converse with one another. And they will take care that their families do not exceed their means; having an eye to poverty or war.

GLAUCON: But you have not given them a relish to their meal.

S: True, I had forgotten; of course they must have a relish—salt, and olives, and cheese, and they will boil roots and herbs such as country people prepare; for a dessert we shall give them figs, and peas, and beans; and they will roast myrtle-berries and acorns at the fire, drinking in moderation. And with such a diet they may be expected to live in peace and health to a good old age, and bequeath a similar life to their children after them.

G: Yes, Socrates, and if you were providing for a city of pigs, how else would you feed the beasts?

S: But what would you have, Glaucon?

G: Why you should give them the ordinary conveniences of life. People who are to be comfortable are accustomed to lie on sofas, and dine off tables, and they should have sauces and sweets in the modern style.

S: Yes, now I understand: the question which you would have me consider is, not only how a city, but how a luxurious city is created; and possibly there is no harm in this, for in such a city we shall be more likely to see how justice and injustice originate. In my opinion the true and healthy constitution of the city is the one which I have described. But if you wish also to see a city at fever-heat, I have no objection. For I suspect that many will not be satisfied with the simpler way of life. They will be for adding sofas, and tables, and other furniture; also dainties, and perfumes, and incense, and courtesans, and cakes, all these not of one sort only, but in every variety; we must go beyond the necessaries of which I was at first speaking, such as houses, and clothes, and shoes: the arts of the painter and the embroiderer will have to be set in motion, and gold and ivory and all sorts of materials must be procured.

G: True.

S: Then we must enlarge our borders; for the original healthy city is no longer sufficient. Now will the city have to fill and swell with a multitude of callings which are not required by any natural want; such as the whole tribe of hunters and actors, of whom one large class have to do with forms and colors; another will be the votaries of music—poets and their attendant train of rhapsodists, players, dancers, contractors; also makers of divers kinds of articles, including women's dresses. And we shall want more servants. Will not tutors be also in request, and nurses wet and dry, hairdressers and barbers, as well as confectioners and cooks; and swineherds, too, who were not needed and therefore had no place in the former edition of our City, but are needed now? They must not be forgotten: and there will be animals of many other kinds, if people eat them.

G: Certainly.

S: And living in this way we shall have much greater need of physicians than before?

G: Much greater.

S: And the country which was enough to support the original inhabitants will be too small now, and not enough?

G: Quite true.

S: Then a slice of our neighbours' land will be wanted by us for pasture and tillage, and they will want a slice of ours, if, like ourselves, they exceed the limit of necessity, and give themselves up to the unlimited accumulation of wealth?

G: That, Socrates, will be inevitable.

S: And so we shall go to war, Glaucon. Shall we not?

G: Most certainly, he replied.

S: Then without determining as yet whether war does good or harm, thus much we may affirm, that now we have discovered war to be derived from causes which are also the causes of almost all the evils in Cities, private as well as public.

G: Undoubtedly.

S: And our city must once more enlarge; and this time the enlargement will be nothing short of a whole army, which will have to go out and fight with the invaders for all that we have, as well as for the things and persons whom we were describing above.

Questions for Review and Discussion

    1. According to Socrates in Plato's *Crito* someone accused unjustly has only two legitimate options, what are they?

2. Why does Socrates in Plato's *Crito* argue that escape or banishment is wrong?

3. What, according to Socrates in Plato's *Crito,* has he done that demonstrates his agreement with the city?

4. According to Plato in the *Republic,* what is the difference between a healthy city and a "feverish" one?

5. According to Plato's *Republic,* why is justice a concern for the city?

Aristotle

Aristotle (384 BCE–322 BCE) was a student of Plato, but he developed a political theory that diverges from Plato's in important ways, particularly because of their differing views of metaphysics, or the nature of things. Aristotle's metaphysics defines things by their proper function. So for Aristotle, a city can be defined by its proper function, and function is defined by the end or goal at which a thing aims. In Book I, Aristotle argues that the city is an association aimed at some good. Citizens must come together as a community to achieve that good. The selections from Book III further explore the issues of how to define a city, the character of the city, the diversity of citizens, the function of the city, and how a city can support its citizens in living well. These issues are also raised in selections by Pericles, Plato, Hobbes, More, Weber, Young, Kemmis, West, Mendieta, Gooding-Williams, and Francis.

POLITICS (CIRCA 350 BCE)
(SELECTIONS FROM BOOKS I AND III)

Book I

Chapter 1

Every association is a community of some kind, and every community is established with a view to some good; for mankind always act in order to obtain that which they think good. But, if all communities aim at some good, the city or political community, which is the highest of all, and which embraces all the rest, aims at good in a greater degree than any other, and at the highest good.

Some people think that the qualifications of a city-statesman, king, householder, and master are the same, and that they differ, not in kind, but only in the number of their subjects. For example, the ruler over a few is called a master; over more, the manager of a household; over a still larger number, a city-statesman or king, as if there were no difference between a great household and a small city-state. The distinction which is made between the king and the city-statesman is as follows: When the government is personal, the ruler is a king; when, according to the rules of the political science, the citizens rule and are ruled in turn, then he is called a city-statesman.

But all this is a mistake; for governments differ in kind, as will be evident to any one who considers the matter according to the method

33

which has hitherto guided us. As in other departments of science, so in politics, the compound should always be resolved into the simple elements or least parts of the whole. We must therefore look at the elements of which the city-state is composed, in order that we may see in what the different kinds of rule differ from one another, and whether any scientific result can be attained about each one of them.

Book III

CHAPTER 3

Whether they ought to be so or not is a question which is bound up with the previous inquiry. For a parallel question is raised respecting the city-state, whether a certain act is or is not an act of the city-state; for example, in the transition from an oligarchy or a tyranny to a democracy. In such cases persons refuse to fulfill their contracts or any other obligations, on the ground that the tyrant, and not the city-state, contracted them; they argue that some constitutions are established by force, and not for the sake of the common good. But this would apply equally to democracies, for they too may be founded on violence, and then the acts of the democracy will be neither more nor less acts of the city-state in question than those of an oligarchy or of a tyranny. This question runs up into another: on what principle shall we ever say that the city-state is the same, or different? It would be a very superficial view which considered only the place and the inhabitants (for the soil and the population may be separated, and some of the inhabitants may live in one place and some in another). This, however, is not a very serious difficulty; we need only remark that the word 'city-state' is ambiguous.

It is further asked: When are men, living in the same place, to be regarded as a single city—what is the limit? Certainly not the wall of the city, for you might surround all Peloponnesus with a wall. Like this, we may say, is Babylon, and every city that has the compass of a nation rather than a city; Babylon, they say, had been taken for three days before some part of the inhabitants became aware of the fact. This difficulty may, however, with advantage be deferred to another occasion; the city-statesman has to consider the size of the city-state, and whether it should consist of more than one nation or not.

Again, shall we say that while the race of inhabitants, as well as their place of abode, remain the same, the city is also the same, although the citizens are always dying and being born, as we call rivers and fountains the same, although the water is always flowing away and coming again. Or shall we say that the generations of men, like the rivers, are the same, but that the city-state changes? For, since the city-state is a partnership, and is a partnership of citizens in a constitution, when the form of government changes, and becomes different, then it may be supposed that the city-state is no longer the same, just as a tragic differs from a comic chorus, although the members of both may be identical. And in this manner we speak of every union or composition of elements as different when the form of their composition alters; for example, a scale containing the same sounds is said to be different, accordingly as the Dorian or the Phrygian mode is employed. And if this is true it is evident that the sameness of the city-state consists chiefly in the sameness of the constitution, and it may be called or not called by the same name, whether the inhabitants are the same or entirely different. It is quite another question, whether a city-state ought or ought not to fulfill engagements when the form of government changes.

Chapter 4

There is a point nearly allied to the preceding: Whether the virtue of a good man and a good citizen is the same or not. But, before entering on this discussion, we must certainly first obtain some general notion of the virtue of the citizen. Like the sailor, the citizen is a member of a community. Now, sailors have different functions, for one of them is a rower, another a pilot, and a third a look-out man, a fourth is described by some similar term; and while the precise definition of each individual's virtue applies exclusively to him, there is, at the same time, a common definition applicable to them all. For they have all of them a common object, which is safety in navigation. Similarly, one citizen differs from another, but the salvation of the community is the common business of them all. This community is the constitution; the virtue of the citizen must therefore be relative to the constitution of which he is a member. If, then, there are many forms of government, it is evident that there is not one single virtue of the good citizen which is perfect virtue. But we say that the good man is he who has one single virtue which is perfect virtue. Hence it is evident that the good citizen need not of necessity possess the virtue which makes a good man.

The same question may also be approached by another road, from a consideration of the best constitution. If the city-state cannot be entirely composed of good men, and yet each citizen is expected to do his own business well, and must therefore have virtue, still inasmuch as all the citizens cannot be alike, the virtue of the citizen and of the good man cannot coincide. All must have the virtue of the good citizen—thus, and thus only, can the city-state be perfect; but they will not have the virtue of a good man, unless we assume that in the good city-state all the citizens must be good.

Again, the city-state, as composed of unlikes, may be compared to the living being: as the first elements into which a living being is resolved are soul and body, as soul is made up of rational principle and appetite, the family of husband and wife, property of master and slave, so of all these, as well as other dissimilar elements, the city-state is composed; and, therefore, the virtue of all the citizens cannot possibly be the same, any more than the excellence of the leader of a chorus is the same as that of the performer who stands by his side. I have said enough to show why the two kinds of virtue cannot be absolutely and always the same.

But will there then be no case in which the virtue of the good citizen and the virtue of the good man coincide? To this we answer that the good ruler is a good and wise man, and that he who would be a city-statesman must be a wise man. And some persons say that even the education of the ruler should be of a special kind; for are not the children of kings instructed in riding and military exercises? As Euripides says: "No subtle arts for me, but what the city-state requires."

As though there were a special education needed by a ruler. If then the virtue of a good ruler is the same as that of a good man, and we assume further that the subject is a citizen as well as the ruler, the virtue of the good citizen and the virtue of the good man cannot be absolutely the same, although in some cases they may; for the virtue of a ruler differs from that of a citizen. It was the sense of this difference which made Jason say that 'he felt hungry when he was not a tyrant,' meaning that he could not endure to live in a private station. But, on the other hand, it may be argued that men are praised for knowing both how to rule and how to obey, and he is said to be a citizen of approved virtue who is able to do both. Now if we suppose the virtue of a good man to be that which rules, and the virtue of the citizen to include ruling and obeying, it cannot be said that they are equally worthy of praise. Since, then, it is sometimes thought that the ruler and the ruled must learn different things and not the same, but that the citizen must know and share in them both, the inference is obvious. There is, indeed, the rule of a master, which is concerned with menial offices—the master need not know how to perform these, but may employ others in the execution of them: the other would be degrading; and by the other I mean the power actually to do menial duties, which vary much in character and are executed by various classes of slaves, such, for example, as handicrafts-men, who, as their name signifies, live by the labor of their hands: under these the mechanic is included. Hence in ancient times, and among some nations, the working classes had no share in the government—a privilege which they only acquired under the extreme democracy. Certainly the good man and the city-statesman and the good citizen ought not to learn the crafts of inferiors except for their own occasional use; if they habitually practice them, there will cease to be a distinction between master and slave.

This is not the rule of which we are speaking; but there is a rule of another kind, which is exercised over freemen and equals by birth— a constitutional rule, which the ruler must learn by obeying, as he would learn the duties of a general of cavalry by being under the orders of a general of cavalry, or the duties of a general of infantry by being under the orders of a general of infantry, and by having had the command of a regiment and of a company. It has been well said that 'he who has never learned to obey cannot be a good commander.' The two are not the same, but the good citizen ought to be capable of both; he should know how to govern like a freeman, and how to obey like a freeman—these are the virtues of a citizen. And, although the temperance and justice of a ruler are distinct from those of a subject, the virtue of a good man will include both; for the virtue of the good man who is free and also a subject, e.g., his justice, will not be one but will comprise distinct kinds, the one qualifying him to rule, the other to obey, and differing as the temperance and courage of men and women differ. For a man would be thought a coward if he had no more courage than a courageous woman, and a woman would be thought loquacious if she imposed no more restraint on her conversation than the good man; and indeed their part in the management of the household is different, for the duty of the one is to acquire, and of the other to preserve. Practical wisdom only is characteristic of the ruler: it would seem that all other virtues must equally belong to ruler and subject. The virtue of the subject is certainly not wisdom, but only true opinion; he may be compared to the maker of the flute, while his master is like the flute-player or user of the flute.

From these considerations may be gathered the answer to the question, whether the virtue of the good man is the same as that of the good citizen, or different, and how far the same, and how far different.

CHAPTER 6

Having determined these questions, we have next to consider whether there is only one form of government or many, and if many, what they are, and how many, and what are the differences between them.

A constitution is the arrangement of magistracies in a city-state, especially of the highest of all. The government is everywhere sovereign in the city-state, and the constitution is in fact the government. For example, in democracies the people are supreme, but in oligarchies, the few; and, therefore, we say that these two forms of government also are different: and so in other cases.

First, let us consider what is the purpose of a city-state, and how many forms of government there are by which human society is regulated.

We have already said, in the first part of this treatise, when discussing household management and the rule of a master, that man is by nature a political animal. And therefore, men, even when they do not require one another's help, desire to live together; not but that they are also brought together by their common interests in proportion as they severally attain to any measure of well-being. This is certainly the chief end, both of individuals and of city-states. And also for the sake of mere life (in which there is possibly some noble element so long as the evils of existence do not greatly overbalance the good) mankind meet together and maintain the political community. And we all see that men cling to life even at the cost of enduring great misfortune, seeming to find in life a natural sweetness and happiness.

There is no difficulty in distinguishing the various kinds of authority; they have been often defined already in discussions outside the school. The rule of a master, although the slave by nature and the master by nature have in reality the same interests, is nevertheless exercised primarily with a view to the interest of the master, but accidentally considers the slave, since, if the slave perish, the rule of the master perishes with him. On the other hand, the government of a wife and children and of a household, which we have called household management, is exercised in the first instance for the good of the governed or for the common good of both parties, but essentially for the good of the governed, as we see to be the case in medicine, gymnastic, and the arts in general, which are only accidentally concerned with the good of the artists themselves. For there is no reason why the trainer may not sometimes practice gymnastics, and the helmsman is always one of the crew. The trainer or the helmsman considers the good of those committed to his care. But, when he is one of the persons taken care of, he accidentally participates in the advantage, for the helmsman is also a sailor, and the trainer becomes one of those in training. And so in politics: when the city-state is framed upon the principle of equality and likeness, the citizens think that they ought to hold office by turns. Formerly, as is natural, every one would take his turn of service; and then again, somebody else would look after his interest, just as he, while in office, had looked after theirs. But nowadays, for the sake of the advantage which is to be gained from the public revenues and from office, men want to be always in office. One might imagine that the rulers, being sickly, were only kept in health while they continued in office; in that case we may be sure that they would be hunting after places. The conclusion is evident: that governments which have a regard to the common interest are constituted in accordance with strict principles of justice, and are therefore true forms; but those which regard only the interest of the rulers are all defective and perverted forms, for they are despotic, whereas a city-state is a community of freemen.

Questions for Review and Discussion

1. Identify two major questions that Aristotle raises in the assigned reading selections from his *Politics*.

2. According to Aristotle, what is the criterion that determines if a polis (city-state) is the same or different?

3. According to Aristotle, is the goodness of man the same as the goodness of a citizen? Why or why not?

4. How does Aristotle define the goodness of a citizen?

5. How does Aristotle define the goodness of a man?

6. What, according to Aristotle, is the purpose of the polis (city-state)?

Augustine

Augustine (AD 354–AD 430) was a medieval Christian philosopher heavily influenced by Plato. While early Christians believed that the Holy Roman Empire was eternal and an instrument of divine providence, the sacking of Rome by the Visigoths in 410 shook such beliefs. Many Romans began to blame Christians for the city's decline. Augustine therefore reappraises the relationship between the city and Christianity. In this selection from *City of God*, Augustine reflects on the ancient Roman Cicero's understanding of the city as a republic, arguing that we must take his definition seriously if we are to understand the city and the cause of its decline. He defends Christians from blame for the fall of Rome, arguing that Rome was never a just republic in the first place. For Augustine, the justice of the city of man depends on the justice of the city of God. The reading deals with the nature of the city and issues of justice, and can be compared productively with Plato, Aristotle, Mumford, Young, Engels, and Light.

CITY OF GOD (426 AD)

Book II

CHAPTER 21

If our enemies scorn the author who said that the Roman republic was the "worst and the most disgraceful," and if they do not care about the great shame and degradation of the "worst and most disgraceful" morals that fill it, but care only that it stand firm and survive, then let them hear no more about how it became the worst and most disgraceful, as Sallust narrates. Instead, let them hear that, as Cicero argues,[1] the republic had already at that time utterly perished and no longer existed at all.

---

1. Cicero (106–43 B.C.): a Roman rhetorician, politician, and philosopher, famous for his eloquence and mastery of the Latini language. His works occupied a major position in Roman education in general and in Augustine's life in particular. In his *Confessions*, Augustine describes how reading Cicero's *Hortensius* inflamed him with a desire for wisdom (III. 4.7–8). In the present chapter Augustine relates the discussion of Cicero's dialogue entitled *The Republic*, only part of which is extant. See also Augustine's remarks on Cicero in III, 30.

Cicero brings forth Scipio, the destroyer of Carthage himself,[2] discussing the republic at a time when there was already foreboding that it was about to perish through the corruption described by Sallust. . . . At the end of the second book, Scipio says,

> Among lyres and flutes or singing voices, a certain harmony must be maintained out of the different sounds. Trained ears cannot bear false or discordant notes. This harmony, full of concord and agreement, is produced from the regulation of the most dissimilar voices. In the same way, the city, having been regulated by reason, harmonizes through a consensus of dissimilar elements from the upper, lower, and middle classes, just like musical notes. What the musicians call "harmony" in music, is "concord" in a city, a bond of preservation that is the tightest and the best of all in a republic, and in no way can it exist without justice.[3]

After Scipio discusses somewhat more broadly and fully how great an advantage justice is to a city and how great a disadvantage is its absence, Philus, one of those present at the discussion, wades in and demands that this question be treated more thoroughly and that more be said about justice on account of what was then commonly supposed, namely, that a republic cannot be ruled without injustice. Scipio accordingly agrees that this question must be discussed and explicated. He replies that he thinks there is nothing that has already been said about a republic that could serve as a basis for proceeding further, unless it can be firmly established not only that it is false that a republic cannot be ruled without injustice, but also that it is most true that a republic cannot be ruled without supreme justice.[4]

The explication of this question is put off until the following day, when it is argued out with great conflict in the third book. Philus himself takes up the cause of those who think that without injustice a republic cannot be governed. Above all else, he apologizes for doing so, in order

---

2. Scipio Africanus the Younger (c. 185–129 B.C.): a famous Roman general who captured the city of Carthage in 146 B.C., thereby ending the third and final Punic War. Cicero casts Scipio as one of the interlocutors in his dialogue, and it would seem that he speaks for Cicero himself in that conversation. This Scipio is not to be confused with Scipio Africanus the Greater, who defeated the great Cathaginian general Hannibal in 202 to bring about an end to the Second Punic War.

3. *Republic* II. 42.

4. *Republic* II. 44.

that it would not be believed that he himself actually held this position. He zealously pleads the cause of injustice against justice. Using arguments and examples resembling the truth, he undertakes to show that injustice is useful for a republic and justice useless.[5] Then Laelius, at the request of all the others, sets forth to defend justice and protects, to the extent that he is able, the position that nothing is so inimical to a city as injustice and that a republic cannot be governed or stand firm at all without a great deal of justice.[6]

After this question is treated to an extent that is viewed as sufficient, Scipio returns to the point where the discussion was interrupted. He repeats and recommends his brief definition of a republic, stating that a republic is "the affair of the people."[7] However, he defines a "people" to be not every fellowship of a multitude, but a "fellowship united through a consensus concerning right and a sharing of advantage." Next, he shows the great advantage of definition in argumentation, and from his own definitions he then concludes that a republic, i.e. the affair of a people, exists when a people is governed well and justly, whether it is by a single king, a few aristocrats, or the whole people. However, when a king is unjust, he calls him, according to the Greek usage, a tyrant; when the aristocrats are unjust, he says their fellowship is a faction; when the people itself is unjust, he finds no customary name for it, unless it would also be called tyranny. In these latter three cases, he does not show that such a republic is then corrupt, as he had argued on the previous day. Rather, reasoning from his definitions, he teaches that a republic does not exist at all, because there is no "affair of the people" when a tyrant or a faction seize it. Nor is the people then a people if it is unjust, because there is no multitude united through a consensus concerning right and a sharing of advantage, as "people" was defined.

Therefore, when the Roman republic was of the quality described by Sallust, it was not then "the worst and most disgraceful," as he had said, but it did not exist at all according to this line of reasoning, which this dialogue on the republic conducted among the great leaders of that age makes clear. Also, Cicero himself, speaking in his own name and not in the person of Scipio or anyone else, quotes a verse from the poet

---

5. *Republic* III. 5–20.

6. *Republic* III. 21–29.

7. *Republic* I. 25; III. 31. With this definition, Scipio puns on the word "republic," saying that the *res publica* (republic) is the *res populi* (the thing, affair, or property of the people). Perhaps the English word "commonwealth" more closely approximates Scipio's point: the commonwealth is the weal (or well-being) of the community. However, translating *res publica* as "commonwealth" would obscure the connection to the Roman republic of which Scipio (and Augustine) are speaking; moreover, the English word has lost much of its original force. Hence, *res publica* has been translated as "republic" throughout.

Ennius at the beginning of Book 5: "The Roman republic stands firm on the morals and men of yesteryear."[8] Cicero goes on to say,

> This verse, through both its brevity and truth, seems to me to be just like a statement from some oracle. If the city had not had such morals, the men could not have founded or preserved for so long a republic ruling so far and wide; nor could the morals have done so, if these men had not been leaders. Thus, before our time, the morality of the forefathers brought forth outstanding men, and superior men maintained the old morality and the ways of our ancestors. Our age, however, has received the republic like a remarkable painting which is fading with age, and not only has it neglected to restore its original colors, but it has not even bothered to preserve, so to speak, its shape and basic outlines. What remains from the ancient morals upon which Ennius said the Roman republic stands firm? We see that they have fallen into such oblivion that not only are they not practised, but they are not even known. What shall I say of the men of our time? The morals themselves perished because of a lack of men. Not only must we answer for such a crime, but we must, as it were, plead our case against a capital charge. We preserve the republic in word, but the thing itself we lost long ago, and this is due not to some accident, but to our own vices.

Indeed, Cicero was confessing these things long after the death of Africanus, whom he portrays in the argument in his books *On the Republic;*[9] nevertheless, this was still before the coming of Christ. If these views had been thought and stated while the Christian religion was growing strong, who among our enemies would not have been of the opinion that the Christians should be blamed for them? Why, then, did their gods not bother to prevent the ruin and loss of the republic that Cicero, long before Christ came in the flesh, so mournfully laments as lost? Those who praise that republic even for those "men and morals of yesteryear" must consider whether true justice flourished in it or whether perhaps even then it was something that did not live through morals but was depicted through colors. Cicero himself unwittingly expresses this when he commends the painting.

However, we will examine this elsewhere, if God is willing.[10] In the appropriate place, I will attempt to show that according to the definitions

---

8. Ennius (239–c. 269 B.C.) was an influential Latin poet, though little of his work is extant.

9. Scipio Africanus the Younger died in 129 B.C.; Cicero is thought to have begun the *Republic* in about 54 B.C.

10. See XIX. 21 and 24.

of Cicero concerning what a "republic" is and what a "people" is, which were succinctly set forth in the speeches of Scipio (and also confirmed by many statements either of Cicero's own or of other speakers who are portrayed in the same dialogue), the republic never existed because true justice was never present in it. According to more accepted definitions, however, a certain sort of republic did exist, and it was directed better by the earlier Romans than by the later ones. Nevertheless, true justice does not exist except in that republic whose founder and ruler is Christ— if it is admitted that it, too, may be called a "republic," since we cannot deny that it is "the affair of the people." Yet even if such a use of this name "republic," which is commonly used for other things and in other ways, is perhaps too far removed from normal usage, certainly there is true justice in that city of which the Sacred Scripture says, "Glorious things are said about you, O city of God" (Ps 87:3).

Book XIX

Chapter 21

It is at this place that I will explain, as briefly and clearly as I can, what in the second book of this work I promised that I would demonstrate; namely, that, according to the definition that Scipio uses in the *Republic* of Cicero, there never was a Roman republic.[11] He succinctly defines a "republic" as "the affair of a people." If this definition is true, there never was a Roman republic, because Rome never was the affair of a people, which is Scipio's definition of a republic.

The reason for this is that he defined "a people" as "a fellowship of a multitude united through a consensus concerning right and a sharing of advantage." What he calls "a consensus concerning right" he explains in the dialogue by making it clear that it is not possible for a republic to be managed without justice. Therefore, where there is no true justice, there can be no right. What is done by right is indeed done justly; what is done unjustly, however, cannot be done by right. The iniquitous institutions of human beings must not be said or thought to exist by right, because even those institutions say that right flows from the fountain of justice, and that what is customarily said by those who do not understand right correctly—i.e. that right is the advantage of the strongest—is false.[12]

---

11. See II. 21.

12. In Book I of Plato's *Republic*, Thrasymachus defines justice as "the advantage of the strongest."

Accordingly, where there is no true justice, there can be no fellow-ship of men united through a consensus concerning right, and therefore there can be no people according to the definition of Scipio or Cicero. Moreover, if there is no people, neither can there be an affair of a people, but only of some sort of a multitude which is not worthy of the name of "a people." Consequently, if a republic is "the affair of a people," and there is no people which is not "united by means of a consensus concern-ing right," and there is no right where there is no justice, without doubt it must be concluded that where there is no justice, there is no republic.

Furthermore, justice is that virtue which distributes to everyone his due. What sort of justice is it, then, that takes a man away from the true God and subjects him to unclean demons? Is *this* to distribute to each his due? Or, is he who takes the ground purchased by someone and gives it to another who has no right to it unjust, but he who takes himself away from the dominion of the God who made him and enslaves himself to malicious spirits just?

Certainly, the cause of justice against injustice is argued very ener-getically and forcefully in that very same book, *The Republic*. Earlier, the case of injustice against justice was considered and it was said that the republic could not stand firm or be managed except through injustice. It was set down as the most powerful part of the argument that it was unjust for men to serve other men as their masters, but that unless the imperial city to whom the great republic belongs follows such injustice it is not able to rule its provinces. The response from the side of justice was that this rule over the inhabitants of the provinces is just because servitude is advantageous for such men and is done for their benefit when it is done correctly—that is, when the license for wrongdoing is taken away from the wicked. Also, it was argued that they will be in a better condition as a result of having been subdued, because they were in a worse condition before being subdued.

In order to strengthen this reasoning, a famous example was stated as though it was borrowed from nature: "Why, then, does God rule man, the soul rule the body, the reason rule lust and the rest of the corrupt parts of the soul?"[13] Plainly, this example teaches well that servitude is advantageous to some and that serving God is indeed advantageous to all. In serving God, the soul correctly rules the body, and the reason in the soul subordinated to the Lord God correctly rules lust and the rest of the corrupt parts of the soul. Thus, when a man does not serve God, what in him can be reckoned to belong to justice? Indeed, when not serving God, the soul can in no way justly rule the body, or human

---

13. *Republic* III. 25.

reason the vices. Furthermore, if there is not any justice in such a man, without doubt neither is there any in a fellowship of human beings which consists of such men. Therefore, this is not that "consensus concerning right" which makes a multitude of human beings a "people," whose affair is called a "republic."

What shall I say concerning the "advantage," the sharing of which also unites a fellowship of men so that it is named "a people," as stipulated by the definition? If you carefully direct your attention, you will see that there is no advantage to any who live impiously, as do all who do not serve God but serve the demons who, the more impious they are, the more they want to receive sacrifice as gods, even though they are the most unclean spirits of all. Yet, what we have said about the consensus concerning right I think is sufficient to make it apparent that, according to this definition, there is no people which might be said to be a republic in which there is no justice.

If our enemies say that the Romans have not served unclean spirits but good and holy gods in their republic, must what we have already said sufficiently, indeed more than sufficiently, be repeated yet again? Who, except the excessively stupid or the shamelessly contentious, having arrived at this point after reading the earlier books of this work, finds it possible to doubt but that the Romans have up to this point served evil and impure demons? Nevertheless, in order to say no more about the sort of gods they are worshipping with sacrifices, I instead cite what is written in the law of the true God: "Anyone sacrificing to the gods, except only to the Lord, will be eradicated" (Ex 22:20). Thus, he who admonishes with such a threat did not want either good gods or evil ones to receive sacrifice.

CHAPTER 23

. . . We ourselves—his city—are the best and most radiant sacrifice. We celebrate this mystery through our offerings, which are known to the faithful, as we have argued in the preceding books.[14] Indeed, through the Hebrew prophets the divine oracles thundered that the offering of sacrificial victims by the Jews, a foreshadowing of the future, would cease, and that peoples from the rising of the sun to its setting would offer one sacrifice, as we see happening now.[15] From these oracles we have taken as much as seemed sufficient and have already sprinkled them throughout this work.

---

14. Augustine treats this especially well in X. 6, which is not included in this volume.

15. Augustine may have in mind Malachi 1:11.

Thus, justice exists when the one and supreme god rules his obedient city according to his grace, so that it does not sacrifice to any whatsoever except Him alone. As a result, in everyone belonging to that same city and obeying God, the soul faithfully commands the body, and reason the corrupt parts of the soul, in accord with the lawful order. Consequently, just like a single just man, a fellowship and a people of just men lives by faith, which works through love, by which man loves God as God ought to be loved, and his neighbor as himself. Where that justice does not exist, truly there is no "fellowship of men united through a consensus concerning right and a sharing of advantage." If this justice does not exist, then a people does not exist, if this is the true definition of a people. Therefore, neither does a republic exist, for there is no affair of a people where there is no people.

CHAPTER 24

If, however, a people is not defined in that way, but in another—if, for example, it is said that a people is "a fellowship of a multitude of rational beings united through sharing in an agreement about what it loves"— then truly, in order to see the character of a people, what it loves must be considered. If it is not a fellowship of a multitude of beasts, but of rational creatures, and is united through sharing in an agreement about what it loves, then, no matter what it loves, it is not unreasonable to call it "a people." It is a better people if it agrees in loving better things; a worse one if it agrees in loving worse things. According to this definition, the Roman people is a people, and its affair is without doubt a republic. However, history gives witness to what that people loved originally and subsequently, and by what morals it arrived at the bloodiest revolutions and then at social and civil wars, utterly shattering and annihilating concord itself, which is, in a certain sense, the well-being of a people. Of this we have said much in the preceding books. [. . .]

Questions for Review and Discussion

1. What metaphor of the city does Augustine approvingly cite from Cicero?

2. According to Augustine, what is Cicero's complete definition of a "republic"?

3. Why is such a definition crucial to Augustine's argument?

4. What reasons does Augustine give to defend Christians from blame for Rome's downfall?

Modern Readings (1500–1899)

Niccolò Machiavelli

Niccolò Machiavelli (1469–1527) is the last of the philosophers anthologized in this text who lived in a city-state rather than a modern
nation. A native of Florence, Italy, Machiavelli wrote *The Prince* to
impress the powerful ruling family of the Medici. Machiavelli argues
that the prince must maximize his skills and use those skills to capitalize on what luck (*fortuna*) brings him. Machiavelli defines the success of the prince in terms of what he ultimately accomplishes (hence
the term "Machiavellian," which means acting as if the ends justify
the means). In the passage selected here, Machiavelli advises the
prince on how cities that have been acquired or conquered should
be handled. Implicit in his discussion are assumptions about what
defines a city. In *The Discourses*, Machiavelli analyzes Livy's history
of ancient Rome. Machiavelli argues that we can learn much from
Rome about how to establish a good republican government. The
passage addresses the universal origins of cities and the specific
case of Rome. Although Machiavelli's work lends itself to multiple
interpretations, it has often been read by later thinkers as working in
stark contrast to the ideas of his contemporary Thomas More.
Machiavelli appears to reject political philosophy built on assumptions
about the good society and instead develops a model drawn on historical experience and assessment about "what works." These readings might be compared with Plato, Aristotle, Augustine, Hobbes, More,
Mumford, and Weber on the development and function of the city.

THE PRINCE (1512/1513)

CHAPTER V: CONCERNING THE WAY TO GOVERN CITIES OR PRINCIPALITIES
WHICH LIVED UNDER THEIR OWN LAWS BEFORE THEY WERE ANNEXED

Whenever those states which have been acquired as stated have been
accustomed to live under their own laws and in freedom, there are three
courses for those who wish to hold them: the first is to ruin them, the
next is to reside there in person, the third is to permit them to live under
their own laws, drawing a tribute, and establishing within it an oligarchy
which will keep it friendly to you. Because such a government, being
created by the prince, knows that it cannot stand without his friendship
and interest, and does its utmost to support him; and therefore he who
would keep a city accustomed to freedom will hold it more easily by the
means of its own citizens than in any other way.

There are, for example, the Spartans and the Romans. The Spartans held Athens and Thebes, establishing there an oligarchy, nevertheless they lost them. The Romans, in order to hold Capua, Carthage, and Numantia, dismantled them, and did not lose them. They wished to hold Greece as the Spartans held it, making it free and permitting its laws, and did not succeed. So to hold it they were compelled to dismantle many cities in the country, for in truth there is no safe way to retain them otherwise than by ruining them. And he who becomes master of a city accustomed to freedom and does not destroy it, may expect to be destroyed by it, for in rebellion it has always the watch-word of liberty and its ancient privileges as a rallying point, which neither time nor benefits will ever cause it to forget. And what ever you may do or provide against, they never forget that name or their privileges unless they are disunited or dispersed but at every chance they immediately rally to them, as Pisa after the hundred years she had been held in bondage by the Florentines.

But when cities or countries are accustomed to live under a prince, and his family is exterminated, they, being on the one hand accustomed to obey and on the other hand not having the old prince, cannot agree in making one from amongst themselves, and they do not know how to govern themselves. For this reason they are very slow to take up arms, and a prince can gain them to himself and secure them much more easily. But in republics there is more vitality, greater hatred, and more desire for vengeance, which will never permit them to allow the memory of their former liberty to rest; so that the safest way is to destroy them or to reside there.

DISCOURSES Upon The First Ten (Books) of Titus Livy (Book I, ch. 1) (1517)

Those who read what the beginning of the City of Rome was, and of her Law-givers and how it was organized, do not wonder that so much excellence had been maintained for so many centuries in that City, and that afterward there should have been born that Empire to which that Republic was joined.

And wanting first to discuss its origin, that all cities have been founded either by the people of the country in which they stand, or by foreigners. Cities have their origins in the former of these two ways when the inhabitants of a country find that they cannot live securely if they live dispersed in many and small societies, each of them unable, whether from its situation or its slender numbers, to stand alone against the attacks of its enemies; on whose approach there is no time left to unite for defense without abandoning many strongholds, and thus becoming an easy prey to the invader. To escape those dangers, whether of their own motion or at the instance of some of greater authority among them, they restrict themselves to dwell together in certain places, which they think will be more convenient to live in and easier to defend.

Among many cities taking their origin in this way were Athens and Venice; the former of which, for reasons like those just now mentioned, was built by a scattered population under the direction of Theseus. To escape the wars which were everyday arising in Italy because of the coming of new barbarians after the decline of the Roman Empire, numerous refugees, sheltering in certain little islands in a corner of the Adriatic Sea, gave beginning to Venice; where, without any recognized leader to direct them, they agreed to live together under such laws as they thought best suited to maintain them. And by reason of the prolonged tranquility which their position secured, they being protected by the narrow sea and by the circumstance that the tribes who then harassed Italy had no ships wherewith to molest them, they were able from very small beginnings to come to that greatness they now enjoy.

In the second case, namely of a city being founded by foreigners, the settlers are either wholly independent, or they are controlled by others, as where colonies are sent forth either by a prince or by a republic, to relieve their countries of an excessive population, or to defend newly acquired territories which it is sought to secure at small cost. Of this sort many cities were settled by the Romans, and in all parts of their dominions. It may also happen that such cities are founded by a prince merely to add to his renown, without any intention on his part to dwell there, as Alexandria was built by Alexander the Great. Cities like these, not having had their beginning in freedom, seldom make such progress as to rank among the chief towns of kingdoms.

The city of Florence belongs to that class of towns which has not been independent from the first; for whether we ascribe its origin to the soldiers of Sylla, or, as some have conjectured, to the mountaineers of Fiesole (who, emboldened by the long peace which prevailed throughout the world during the reign of Octavianus, came down to occupy the plain on the banks of the Arno), in either case, it was founded under the auspices of Rome and could not in the beginning have any other growth than what was permitted by the grace of the sovereign State.

The origin of cities may be said to be independent when a people, either by themselves or under some prince, are constrained by famine, pestilence, or war to leave their native land and seek a new habitation. Settlers of this sort either establish themselves in cities which they find ready to their hand in the countries of which they take possession, as did Moses; or they build new ones, as did Aeneas. It is in this last case that the merits of a founder and the good fortune of the city founded are best seen; and this good fortune will be more or less remarkable according to the greater or less capacity of him who gives the city its beginning.

The capacity of a city's founder is known in two ways: by his choice of a site and by the laws he frames. And since men act either of necessity or from choice, and merit may seem greater where choice is more restricted, we have to consider whether it may not be well to choose a sterile district as the site of a new city, in order that the inhabitants, being constrained to industry, and less corrupted by ease, may live in closer union, finding less cause for division in the poverty of their land; as was the case in Ragusa, and in many other cities built in similar situations. Such a choice would be certainly the wisest and the most advantageous, could men be content to enjoy what is their own without seeking to lord it over others. But since to be safe they must be strong, they are compelled to avoid these barren districts, and to plant themselves in more fertile regions; where, the fruitfulness of the soil enabling them to increase and multiply, they may defend themselves against any who attack them, and overthrow any who would withstand their power.

And as for that idleness which the situation might encourage, care must be had that hardships which the site does not enforce, shall be enforced by the laws; and that the example of those wise nations be imitated, who, inhabiting most fruitful and delightful countries, and such as were likely to rear a listless and effeminate race, unfit for all manly exercises, in order to obviate the mischief wrought by the amenity and relaxing influence of the soil and climate, subjected all who were to serve as soldiers to the severest training; whence it came that better soldiers were raised in these countries than in others by nature rugged and barren. Such, of old, was the kingdom of the Egyptians, which, though of all lands the most bountiful, yet, by the severe training which its laws enforced, produced most valiant soldiers, who, had their names not been lost in antiquity, might be thought to deserve more praise than Alexander the Great and many besides, whose memory is still fresh in men's minds. And even in recent times, any one contemplating the kingdom of the Soldan, and the military order of the Mamelukes before they were destroyed by Selim the Grand Turk, must have seen how carefully they trained their soldiers in every kind of warlike exercise; showing thereby how much they dreaded that indolence to which their genial soil and climate might have disposed them, unless neutralized by strenuous laws. I say, then, that it is a prudent choice to found your city in a fertile region when the effects of that fertility are duly balanced by the restraint of the laws.

When Alexander the Great thought to add to his renown by founding a city, Dinocrates the architect came and showed him how he might build it on Mount Athos, which offered not only a strong position, but

could be arranged in such a way that would give the city built there a
semblance of the human form, which would be a thing strange and striking, and worthy of so great a monarch. But on Alexander asking how the
inhabitants were to live, Dinocrates answered that he had not thought of
that. Whereupon, Alexander laughed, and leaving Mount Athos as it stood,
built Alexandria; where, the fruitfulness of the soil, and the vicinity of the
Nile and the sea, might attract many to take up their abode.

To him, therefore, who inquires into the origin of Rome, if he assign
its beginning to Aeneas, it will seem to be of those cities which were
founded by strangers if to Romulus, then of those founded by the natives
of the country. But in whichever class we place it, it will be seen to have
had its beginning in freedom, and not in subjection to another State. It
will be seen, too, as hereafter shall be noted, how strict was the discipline
which the laws instituted by Romulus, Numa, and its other founders made
compulsory upon it; so that neither its fertility, the proximity of the sea,
the number of its victories, nor the extent of its dominion, could for many
centuries corrupt it, but, on the contrary, maintained it replete with such
virtues as were never matched in any other commonwealth.

And because the things done by Rome, and which Titus Livius has
celebrated, were effected at home or abroad by public or by private
wisdom, I shall begin by treating, and noting the consequences of those
things done at home in accordance with the public voice, which seem
most to merit attention; and to this object the whole of this first Book
or first Part of my Discourses, shall be directed.

Questions for Review and Discussion

1. What, according to Machiavelli in *The Prince*, are the three
   options a prince might exercise in attempting to hold on to
   newly acquired cities?

2. Why does Machiavelli argue that the destruction of cities is
   often the best way to hold on to them?

3. In the *Discourses*, Machiavelli describes two origins for cities.
   What are they?

4. In the *Discourses*, Machiavelli notes that cities are "more or
   less remarkable," depending on how talented those who founded
   the cities are. On what two things can we judge the ability of the
   men who build cities?

5. In the *Discourses*, Machiavelli tells the story of how Alexander
   the Great chose the site for Alexandria. Summarize the story;
   what are we to learn from it?

St. Thomas More

St. Thomas More (1478–1535) lived during the transition from the medieval feudal societies in which the primary form of government was the city-state to the creation of modern nation-states. During his lifetime, he witnessed the discovery of the "new world," the publication of Machiavelli's *Prince*, and Luther's Reformation. More's *Utopia* describes a fictitious "perfect society," although interpretations differ on whether More actually believed that the cities he describes are ideal. *Utopia* set an example for philosophical utopian writings of the eighteenth and nineteenth centuries. The ideals presented in utopias provide either a point of departure for a critique of existing social political orders and/or offer the opportunity to imagine new pos ties. The selection that follows addresses economic, governance social arrangements of the cities. Residents of Utopia adhere system of relative equality among citizens, although More grants g privileges to the scholar-leaders and shifts burdensome work to s Readers might compare this reading to conceptions of ideal c Plato, Aristotle and Young and to the apparent rejection of i views by Machiavelli and Hobbes. Consider this reading also i of social justice issues raised by Addams, West, Bickford, E Light, and Hayek.

· *UTOPIA* (1516)

There are fifty-four cities in the island, all large and well built, the manners, customs, and laws of which are the same, and they are all contrived as near in the same manner as the ground on which they stand will allow. The nearest lie at least twenty-four miles' distance from one another, and the most remote are not so far distant but that a man can go on foot in one day from it to that which lies next it.

Every city sends three of its wisest Senators once a year to Amaurot, to consult about their common concerns; for that is the chief town of the island, being situated near the centre of it, so that it is the most convenient place for their assemblies. The jurisdiction of every city extends at least twenty miles: and where the towns lie wider, they have much more ground: no town desires to enlarge its bounds, for the people consider themselves rather as tenants than landlords.

[. . .] He that knows one of their towns knows them all, they are so like one another, except where the situation makes some difference. I shall therefore describe one of them; and none is so proper as Amaurot; for as none is more eminent, all the rest yielding in precedence to this,

because it is the seat of their Supreme Council, so there was none of
them better known to me, I having lived five years altogether in it.

It lies upon the side of a hill, or rather a rising ground: its figure
is almost square, for from the one side of it, which shoots up almost to
the top of the hill, it runs down in a descent for two miles to the river
Anider; but it is a little broader the other way that runs along by the
bank of that river. [. . .]

The town is compassed with a high and thick wall, in which there
are many towers and forts; there is also a broad and deep dry ditch, set
thick with thorns, cast round three sides of the town, and the river is
instead of a ditch on the fourth side. The streets are very convenient for
all carriage, and are well sheltered from the winds. Their buildings are
good, and are so uniform that a whole side of a street looks like one
house. The streets are twenty feet broad; there lie gardens behind all
their houses; these are large but enclosed with buildings that on all hands
face the streets; so that every house has both a door to the street, and
a back door to the garden. Their doors have all two leaves, which, as they
are easily opened, so they shut of their own accord; and there being no
property among them, every man may freely enter into any house whatsoever. At every ten years' end they shift their houses by lots.

They cultivate their gardens with great care, so that they have vines,
fruits, herbs, and flowers in them; and all is so well ordered, and so finely
kept, that I never saw gardens anywhere that were both so fruitful and
so beautiful as theirs. And this humor of ordering their gardens so well
is not only kept up by the pleasure they find in it, but also by an
emulation between the inhabitants of the several streets, who vie with
each other; and there is indeed nothing belonging to the whole town
that is both more useful and more pleasant. So that he who founded the
town seems to have taken care of nothing more than of their gardens;
for they say, the whole scheme of the town was designed at first by
Utopus, but he left all that belonged to the ornament and improvement
of it to be added by those that should come after him, that being too
much for one man to bring to perfection. [. . .]

[Now for their system of government.] Thirty families choose every
year a magistrate, who was anciently called the syphogrant, but is now
called the philarch; and over every ten syphogrants, with the families
subject to them, there is another magistrate, who was anciently called the
tranibor, but of late the archphilarch. All the syphogrants, who are in
number 200, choose the Prince out of a list of four, who are named by
the people of the four divisions of the city; but they take an oath before
they proceed to an election, that they will choose him whom they think
most fit for the office. They give their voices secretly, so that it is not

known for whom everyone gives his suffrage. The Prince is for life, unless he is removed upon suspicion of some design to enslave the people. The tranibors are new-chosen every year, but yet they are for the most part continued. All their other magistrates are only annual.

The tranibors meet every third day, and oftener if necessary, and consult with the prince, either concerning the affairs of the State in general or such private differences as may arise sometimes among the people; though that falls out but seldom. There are always two syphogrants called into the council-chamber, and these are changed every day. It is a fundamental rule of their government that no conclusion can be made in anything that relates to the public till it has been first debated three days in their Council. It is death for any to meet and consult concerning the State, unless it be either in their ordinary Council, or in the assembly of the whole body of the people.

These things have been so provided among them, that the prince and the tranibors may not conspire together to change the government and enslave the people; and therefore when anything of great importance is set on foot, it is sent to the syphogrants; who after they have communicated it to the families that belong to their divisions, and have considered it among themselves, make report to the Senate; and upon great occasions, the matter is referred to the Council of the whole island. One rule observed in their Council, is, never to debate a thing on the same day in which it is first proposed; for that is always referred to the next meeting, that so men may not rashly, and in the heat of discourse, engage themselves too soon, which might bias them so much, that instead of consulting the good of the public, they might rather study to support their first opinions, and by a perverse and preposterous sort of shame, hazard their country rather than endanger their own reputation, or venture the being suspected to have wanted foresight in the expedients that they at first proposed. And therefore to prevent this, they take care that they may rather be deliberate than sudden in their motions.

Let us now discuss their work and living conditions. Agriculture is that which is so universally understood among them that no person, either man or woman, is ignorant of it; they are instructed in it from their childhood, partly by what they learn at school and partly by practice; they being led out often into the fields, about the town, where they not only see others at work, but are likewise exercised in it themselves. Besides agriculture, which is so common to them all, every man [and woman] has some peculiar trade to which he applies himself, such as the manufacture of wool, or flax, masonry, smith's work, or carpenter's work; for there is no sort of trade that is not in great esteem among them.

Throughout the island they wear the same sort of clothes without
any other distinction, except what is necessary to distinguish the two
sexes, and the married and unmarried. The fashion never alters; and as
it is neither disagreeable nor uneasy, so it is suited to the climate, and
calculated both for their summers and winters. Every family makes their
own clothes; but all among them, women as well as men, learn one or
other of the trades formerly mentioned. Women, for the most part, deal
in wool and flax, which suit best with their weakness, leaving the ruder
trades to the men.

The same trade generally passes down from father to son, inclinations often following descent; but if any man's genius lies another way,
he is by adoption translated into a family that deals in the trade to which
he is inclined: and when that is to be done, care is taken not only by his
father, but by the magistrate, that he may be put to a discreet and good
man. And if after a person has learned one trade, he desires to acquire
another, that is also allowed, and is managed in the same manner as the
former. When he has learned both, he follows that which he likes best,
unless the public has more occasion for the other.

The chief, and almost the only business of the syphogrants, is to
take care that no man may live idle, but that every one may follow his
trade diligently: yet they do not wear themselves out with perpetual toil,
from morning to night, as if they were beasts of burden, which, as it is
indeed a heavy slavery, so it is everywhere the common course of life
among all mechanics except the Utopians; but they dividing the day and
night into twenty-four hours, appoint six of these for work; three of
which are before dinner, and three after. They then sup, and at eight
o'clock, counting from noon, go to bed and sleep eight hours. The rest
of their time besides that taken up in work, eating and sleeping, is left
to every man's discretion; yet they are not to abuse that interval to
luxury and idleness, but must employ it in some proper exercise according to their various inclinations, which is for the most part reading. It is
ordinary to have public lectures every morning before daybreak; at which
none are obliged to appear but those who are marked out for literature;
yet a great many, both men and women of all ranks, go to hear lectures
of one sort of other, according to their inclinations. But if others, that
are not made for contemplation, choose rather to employ themselves at
that time in their trades, as many of them do, they are not hindered, but
are rather commended, as men that take care to serve their country.

After supper, they spend an hour in some diversion, in summer in
their gardens, and in winter in the halls where they eat; where they
entertain each other, either with music or discourse. They do not so
much as know dice, or any such foolish and mischievous games: they

have, however, two sorts of games not unlike our chess; the one is between several numbers, [. . .] the other resembles a battle between the virtues and the vices [. . .] But the time appointed for labor is to be narrowly examined, otherwise you may imagine, that since there are only six hours appointed for work, they may fall under a scarcity of necessary provisions. But it is so far from being true, that this time is not sufficient for supplying them with plenty of all things, either necessary or convenient, that it is rather too much; and this you will easily apprehend, if you consider how great a part of all other nations is quite idle.

First, women generally do little, who are the half of mankind; and if some few women are diligent, their husbands are idle: then consider the great company of idle priests, and of those that are called religious men; add to these all rich men, chiefly those that have estates in land, who are called noblemen and gentlemen, together with their families, made up of idle persons, that are kept more for show than use; add to these, all those strong and lusty beggars, that go about pretending some disease, in excuse for their begging; and upon the whole account you will find that the number of those by whose labors mankind is supplied, is much less than you perhaps imagined. Then consider how few of those that work are employed in labors that are of real service; for we who measure all things by money, give rise to many trades that are both vain and superfluous, and serve only to support riot and luxury. For if those who work were employed only in such things as the conveniences of life require, there would be such an abundance of them that the prices of them would so sink that tradesmen could not be maintained by their gains; if all those who labor about useless things were set to more profitable employments, and if all they that languish out their lives in sloth and idleness, every one of whom consumes as much as any two of the men that are at work, were forced to labor, you may easily imagine that a small proportion of time would serve for doing all that is either necessary, profitable, or pleasant to mankind, especially while pleasure is kept within its due bounds.

This appears very plainly in Utopia, for there, in a great city, and in all the territory that lies round it, you can scarce find 500, either men or women, by their age and strength, who are capable of labor, that are not engaged in it; even the syphogrants, though excused by the law, yet do not excuse themselves, but work, that by their examples they may excite the industry of the rest of the people. The like exemption is allowed to those who, being recommended to the people by the priests, are by the secret suffrages of the syphogrants privileged from labor, that they may apply themselves wholly to study; and if any of these fall short of those hopes that they seemed at first to give, they are obliged to return to work. And sometimes a mechanic, that so employs his leisure hours, as to make a considerable advancement in learning, is eased from being a tradesman, and ranked among their learned men. Out of these they choose their ambassadors, their priests, their tranibors, and the prince himself, anciently called their Barzenes, but is called of late their Ademus.

And thus from the great numbers among them that are neither suffered to be idle, nor to be employed in any fruitless labor, you may easily make the estimate how much may be done in those few hours in which they are obliged to labor. But besides all that has been already said, it is to be considered that the needful arts among them are managed with less labor than anywhere else.

But it is now time to explain to you the mutual intercourse of this people, their commerce, and the rules by which all things are distributed among them.

As their cities are composed of families, so their families are made up of those that are nearly related to one another. Their women, when they grow up, are married out; but all the males, both children and grandchildren, live still in the same house, in great obedience to their common parent, unless age has weakened his understanding: and in that case, he that is next to him in age comes in his room. But lest any city should become either too great, or by any accident be dispeopled, provision is made that none of their cities may contain above 6,000 families, besides those of the country round it. No family may have less than ten and more than sixteen persons in it; but there can be no determined number for the children under age. This rule is easily observed, by removing some of the children of a more fruitful couple to any other family that does not abound so much in them.

By the same rule, they supply cities that do not increase so fast, from others that breed faster; and if there is any increase over the whole island, then they draw out a number of their citizens out of the several towns, and send them over to the neighboring continent; where, if they find that the inhabitants have more soil than they can well cultivate, they fix a colony, taking the inhabitants into their society, if they are willing to live with them; and where they do that of their own accord, they quickly enter into their method of life, and conform to their rules, and this proves a happiness to both nations; for according to their constitution, such care is taken of the soil that it becomes fruitful enough for both, though it might be otherwise too narrow and barren for any one of them. But if the natives refuse to conform themselves to their laws, they drive them out of those bounds which they mark out for themselves, and use force if they resist. For they account it a very just cause of war, for a nation to hinder others from possessing a part of that soil of which they make no use, but which is suffered to lie idle and uncultivated; since every man has by the law of nature a right to such a waste portion of the earth as is necessary for his subsistence. If an accident has so lessened the number of the inhabitants of any of their towns that it cannot be made up from the other towns of the island, without diminishing them too much, which is said to have fallen out but twice since they were first a people, when great numbers were carried off by the plague, the loss is then supplied by recalling as many as are wanted from their colonies; for they will abandon these, rather than suffer the towns in the island to sink too low.

But to return to their manner of living in society, the oldest man of every family, as has been already said, is its governor. Wives serve their husbands, and children their parents, and always the younger serves the elder. Every city is divided into four equal parts, and in the middle of each there is a marketplace: what is brought thither, and manufactured by the several families, is carried from thence to houses appointed for that purpose, in which all things of a sort are laid by themselves; and thither every father goes and takes whatsoever he or his family stand in need of, without either paying for it or leaving anything in exchange. There is no reason for giving a denial to any person, since there is such plenty of everything among them; and there is no danger of a man's asking for more than he needs; they have no inducements to do this, since they are sure that they shall always be supplied. It is the fear of want that makes any of the whole race of animals either greedy or ravenous; but besides fear, there is in man a pride that makes him fancy it a particular glory to excel others in pomp and excess. But by the laws of the Utopians, there is no room for this. Near these markets there are others for all sorts of provisions, where there are not only herbs, fruits, and bread, but also fish, fowl, and cattle.

There are also, without their towns, places appointed near some running water, for killing their beasts, and for washing away their filth, which is done by their slaves: for they suffer none of their citizens to kill their cattle, because they think that pity and good-nature, which are among the best of those affections that are born with us, are much impaired by the butchering of animals: nor do they suffer anything that is foul or unclean to be brought within their towns, lest the air should be infected by ill-smells which might prejudice their health. In every street there are great halls that lie at an equal distance from each other, distinguished by particular names. The syphogrants dwell in those that are set over thirty families, fifteen lying on one side of it, and as many on the other. In these halls they all meet and have their repasts. The stewards of every one of them come to the market-place at an appointed hour; and according to the number of those that belong to the hall, they carry home provisions. But they take more care of their sick than of any others: these are lodged and provided for in public hospitals they have belonging to every town four hospitals, that are built without their walls, and are so large that they may pass for little towns: by this means, if they had ever such a number of sick persons, they could lodge them conveniently, and at such a distance, that such of them as are sick of infectious diseases may be kept so far from the rest that there can be no danger of contagion. The hospitals are furnished and stored with all things that are convenient for the ease and recovery of the sick; and those that are put in them are looked after with such tender and watchful care, and are so constantly attended by their skillful physicians, that as none is sent to them against their will, so there is scarce one in a whole town that, if he should fall ill, would not choose rather to go thither than lie sick at home.

After the steward of the hospitals has taken for the sick whatsoever the physician prescribes, then the best things that are left in the market are distributed equally among the halls, in proportion to their numbers, only, in the first place, they serve the Prince, the chief priest, the tranibors, the ambassadors, and strangers, if there are any, which indeed falls out but seldom, and for whom there are houses well furnished, particularly appointed for their reception when they come among them. At the hours of dinner and supper, the whole syphogranty being called together by sound of trumpet, they meet and eat together, except only such as are in the hospitals or lie sick at home. Yet after the halls are served, no man is hindered to carry provisions home from the market-place; for they know that none does that but for some good reason; for though any that will may eat at home, yet none does it willingly, since it is both ridiculous and foolish for any to give themselves the trouble to make ready an ill dinner at home, when there is a much more plentiful one made ready for him so near at hand. All the uneasy and sordid services about these halls are performed by their slaves; but the dressing and cooking their meat, and the ordering their tables, belong only to the women, all those of every family taking it by turns. They sit at three or more tables, according to their number; the men sit toward the wall, and the women sit on the other side, that if any of them should be taken suddenly ill, which is no uncommon case among women with child, she may, without disturbing the rest, rise and go to the nurses' room, who are there with the sucking children, where there is always clean water at hand, and cradles in which they may lay the young children, if there is occasion for it, and a fire that they may shift and dress them before it.

Every child is nursed by its own mother, if death or sickness does not intervene; and in that case the syphogrants' wives find out a nurse quickly, which is no hard matter; for anyone that can do it offers herself cheerfully; for as they are much inclined to that piece of mercy, so the child whom the nurse considers the nurse as its mother. All the children under five years old sit among the nurses, the rest of the younger sort of both sexes, till they are fit for marriage, either serve those that sit at table or, if they are not strong enough for that, stand by them in great silence, and eat what is given them; nor have they any other formality of dining. In the middle of the first table, which stands across the upper end of the hall, sit the syphogrant and his wife; for that is the chief and most conspicuous place: next to him sit two of the most ancient, for there go always four to a mess. If there is a temple within that syphogranty, the priest and his wife sit with the syphogrant above all the rest: next them there is a mixture of old and young, who are so placed, that as the young are set near others, so they are mixed with the more ancient; which they say was appointed on this account, that the gravity of the old people, and the reverence that is due to them, might restrain the younger from all indecent words and gestures. Dishes are not served up to the whole table at first, but the best are first set before the old, whose seats are distinguished from the young, and after them all the rest are served alike. The old men distribute to the younger any curious meats that happen to be set before them, if there is not such an abundance of them that the whole company may be served alike.

Thus old men are honored with a particular respect; yet all the rest fare as well as they. Both dinner and supper are begun with some lecture of morality that is read to them; but it is so short, that it is not tedious nor uneasy to them to hear it: from hence the old men take occasion to entertain those about them with some useful and pleasant enlargements; but they do not engross the whole discourse so to themselves, during their meals, that the younger may not put in for a share: on the contrary, they engage them to talk, that so they may in that free way of conversation find out the force of everyone's spirit and observe his temper. They despatch their dinners quickly, but sit long at supper; because they go to work after the one, and are to sleep after the other, during which they think the stomach carries on the concoction more vigorously. They never sup without music; and there is always fruit served up after meat; while they are at table, some burn perfumes and sprinkle about fragrant ointments and sweet waters: in short, they want nothing that may cheer up their spirits: they give themselves a large allowance that way, and indulge themselves in all such pleasures as are attended with no inconvenience.

[. . .] [T]he slaves among them are only such as are condemned to that state of life for the commission of some crime, or, which is more common, such as their merchants find condemned to die in those parts to which they trade, whom they sometimes redeem at low rates; and in other places have them for nothing. They are kept at perpetual labor, and are always chained, but with this difference, that their own natives are treated much worse than others; they are considered as more profligate than the rest, and since they could not be restrained by the advantages of so excellent an education, are judged worthy of harder usage.

[. . .] As they fright men from committing crimes by punishments, so they invite them to the love of virtue by public honors: therefore they erect statues to the memories of such worthy men as have deserved well of their country, and set these in their market-places, both to perpetuate the remembrance of their actions, and to be an incitement to their posterity to follow their example.

If any man aspires to any office, he is sure never to compass it: they all live easily together, for none of the magistrates are either insolent or cruel to the people: they affect rather to be called fathers, and by being really so, they well deserve the name; and the people pay them all the marks of honor the more freely, because none are exacted from them. The Prince himself has no distinction, either of garments or of a crown; but is only distinguished by a sheaf of corn carried before him; as the high-priest is also known by his being preceded by a person carrying a wax light.

They have but few laws, and such is their constitution that they need not many. They very much condemn other nations, whose laws, together with the commentaries on them, swell up to so many volumes; for they think it an unreasonable thing to oblige men to obey a body of laws that are both of such a bulk and so dark as not to be read and understood by every one of the subjects.

Questions for Review and Discussion

1. Describe the work and economic organization of Utopia.

2. Describe the political/governance arrangements of the cities.

3. Describe the social and familial arrangements of the cities.

4. What is the rationale for treating most people the same?

5. Do you think that More's city is a utopia? Which of More's proposals reflect your concept of urban ideals? Which city ideals (if any) do you think More's city lacks?

Thomas Hobbes

Hobbes (1558–1679) was a political philosopher who lived during a time of great political strife in England. As cities were joined to form nation-states and feudal traditions were overthrown, Hobbes became focused on the question of how to conceptualize the relationship between the government and the individual citizen. Hobbes developed a social contract theory to explain how government is legitimized in the absence of traditional authority. Hobbes believed that the state of nature, that is, the conditions for individuals living without civil authority, is "nasty, brutish, and short." He therefore argues that as a matter of survival it is rational for individual citizens to sign over their power to an absolute monarch who can uphold order and protect them. The first selection from Hobbes raises the same issues discussed in the previous passage by Machiavelli, namely, how cities got started. Hobbes then moves on to discuss power, civil laws, and the functions of cities. These readings might be compared with Plato, Aristotle, Machiavelli, More, and Weber on the development and function of the city. See also Grosz on Hobbes's use of the metaphor of the body politic.

EXCERPTS FROM *DE CIVE* (1642)

CHAPTER V. OF THE CAUSES, AND FIRST BEGINNING OF CIVIL GOVERNMENT
SEC. 7–12

7. This submission of the wills of all those men to the will of one man, or one council, is then made, when each one of them obliges himself by contract to every one of the rest, not to resist the will of that one man, or council, to which he hath submitted himself; that is, that he refuse him not the use of his wealth, and strength, against any others whatsoever (for he is supposed still to retain a right of defending himself against violence) and this is called UNION. But we understand that to be the will of the council, which is the will of the major part of those men of whom the council consists.

8. But though the will itself be not voluntary, but only the beginning of voluntary actions (for we will not to will, but to act) and therefore falls least of all under deliberation, and compact; yet he who submits his will to the will of another, conveys to that other the right of his strength and faculties. Insomuch as when the rest have done the same, he to whom they have submitted hath so much power, as by the terror of it he can conform the wills of particular men unto unity, and concord.

9. Now union thus made is called a city, or civil society, and also a civil person. For when there is one will of all men, it is to be esteemed for one person, and by the word (one) it is to be known, and distinguished from all particular men, as having its own rights and properties. Insomuch as neither any one citizen, nor all of them together (if we except him, whose will stands for the will of all) is to be accounted the city. A CITY therefore (that we may define it) is one person, whose will, by the compact of many men, is to be received for the will of them all; so as he may use all the power and faculties of each particular person, to the maintenance of peace, and for common defense.

10. But although every city be a civil person, yet every civil person is not a city; for it may happen that many citizens, by the permission of the city, may join together in one person, for the doing of certain things. These now will be civil persons, as the companies of merchants, and many other convents; but cities they are not, because they have not submitted themselves to the will of the company simply, and in all things, but in certain things only determined by the city; and on such terms as it is lawful for any one of them to contend in judgment against the body itself of the sodality; which is by no means allowable to a citizen against the city. Such like societies therefore are civil Persons subordinate to the city.

11. In every city, that man, or council, to whose will each particular man hath subjected his will (so as hath been declared) is said to have the SUPREME POWER, or CHIEF COMMAND, or DOMINION; which power, and right of commanding, consists in this, that each citizen hath conveyed all his strength and power to that man, or council; which to have done (because no man can transfer his power in a natural manner) is nothing else than to have parted with his right of resisting. Each citizen, as also every subordinate civil person, is called the SUBJECT of him who hath the chief command.

12. By what hath been said, it is sufficiently shown, in what manner, and by what degrees many natural persons, through desire of preserving themselves, and by mutual fear, have grown together into a civil person, whom we have called a city. But they who submit themselves to another for fear, either submit to him whom they fear, or some other whom they confide in for protection; They act according to the first manner who are vanquished in war, that they may not be slain; they according to the second, who are not yet overcome, that they may not be overcome. The first manner receives its beginning from natural power, and may be called the natural beginning of a city; the latter from the council, and constitution of those who meet together, which is a beginning by institution. Hence it is, that there are two kinds of cities, the one

natural, such as is the paternal, and despotic; the other institutive, which may be also called political. In the first the lord acquires to himself such citizens as he will; in the other the citizens by their own wills appoint a lord over themselves, whether he be one man, or one company of men endued with the command in chief. But we will speak in the first place of a city political or by institution, and next of a city natural.

CHAPTER VI. OF THE RIGHT OF HIM, WHETHER COUNCIL, OR ONE MAN ONLY, WHO HATH THE SUPREME POWER IN THE CITY, SEC. 1, 9, 15, 18–20

1. We must consider first of all what a multitude of men (gathering themselves of their own free wills into society) is, namely, that it is not any one body, but many men, whereof each one hath his own will, and his peculiar judgment concerning all things that may be proposed. And though by particular contracts each single man may have his own right, and propriety, so as one may say *This is mine*, the other, *That is his*; yet will there not be any thing of which the whole multitude, as a person distinct from a single man, can rightly say, This is *mine*, more than another's. Neither must we ascribe any action to the multitude, as it's one, but (if all, or more of them do agree) it will not be an action, but as many actions, as men. For although in some great sedition, it is commonly said, that the people of that city have taken up arms; yet is it true of those only who are in arms, or who consent to them. For the city, which is one person, cannot take up arms against itself. Whatsoever therefore is done by the multitude, must be understood to be done by every one of those by whom it is made up; and that he, who being in the multitude, and yet consented not, nor gave any helps to the things that were done by it, must be judged to have done nothing. Besides, in a multitude not yet reduced into one person, in that manner as hath been said, there remains that same state of nature in which all things belong to all men and there is no place for *Meum* & *Tuum*, which is called Dominion, and Propriety, by reason that that security is not yet extant which we have declared above to be necessarily requisite for the practice of the Natural Laws.

9. Furthermore, since it no less, nay it much more conduceth to peace to prevent brawls from arising, than to appease them being risen; and that all controversies are bred from hence, that the opinions of men differ concerning Meum & Tuum, just and unjust, profitable and unprofitable, good and evil, honest and dishonest, and the like, which every man esteems according to his own judgment; it belongs to the same chief power to make some common Rules for all men, and to declare them publicly, by which every man may know what may be called

his, what another's, what just, what unjust, what honest, what dishonest, what good, what evil, that is summarily, what is to be done, what to be avoided in our common course of life. But those rules and measures are usually called the civil laws, or the laws of the city, as being the commands of him who hath the supreme power in the city. And the CIVIL LAWS (that we may define them) are nothing else but the commands of him who hath the chief authority in the city, for direction of the future actions of his citizens.

15. Now because (as hath been shown above) before the constitution of a city all things belonged to all men, nor is there that thing which any man can so call his, as any other may not, by the same right, claim as his own, (for where all things are *common*, there can be nothing *proper* to any man) it follows, that *propriety* received its beginning when cities received theirs, and that that only is *proper* to each man which he can keep by the laws, and the power of the whole city, (that is) of him on whom its chief command is conferred. Whence we understand, that each particular citizen hath a *propriety*, to which none of his fellow-citizens hath right, because they are tied to the same laws; but he hath no propriety in which the chief ruler (whose commands are the laws, whose will contains the will of each man, and who, by every single person, is constituted the supreme judge) hath not a right. But although there be many things which the city permits to its citizens, and therefore they may sometimes go to law against their chief; yet is not that action belonging to civil right, but to natural equity; neither is it concerning what by right he may do who hath the supreme power, but what he hath been willing should be done, and therefore he shall be judge himself, as though (the equity of the cause being well understood) he could not give wrong judgment.

18. It is therefore manifest, that in every city there is some one man, or council, or court, who by right hath as great a power over each single citizen, as each man hath over himself considered out of that civil state, that is, supreme and absolute, to be limited only by the strength and forces of the city itself, and by nothing else in the world: for if his power were limited, that limitation must necessarily proceed from some greater power; For he that prescribes limits, must have a greater power than he who is confined by them; now that confining power is either without limit, or is again restrained by some other greater than itself, and so we shall at length arrive to a power which hath no other limit, but that which is the *terminus ultimus* of the forces of all the citizens together. That same is called the supreme command, and if it be committed to a council, a supreme council, but if to one man, the supreme lord of the city. Now the notes of supreme command are these, to make and

abrogate laws. To determine war and peace, to know, and judge of all controversies, either by himself, or by judges appointed by him; to elect all magistrates; ministers, and councilors. Lastly, if there be any man who by right can do someone action which is not lawful for any citizen or citizens to do beside himself, that man hath obtained the supreme power: For those things which by Right may not be done by any one or many citizens, the city itself can only do: He therefore that doth those things useth the city's right, which is the supreme power.

19. They who compare a city and its citizens, with a man and his members, almost all say, that he who hath the supreme power in the city, is in relation to the whole city, such as the head is to the whole man; But it appears by what hath been already said, that he who is endued with such a power, (whether it be a man, or a court) hath a relation to the city, not as that of the head, but of the soul to the body. For it is the soul by which a man hath a will, that is, can either will, or nil; so by him who hath the supreme power, and no otherwise, the city hath a will, and can either will or nil. A court of counsellors is rather to be compared with the head, or one counsellor, whose only counsel (if of any one alone) the chief ruler makes use of in matters of greatest moment: for the office of the head is to counsel, as the soul's is to command.

20. For as much as the supreme command is constituted by virtue of the compacts which each single citizen, or subject, mutually makes with the other; but all contracts, as they receive their force from the contractors, so by their consent they lose it again, and are broken; perhaps some may infer hence, that by the consent of all the subjects together, the supreme authority may be wholly taken away. Which inference if it were true, I cannot discern what danger would thence by right arise to the supreme commanders. For since it is supposed, that each one hath obliged himself to each other, if any one of them shall refuse, whatsoever the rest shall agree to do, he is bound notwithstanding; neither can any man without injury to me, doe that which by contract made with me, he hath obliged himself not to doe. But it is not to be imagined that ever it will happen, that all the subjects together, not so much as one excepted, will combine against the supreme power; wherefore there is no fear for rulers in chief, that by any right they can be despoiled of their authority. If notwithstanding it were granted, that their right depended only on that contract which each man makes with his fellow-citizen, it might very easily happen, that they might be robbed of that dominion under pretence of right; for subjects being called either by the command of the city, or seditiously flocking together, most men think that the consents of all are contained in the votes of the greater part. Which in

truth is false; for it is not from nature that the consent of the major part should be received for the consent of all, neither is it true in tumults, but it proceeds from civil institution, and is then only true, when that man or court which hath the supreme power, assembling his subjects, by reason of the greatness of their number, allows those that are elected a power of speaking for those who elected them, and will have the major part of voices, in such matters as are by him propounded to be discussed, to be as effectual as the whole. But we cannot imagine that he who is chief, ever convened his subjects with intention that they should dispute his right, unless, weary of the burden of his charge, he declared in plain terms, that he renounces and abandons his government. Now because most men through ignorance esteem not the consent of the major part of citizens only, but even of a very few, provided they be of their opinion, for the consent of the whole city, it may very well seem to them, that the supreme authority may by right be abrogated, so it be done in some great assembly of citizens by the votes of the greater number; But though a government be constituted by the contracts of particular men with particulars, yet its right depends not on that obligation only; there is another tie also toward him who commands; for each citizen compacting with his fellow, says thus, *I convey my right on this party, upon condition, that you pass yours to the same*; by which means, that right which every man had before to use his faculties to his own advantage, is now wholly translated on some certain man, or council, for the common benefit; wherefore what by the mutual contracts each one hath made with the other, what by the donation of right which every man is bound to ratify to him that commands, the government is upheld by a double obligation from the citizens, first that which is due to their fellow citizens, next that which they owe to their prince. Wherefore no subjects how many soever they be, can with any Right despoil him who bears the chief rule, of his authority, even without his own consent.

CHAPTER X. A COMPARISON BETWEEN THREE KINDS OF GOVERNMENT, ACCORDING TO THEIR SEVERAL INCONVENIENCES, SEC. 1

1. What *democracy*, *aristocracy*, and *monarchy* are, hath already been spoken, but which of them tends most to the preservation of the subject's peace, and procuring their advantages, we must see by comparing them together. But first let us set forth the advantages, and disadvantages of a city in general, lest some perhaps should think it better, that every man be left to live at his own will, than to constitute any civil society at all. Every man indeed out of the state of civil government hath a most

entire, but unfruitful liberty; because that he who by reason of his own liberty acts all at his own will, must also by reason of the same liberty in others, suffer all at another's will; but in a constituted city, every subject retains to himself as much freedom as suffices him to live well, and quietly, & there is so much taken away from others, as may make them not to be feared. Out of this state, every man hath such a right to all, as yet he can enjoy nothing; in it, each one securely enjoys his limited right; out of it, any man may rightly spoil, or kill one another; in it, none but one. Out of it we are protected by our own forces; in it, by the power of all. Out of it no man is sure of the fruit of his labors; in it, all men are. Lastly, out of it, there is a dominion of passions, war, fear, poverty, slovenliness, solitude, barbarism, ignorance, cruelty. In it, the dominion of reason, peace, security, riches, decency, society, elegancy, sciences, and benevolence.

Questions for Review and Discussion

1. How does Hobbes define the city?

2. How does Hobbes define "citizen"?

3. According to Hobbes, what motivates people to join together by contract to form a city?

4. What powers does the supreme power of the city (whether it be ruler or rulers) have?

5. According to Hobbes, what is the difference between the state of nature and the city in regard to property?

Jean-Jacques Rousseau

Jean Jacques Rousseau (1712–1778) was born in the city-state of Geneva (now in Switzerland). Rousseau wrote a wide range of works, especially in political philosophy and philosophy of education, and developed a more democratic social contract theory than that of Hobbes. Although he left Geneva as a young man to escape apprenticeship as an engraver and pursue an intellectual career, he was disappointed with his adopted home of Paris, which he thought was corrupt. Many of Rousseau's political ideals are based on his imaginings of Geneva. In this passage, Rousseau argues that theaters corrupt the morals of citizens in ideal cities (such as Geneva). His letter therefore posits an ideal of the city as pastoral. The essay addresses ideals of citizenship, and may be effectively compared with Pericles, Plato, Hobbes, West, Bickford, Gooding-Williams, and Kemmis. Rousseau also raises questions about the relationship between rural and urban life and can be compared to Jefferson, Simmel, and Light.

THE LETTER TO M. D'ALEMBERT
ON THE THEATER (1758)*

I hasten to turn to a discussion that is less grave and less serious but which is still of enough concern to us to merit our reflection and which I enter into more willingly as it is somewhat more within my competence. It is that of the project to establish a theatre for the drama at Geneva. I shall not expound here my conjectures about the motives which might have brought you to propose an establishment so contrary to our maxims. Whatever your reasons, I have here to do only with ours; and all that I shall permit myself to say with respect to you is that you will surely be the first philosopher** who ever encouraged a free people, a small city, and a poor state to burden itself with a public theatre.[2]

---

*Reprinted with the permission of The Free Press, a Division of Simon and Schuster Adult Publishing Group, from POLITICS AND THE ARTS: Letter to M. d'Alembert on the Theater by Jean Jacques Rousseau, translated by Allan D. Bloom. Copyright © 1960 by The Free Press. Copyright © renewed 1988 by The Free Press. All rights reserved.

**Of two famous historians, both philosophers, both dear to M. d'Alembert, the modern[1] would be of his opinion, perhaps; but Tacitus, whom he loves, about whom he meditates, whom he deigns to translate, the grave Tacitus, whom he quotes so willingly, and whom he sometimes imitates so well except for his obscurity, would he have agreed?

How many questions I find to discuss in what you appear to have settled! Whether the theatre is good or bad in itself? Whether it can be united with morals [manners]? Whether it is in conformity with republican austerity? Whether it ought to be tolerated in a little city? Whether the actor's profession can be a decent one? Whether actresses can be as well behaved as other women? Whether good laws suffice for repressing the abuses? Whether these laws can be well observed? etc. Everything is still problematic concerning the real effects of the theatre; for, since the disputes that it occasions are solely between the men of the church and the men of the world, each side views the problem only through its prejudices. Here, Sir, are studies that would not be unworthy of your pen. As for me, without believing that what I might do could serve as a substitute for your efforts, I shall limit myself in this essay to seeking those clarifications that you have made necessary. I beg you to take into consideration that in speaking my opinion in imitation of your example, I am fulfilling a duty toward my country, and that, if my sentiments are mistaken, at least this error can hurt no one.

At the first glance given to these institutions I see immediately that the theatre is a form of amusement; and if it is true that amusements are necessary to man, you will at least admit that they are only permissible insofar as they are necessary, and that every useless amusement is an evil for a being whose life is so short and whose time is so precious. The state of man has its pleasures which are derived from his nature and are born of his labors, his relations, and his needs. And these pleasures, sweeter to the one who tastes them in the measure that his soul is healthier, make whoever is capable of participating in them indifferent to all others. A father, a son, a husband, and a citizen have such cherished duties to fulfil that they are left nothing to give to boredom. The good use of time makes time even more precious, and the better one puts it to use, the less one can find to lose. Thus it is constantly seen that the habit of work renders inactivity intolerable and that a good conscience extinguishes the taste for frivolous pleasures. But it is discontent with one's self, the burden of idleness, the neglect of simple and natural tastes, that makes foreign amusement so necessary. I do not like the need to occupy the heart constantly with the stage as if it were ill at ease inside of us. Nature itself dictated the response of that barbarian* to whom were vaunted the magnificences of the circus and the games established at Rome. "Don't the Romans," asked this fellow, "have wives or children?" The barbarian was right. People think they come together in the theatre, and it is there that they are

---

*Chrysost, in Matth, Homel, 38.

isolated. It is there that they go to forget their friends, neighbors, and relations in order to concern themselves with fables, in order to cry for the misfortunes of the dead, or to laugh at the expense of the living. But I should have sensed that this language is no longer seasonable in our times. Let us try to find another which is better understood.

To ask if the theatre is good or bad in itself is to pose too vague a question; it is to examine a relation before having defined the terms. The theatre is made for the people, and it is only by its effects on the people that one can determine its absolute qualities. There can be all sorts of entertainment.* There is, from people to people, a prodigious diversity of morals [manners], temperaments, and characters. Man is one; I admit it! But man modified by religions, governments, laws, customs, prejudices, and climates becomes so different from himself that one ought not to seek among us for what is good for men in general, but only what is good for them in this time or that country. [...]

When amusements are by their nature indifferent (and I am willing to consider the theatre as such for now), it is the nature of the occupations which they interrupt that causes them to be judged good or bad, especially when the amusements are engaging enough to become occupations themselves and to substitute the taste for them in place of that for work. Reason dictates the encouragement of the amusements of people whose occupations are harmful, and the turning-away from the same amusements of those whose occupations are beneficial. Another general consideration is that it is not good to leave the choice of their amusements to idle and corrupted men lest they think up ones which conform to their vicious inclinations and become as mischievous in their pleasures as in their business. But let a simple and hard-working people relax from its labors when and as it pleases; one need never fear that it will abuse

---

*"There can be entertainments blameable in themselves, like those which are inhuman or indecent and licentious; such were some of the pagan entertainments. But there are also some which are indifferent in themselves and only become bad through their abuse. For example, theatrical plays are not objectionable insofar as in them descriptions are to be found of the characters and actions of men, where agreeable and useful lessons for every station in life can even be presented. But if an easygoing morality is retailed in them; if the people who exercise this profession lead a licentious life and serve to corrupt others; if such shows support vanity, idleness, luxury, and lewdness, it is evident that the thing turns into an abuse; and unless a way is found to correct these abuses or to protect ourselves from them, it is better to give up this form of amusement." (*Instruction chrétienne,*[3] Vol. III, Book iii, ch. 16.)

This is the state of the question when it is well posed. What must be known is whether the morality of the theatre is necessarily easygoing, whether the abuses are inevitable, whether its difficulties are derived from the nature of the thing or whether they come from causes that can be set aside.

this liberty, and one need not trouble oneself looking for agreeable recreations for it. For, just as little preparation is needed for the food that is seasoned by abstinence and hunger, not much is needed for the pleasures of men exhausted by fatigue, for whom repose alone is a very sweet pleasure. In a big city, full of scheming, idle people without religion or principle, whose imagination, depraved by sloth, inactivity, the love of pleasure, and great needs, engenders only monsters and inspires only crimes; in a big city, where morals [manners] and honor are nothing because each, easily hiding his conduct from the public eye, shows himself only by his reputation and is esteemed only for his riches; in a big city, I say, the police can never increase the number of pleasures permitted too much or apply itself too much to making them agreeable in order to deprive individuals of the temptation of seeking more dangerous ones. Since preventing them from occupying themselves is to prevent them from doing harm, two hours a day stolen from the activity of vice prevents the twelfth part of the crimes that would be committed. And all the discussions in cafés and other refuges of the do-nothings and rascals of the place occasioned by plays seen or to be seen are also that much the more gained by family men, either for their daughters' honor or that of their wives, or for their purse or that of their sons.

But in small cities, in less populated places where individuals, always in the public eye, are born censors of one another and where the police can easily watch everyone, contrary maxims must be followed. If there are industry, arts, and manufactures, care must be taken against offering distractions which relax the greedy interest that finds its pleasures in its efforts and enriches the prince from the avarice of his subjects. If the country, without commerce, nourishes its inhabitants in inaction, far from fomenting idleness in them, to which they are already only too susceptible because of their simple and easy life, their life must be rendered insufferable in constraining them, by dint of boredom, to employ time usefully which they could not abuse. I see that in Paris, where everything is judged by appearances because there is no leisure to examine anything, it is believed, on the basis of the apparent inactivity and listlessness which strikes one at first glance in provincial towns, that the inhabitants, plunged in a stupid inactivity, either simply vegetate or only pester one another and quarrel. This is an error which could easily be corrected if it were remembered that most of the literary men who shine in Paris and most of the useful discoveries and new inventions come from these despised provinces. Stay some time in a little town where you had at first believed you would find only automatons; not only will you soon see there men a great deal more sensible than your big-city monkeys, but you will rarely fail to discover in obscurity there some ingenious man who will surprise you by his talents and his works, who you will surprise even more in admiring them, and who, in showing you prodigies of work, patience, and industry, will think he is showing you only what is ordinary at Paris. Such is the simplicity of true genius. It is neither scheming nor busybodyish; it knows not the path of honors and fortune nor dreams of seeking it; it compares itself to no one; all its resources are within itself; indifferent to insult and hardly conscious of praise, if it is aware of itself, it does not assign itself a place and enjoys itself without appraising itself.

In a little town, proportionately less activity is unquestionably to be found than in a capital, because the passions are less intense and the needs less pressing, but more original spirits, more inventive industry, more really new things are found there because the people are less imitative; having few models, each draws more from himself and puts more of his own in everything he does; because the human mind, less spread out, less drowned in vulgar opinions, elaborates itself and ferments better in tranquil solitude; because, in seeing less, more is imagined; finally, because less pressed for time, there is more leisure to extend and digest one's ideas.

I remember having seen in my youth a very pleasant sight, one perhaps unique on earth, in the vicinity of Neufchatel; an entire mountain covered with dwellings each one of which constitutes the center of the lands which belong to it, so that these houses, separated by distances as equal as the fortunes of the proprietors, offer to the numerous inhabitants of this mountain both the tranquillity of a retreat and the sweetness of society. These happy farmers, all in comfortable circumstances, free of poll-taxes, duties, commissioners, and forced labor, cultivate with all possible care lands the produce of which is theirs, and employ the leisure that tillage leaves them to make countless artifacts with their hands and to put to use the inventive genius which nature gave them. In the winter especially, a time when the deep snows prevent easy communication, each, warmly closed up with his big family in his pretty and clean wooden house,* which he has himself built, busies himself with enjoyable labors which drive boredom from his sanctuary and add to his well-being. Never did carpenter, locksmith, glazier, or turner enter this

---

*I can hear a Paris wit, provided he is not himself giving the reading, protesting at this point, as at many others, and learnedly proving to the ladies (for it is chiefly to ladies that these gentlemen make proofs) that it is impossible that a wooden house be warm. Vulgar falsehood! Error in physics! Alas, poor author! As for me, I think the demonstration is irrefutable. All that I know is that the Swiss spend their winter warmly in the midst of snows in wooden houses.

country; each is everything for himself, no one is anything for another. Among the many comfortable and even elegant pieces of furniture which make up their household and adorn their lodgings, none is ever seen which was not made by the hand of the master. They still have leisure time left over in which to invent and make all sorts of instruments of steel, wood, and cardboard which they sell to foreigners; many of these even get to Paris, among others those little wooden clocks that have been seen there during the last few years. They also make some of iron, and even make watches. And, what seems unbelievable, each joins in himself all the various crafts into which watchmaking is subdivided and makes all his tools himself.

This is not all. They have useful books and are tolerably well educated. They reason sensibly about everything and about many things with brilliance.* They make syphons, magnets, spectacles, pumps, barometers, and cameras obscura. Their tapestry consists of masses of instruments of every sort; you would take a farmer's living room for a mechanic's workshop and for a laboratory in experimental physics. All know how to sketch, paint, and calculate a bit; most play the flute, many know something of the principles of music and can sing true. These arts are not taught them by masters but are passed down, as it were, by tradition. Of those I saw who knew music, one would tell me he had learned it from his father, another from his aunt, and a third from his cousin; some thought they had always known it. One of their most frequent amusements is to sing psalms in four parts with their wives and children; and one is amazed to hear issuing from rustic cabins the strong and masculine harmony of Goudimel so long forgotten by our learned artists.

I could no more tire of wandering among these charming dwellings than could the inhabitants of offering me the frankest hospitality. Unhappily I was young; my curiosity was only that of a child, and I thought more of amusing myself than learning. In thirty years the few observations I made have been erased from my memory. I only remember that I continually admired in these singular men an amazing combination of delicacy and simplicity that would be believed to be almost incompatible and that I have never since observed elsewhere. Otherwise I remember nothing of their morals [manners], their society, or characters. Today, when I would bring other eyes to it, am I never again to see that happy land? Alas, it is on the road to my own.

---

*I can cite, as an example, a man of merit well known in Paris and more than once honored by the suffrages of the Academy of Sciences. It is M. Rivaz, an illustrious Valaisan. I know that he does not have many equals among his countrymen; but it was in living as they do that he learned how to surpass them.

After this sketch, let us suppose that at the summit of the mountain of which I have spoken, amidst the dwellings, a standing and inexpensive theatre be established under the pretext, for example, of providing a decent recreation for people otherwise constantly busy and able to bear this little expense. Let us further suppose that they get a taste for this theatre, and let us investigate what will be the results of its establishment.

I see, in the first place, that their labors will cease to be their amusements and that, as soon as they have a new amusement, it will undermine their taste for the old ones; zeal will no longer furnish so much leisure nor the same inventions. Moreover, everyday there will be no real time lost for those who go to the theatre, and they will no longer go right back to work, since their thoughts will be full of what they have just seen; they will talk about it and think about it. Consequently, slackening of work: first disadvantage.

However little is paid at the door, they do pay. It is still an expense that was not previously made. It costs for oneself and for one's wife and children when they are taken along, and sometimes they must be. In addition, a worker does not present himself in an assembly in his working clothes. He must put on his Sunday clothes, change linen, and powder and shave himself more often; all this costs time and money. Increase of expenses: second disadvantage.

Less assiduous work and larger expenses exact a compensation; it will be found in the price of what is produced, which must be made dearer. Many merchants, driven off by this increase, will leave the Mountaineers* and supply themselves from the neighboring Swiss who, being no less industrious, will have no theatre and will not increase their prices. Decrease in trade: third disadvantage.

During bad weather the roads are not passable; and, since the company must live in these seasons too, it will not interrupt its performances. Hence, making the theatre accessible at all seasons cannot be avoided. In the winter, roads must be made in the snow and, perhaps, paved; and God grant that they do not put up lanterns. Now there are public expenses and, in consequence, contributions from individuals. Establishment of taxes: fourth disadvantage.

The wives of the Mountaineers, going first to see and then to be seen, will want to be dressed and dressed with distinction. The wife of the chief magistrate will not want to present herself at the theatre attired like the schoolmaster's. The schoolmaster's wife will strive to be attired like the chief magistrate's. Out of this will soon emerge a competition in

---

*This is the name given to the inhabitants of this mountain in that country.

dress which will ruin the husbands, will perhaps win them over, and which will find countless new ways to get around the sumptuary laws. Introduction of luxury: fifth disadvantage.

All the rest is easy to imagine. Without taking into consideration the other disadvantages of which I have spoken or will speak in what follows, without investigating the sort of theatre and its moral effects, I confine myself to arguments which have to do with work and gain; and I believe I have shown, by an evident inference, how a prosperous people, but one which owes its well-being to its industry, exchanging reality for appearance, ruins itself at the very moment it wants to shine.

Moreover, my supposition ought not to be objected to as chimerical. I present it merely as such and only want to render its inevitable consequences more or less obvious. Take away some circumstances and you will find other Mountaineers elsewhere; and *mutatis mutandis,* the example has its application.

Thus, even if it were true that the theatre is not bad in itself, it would remain to be investigated if it does not become so in respect to the people for which it is destined. In certain places it will be useful for attracting foreigners; for increasing the circulation of money; for stimulating artists; for varying the fashions; for occupying those who are too rich or aspire to be so; for making them less mischievous; for distracting the people from its miseries; for making it forget its leaders in seeing its buffoons; for maintaining and perfecting taste when decency is lost; for covering the ugliness of vice with the polish of forms; in a word, for preventing bad morals [manners] from degenerating into brigandage. In other places it would only serve to destroy the love of work; to discourage industry; to ruin individuals; to inspire them with the taste for idleness; to make them seek for the means of subsistence without doing anything; to render a people inactive and slack; to prevent it from seeing the public and private goals with which it ought to busy itself; to turn prudence to ridicule; to substitute a theatrical jargon for the practice of virtues; to make metaphysic of all morality; to turn citizens into wits, housewives into bluestockings, and daughters into sweethearts out of the drama. The general effect will be the same on all men; but the men thus changed will suit their country more or less. In becoming equals, the bad will gain and the good will lose still more; all will contract a soft disposition and a spirit of inaction which will deprive the good of great virtues but will keep the bad from meditating great crimes.

From these new reflections results a consequence directly opposed to the one I drew from the first, namely, that when the people is corrupted, the theatre is good for it, and bad for it when it is itself good. It would, hence, seem that these two contrary effects would destroy one another and the theatre remain indifferent to both. But there is this difference: the effect which reenforces the good and the bad, since it is drawn from the spirit of the plays, is subject, as are they, to countless modifications which reduce it to practically nothing, while the effect which changes the good into bad and the bad into good, resulting from the very existence of a theatre, is a real, constant one which returns every day and must finally prevail.

It follows from this that, in order to decide if it is proper or not to establish a theatre in a certain town, we must known in the first place if the morals [manners] are good or bad there, a question concerning which it is perhaps not for me to answer with regard to us. However that may be, all that I can admit about this is that it is true that the drama will not harm us if nothing at all can harm us any more.

TRANSLATOR'S NOTES

1. David Hume.
2. The French word here translated by *theatre* is *spectacle* and has a much broader and richer meaning than the word *theatre* would imply. It is literally anything that one goes to see, and hence entertainment in general. Unfortunately, to translate *spectacle* in a more general way would render its specific sense of *theater* unintelligible in English. But the reader should keep the other connotations in mind, for Rousseau does not limit himself to a discussion of the theatre narrowly conceived, but is investigating the moral effects and correctness of all the pleasures of the eyes and ears with particular reference to their most sophisticated form, the drama. For this purpose the French word is propitious in that its more specific meaning can always be broadened to include its generic sense, and hence the drama can be compared to other forms of entertainment. The very word *spectacle* has been translated by *theatre*, but where impossible, *entertainment* has been used. *Spectacle* is the word used by Rousseau in the title of the work.
3. (Geneva 1752) by Jacob Vernet.

Questions for Review and Discussion

1. What distinctions does Rousseau make between large and small cities (like Paris and Geneva)?

2. How does Rousseau's argument about theaters depend on that distinction?

3. What, according to Rousseau, is the ultimate criterion for deciding whether we should establish a theater in a city?

4. How would you argue against Rousseau's views on theaters? Is it possible that theaters could promote citizenship?

Thomas Jefferson

Thomas Jefferson (1743–1826) is best known as one of the founding fathers of the United States and a drafter of the Declaration of Independence. He was both a political and an intellectual leader who was profoundly influenced by Enlightenment philosophers such as Rousseau. Jefferson's own philosophy focused on political liberalism. His country roots in Virginia, combined with an Enlightenment romantic view of rural life, caused Jefferson to develop a decidedly anti-city view. In a letter to Rush (1800), for example, Jefferson argued that cities are "pestilential to the morals, the health and liberties of man." In a letter to Pictet (1803), he wrote that agrarian life affords "more health, virtue and freedom." While Jefferson's visit to Paris engaged his artistic and intellectual sensibilities, he nevertheless thought country life best. The reading below is excerpted from his *Notes on the State of Virginia* (1787). He argues that the new United States should keep manufacturing at bay. After the War of 1812, Jefferson softened his view on cities, recognizing that, as a matter of national security, cities and domestic industry might be necessary to keep the United States free and independent (see his letter to Austin [1816]). Yet such a concession was motivated by practical considerations; he still thought that the distinguishing mark of the United States would and should be its rural character. Compare Jefferson's views to those of Plato, More, Rousseau, Simmel, and Mumford as well as those of contemporary thinkers like Conlon, Young, and Kemmis who argue in favor of city life, and Light who discusses city/nature distinctions.

"MANUFACTURES" (1787)

*The present state of manufactures, commerce,
interior and exterior trade?*

We never had an interior trade of any importance. Our exterior commerce has suffered very much from the beginning of the present contest. During this time we have manufactured within our families the most necessary articles of cloathing. Those of cotton will bear some comparison with the same kinds of manufacture in Europe; but those of wool, flax and hemp are very coarse, unsightly, and unpleasant: and such is our attachment to agriculture, and such our preference for foreign manufactures, that be it wise or unwise, our people will certainly return as soon as they can, to the raising raw materials, and exchanging them for finer manufactures than they are able to execute themselves.

The political œconomists of Europe have established it as a principle that every state should endeavour to manufacture for itself: and this principle, like many others, we transfer to America, without calculating the difference of circumstance which should often produce a difference of result. In Europe the lands are either cultivated, or locked up against the cultivator. Manufacture must therefore be resorted to of necessity not of choice, to support the surplus of their people. But we have an immensity of land courting the industry of the husbandman. Is it best then that all our citizens should be employed in its improvement, or that one half should be called off from that to exercise manufactures and handicraft arts for the other? Those who labor in the earth are the chosen people of God, if ever he had a chosen people, whose breasts he has made his peculiar deposit for substantial and genuine virtue. It is the focus in which he keeps alive that sacred fire, which otherwise might escape from the face of the earth. Corruption of morals in the mass of cultivators is a phænomenon of which no age nor nation has furnished an example. It is the mark set on those, who not looking up to heaven, to their own soil and industry, as does the husbandman, for their subsistance, depend for it on the casualties and caprice of customers. Dependance begets subservience and venality, suffocates the germ of virtue, and prepares fit tools for the designs of ambition. This, the natural progress and consequence of the arts, has sometimes perhaps been retarded by accidental circumstances: but, generally speaking, the proportion which the aggregate of the other classes of citizens bears in any state to that of its husbandmen, is the proportion of its unsound to its healthy parts, and is a good-enough barometer whereby to measure its degree of corruption. While we have land to labour then, let us never wish to see our citizens occupied at a work-bench, or twirling a distaff. Carpenters, masons, smiths, are wanting in husbandry: but, for the general operations of manufacture, let our work-shops remain in Europe. It is better to carry provisions and materials, and with them their manners and principles. The loss by the transportation of commodities across the Atlantic will be made up in happiness and permanence of government. The mobs of great cities add just so much to the support of pure government, as sores do to the strength of the human body. It is the manners and spirit of a people which preserves a republic in vigour. A degeneracy in these is a canker which soon eats to the heart of its laws and constitution.[1]

---

1. Jefferson's almost passionate belief in the superiority of a primarily agrarian society of predominantly Anglo-Saxon peoples over any other system was reinforced by his observations in France and later became one of the major areas of disagreement between his own Republican party and the Federalists. Jefferson was to modify but never abandon his distrust of large cities and their inhabitants of diverse nationalities. Subsequent criticism of the views he expressed in this Query led him to consider revising his comments, should he ever find time to rewrite the *Notes on Virginia*. See TJ to J. Lithgow, Jan. 4, 1805; A. Whitney Griswold, *Farming and Democracy* (New York, 1948), chap. 2.

Questions for Review and Discussion

1. Why does Jefferson argue that the United States should remain an agrarian society?

2. What sorts of distinctions (either implicit or explicit) does Jefferson make between country and city life?

3. Do you agree with Jefferson? Why or why not?

4. What policy implications does Jefferson's view hold for the United States and U.S. cities?

Jane Addams

Jane Addams (1860–1935) is often called the first social worker because she founded a settlement house in Chicago in 1889 where she and other women worked with new immigrant families in the impoverished West Side. The settlement house was called Hull House. West Side families could go to Hull House for literacy, parenting, and other classes and social service. Addams also was a staunch advocate for social change in urban politics. Addams was not only a practitioner but also a theorist, and only recently has her work as a philosopher been taken as seriously as it deserves to be. Addams worked with John Dewey and others in the American pragmatist tradition. She was greatly interested in the relationship between theory and practice, especially as it pertains to democratic values and urban problems. Addams lived in Chicago during an unprecedented time of growth. As immigrants came in great numbers to Chicago, the city's gap between the rich and poor grew. In this essay, Addams provides an argument about why privileged young persons should work with those who are less privileged. Addams argues that urban problems are not restricted to particular city neighborhoods; urban problems are everyone's problem. Compare Addams on social justice issues in the city to Augustine, Young, West, Bickford, Mendieta, and Light.

"THE SUBJECTIVE NECESSITY FOR SOCIAL SETTLEMENTS" (1893)

Hull House, which was Chicago's first Settlement, was established in September, 1889. It represented no association, but was opened by two women, backed by many friends, in the belief that the mere foothold of a house, easily accessible, ample in space, hospitable and tolerant in spirit, situated in the midst of the large foreign colonies which so easily isolate themselves in American cities, would be in itself a serviceable thing for Chicago. Hull House endeavors to make social intercourse express the growing sense of the economic unity of society. It is an effort to add the social function to democracy. It was opened on the theory that the dependence of classes on each other is reciprocal; and that as "the social relation is essentially a reciprocal relation, it gave a form of expression that has peculiar value."

This paper is an attempt to treat of the subjective necessity for Social Settlements, to analyze the motives which underlie a movement based not only upon conviction, but genuine emotion. Hull House of

Chicago is used as an illustration, but so far as the analysis is faithful, it obtains wherever educated young people are seeking an outlet for that sentiment of universal brotherhood which the best spirit of our times is forcing from an emotion into a motive.

I have divided the motives which constitute the subjective pressure toward Social Settlements into three great lines: the first contains the desire to make the entire social organism democratic, to extend democracy beyond its political expression; the second is the impulse to share the race life, and to bring as much as possible of social energy and the accumulation of civilization to those portions of the race which have little; the third springs from a certain renaissance of Christianity, a movement toward its early humanitarian aspects.

It is not difficult to see that although America is pledged to the democratic ideal, the view of democracy has been partial, and that its best achievement thus far has been pushed along the line of the franchise. Democracy has made little attempt to assert itself in social affairs. We have refused to move beyond the position of its eighteenth-century leaders, who believed that political equality alone would secure all good to all men. We conscientiously followed the gift of the ballot hard upon the gift of freedom to the Negro, but we are quite unmoved by the fact that he lives among us in a practical social ostracism. We hasten to give the franchise to the immigrant from a sense of justice, from a tradition that he ought to have it, while we dub him with epithets deriding his past life or present occupation, and feel no duty to invite him to our houses. We are forced to acknowledge that it is only in our local and national politics that we try very hard for the ideal so dear to those who were enthusiasts when the century was young. We have almost given it up as our ideal in social intercourse. [. . .]

We are perhaps entering upon the second phase of democracy, as the French philosophers entered upon the first, somewhat bewildered by its logical conclusions. The social organism has broken down through large districts of our great cities. Many of the people living there are very poor, the majority of them without leisure or energy for anything but the gain of subsistence. They move often from one wretched lodging to another. They live for the moment side by side, many of them without knowledge of each other, without fellowship, without local tradition or public spirit, without social organization of any kind. Practically nothing is done to remedy this. The people who might do it, who have the social tact and training, the large houses, and the traditions and custom of hospitality, live in other parts of the city. The club-houses, libraries, galleries, and semi-public conveniences for social life are also blocks away. We find working-men organized into armies of producers because men

of executive ability and business sagacity have found it to their interests
thus to organize them. But these working-men are not organized socially;
although living in crowded tenement-houses, they are living without a
corresponding social contact. The chaos is as great as it would be were
they working in huge factories without foreman or superintendent. Their
ideas and resources are cramped. The desire for higher social pleasure is
extinct. They have no share in the traditions and social energy which make
for progress. Too often their only place of meeting is a saloon, their only
host a bartender; a local demagogue forms their public opinion. Men of
ability and refinement, of social power and university cultivation, stay away
from them. Personally, I believe the men who lose most are those who
thus stay away. But the paradox is here: when cultivated people do stay
away from a certain portion of the population, when all social advantages
are persistently withheld [. . .] the result itself is pointed at as a reason, is
used as an argument, for the continued withholding.

It is constantly said that because the masses have never had social
advantages they do not want them, that they are heavy and dull, and that
it will take political or philanthropic machinery to change them. This
divides a city into rich and poor; into the favored, who express their sense
of the social obligation by gifts of money, and into the unfavored, who
express it by clamoring for a "share"—both of them actuated by a vague
sense of justice. This division of the city would be more justifiable, however, if the people who thus isolate themselves on certain streets and use
their social ability for each other gained enough thereby and added sufficient
to the sum total of social progress to justify the withholding of the pleasures and results of that progress from so many people who ought to have
them. But they cannot accomplish this. "The social spirit discharges itself
in many forms, and no one form is adequate to its total expression." We
are all uncomfortable in regard to the sincerity of our best phrases, because
we hesitate to translate our philosophy into the deed.

It is inevitable that those who feel most keenly this insincerity and
partial living should be our young people, our so-called educated young
people who accomplish little toward the solution of this social problem,
and who bear the brunt of being cultivated into unnourished, over-
sensitive lives. They have been shut off from the common labor by which
they live and which is a great source of moral and physical health. They
feel a fatal want of harmony between their theory and their lives, a lack
of co-ordination between thought and action. I think it is hard for us to
realize how seriously many of them are taking to the notion of human
brotherhood, how eagerly they long to give tangible expression to the
democratic ideal. These young men and women, longing to socialize
their democracy, are animated by certain hopes.

These hopes may be loosely formulated thus: that if in a democratic country nothing can be permanently achieved save through the masses of the people, it will be impossible to establish a higher political life than the people themselves crave; that it is difficult to see how the notion of a higher civic life can be fostered save through common intercourse; that the blessings which we associate with a life of refinement and cultivation can be made universal and must be made universal if they are to be permanent; that the good we secure for ourselves is precarious and uncertain, is floating in mid-air; until it is secured for all of us and incorporated into our common life.

These hopes are responsible for results in various directions, pre-eminently in the extension of educational advantages. We find that all educational matters are more democratic in their political than in their social aspects. The public schools in the poorest and most crowded wards of the city are inadequate to the number of children, and many of the teachers are ill-prepared and overworked; but in each ward there is an effort to secure public education. The schoolhouse itself stands as a pledge that the city recognizes and endeavors to fulfill the duty of educating its children. But what becomes of these children when they are no longer in public schools? Many of them never come under the influence of a professional teacher nor a cultivated friend after they are twelve. Society at large does little for their intellectual development. [. . .]

It is needless to say that a Settlement is a protest against a restricted view of education, and makes it possible for every educated man or woman with a teaching faculty to find out those who are ready to be taught. The social and educational activities of a Settlement are but differing manifestations of the attempt to socialize democracy, as is the existence of the settlement itself.

I find it somewhat difficult to formulate the second line of motives which I believe to constitute the trend of the subjective pressure toward the Settlement. There is something primordial about these motives, but I am perhaps over-bold in designating them as a great desire to share the race life. We all bear traces of the starvation struggle which for so long made up the life of the race. Our very organism holds memories and glimpses of that long life of our ancestors which still goes on among so many of our contemporaries. Nothing so deadens the sympathies and shrivels the power of enjoyment as the persistent keeping away from the great opportunities for helpfulness and a continual ignoring of the starvation struggle which makes up the life of at least half the race. To shut one's self away from that half of the race life is to shut one's self away from the most vital part of it; it is to live out but half the humanity which we have been born heir to and to use but half our faculties. We have all had longings for a fuller life which should include the use of these faculties. These longings are the physical complement of the "Intimations of Immortality" on which no ode has yet been written. To portray these would be the work of a poet, and it is hazardous for any but a poet to attempt it.

You may remember the forlorn feeling which occasionally seizes you when you arrive early in the morning a stranger in a great city. The stream of laboring people goes past you as you gaze through the plate-glass window of your hotel. You see hard-working men lifting great burdens; you hear the driving and jostling of huge carts. Your heart sinks with a sudden sense of futility. [. . .]

We have in America a fast-growing number of cultivated young people who have no recognized outlet for their active faculties. They hear constantly of the great social mal-adjustment, but no way is provided for them to change it, and their uselessness hangs about them heavily. Huxley declares that the sense of uselessness is the severest shock which the human system can sustain, and that, if persistently sustained, it results in atrophy of function. These young people have had advantages of college, of European travel and economic study, but they are sustaining this shock of inaction. They have pet phrases, and they tell you that the things that make us all alike are stronger than the things that make us different. They say that all men are united by needs and sympathies far more permanent and radical than anything that temporarily divides them and sets them in opposition to each other. If they affect art, they say that the decay in artistic expression is due to the decay in ethics, that art when shut away from the human interests and from the great mass of humanity is self-destructive. They tell their elders with all the bitterness of youth that if they expect success from them in business, or politics, or in whatever lines their ambition for them has run, they must let them consult all of humanity, that they must let them find out what the people want and how they want it. It is only the stronger young people, however, who formulate this. Many of them dissipate their energies in so-called enjoyment. Others, not content with that, go on studying and go back to college for their second degrees, not that they are especially fond of study, but because they want something definite to do, and their powers have been trained in the direction of mental accumulation. Many are busied beneath mere mental accumulation with lowered vitality and discontent. Walter Besant says they have had the vision that Peter had when he saw the great sheet let down from heaven, wherein was neither clean nor unclean. He calls it the sense of humanity. It is not philanthropy nor benevolence. It is a thing fuller and wider than either of these. This young life, so sincere in its emotion and good phrases and yet so undirected, seems to me as pitiful as the other great mass of destitute lives. [. . .] It is easy to see why the Settlement movement originated in England, where the years of education are more constrained and definite than they are here, where class distinctions are more rigid. The necessity of it was greater there, but we are fast feeling the pressure of the need and meeting the necessity for Settlements in America. Our young people feel nervously the need of putting theory into action, and respond quickly to the Settlement form of activity.

The third division of motives which I believe make toward the Settlement is the result of a certain renaissance going forward in Christianity [. . .] That Christianity has to be revealed and embodied in the line of social progress is a corollary to the simple proposition that man's action is found in his social relationships in the way in which he connects with his fellows, that his motives for action are the zeal and affection with which he regards his fellows. By this simple process was created a deep enthusiasm for humanity, which regarded man as at once the organ and object of revelation; and by this process came about that wonderful fellowship, that true democracy of the early Church, that so captivates the imagination. The early Christians were pre-eminently non-resistant. They believed in love as a cosmic force. There was no iconoclasm during the minor peace of the Church. They did not yet denounce, nor tear down temples, nor preach the end of the world. They grew to a mighty number, but it never occurred to them, either in their weakness or their strength, to regard other men for an instant as their foes or as aliens. The spectacle of the Christians loving all men was the most astounding Rome had ever seen. They were eager to sacrifice themselves for the weak, for children and the aged. They identified themselves with slaves and did not avoid the plague. They longed to share the common lot that they might receive the constant revelation. It was a new treasure which the early Christians added to the sum of all treasures, a joy hitherto unknown in the world—the joy of finding the Christ which lieth in each man, but which no man can unfold save in fellowship. A happiness ranging from the heroic to the pastoral enveloped them. They were to possess a revelation as long as life had new meaning to unfold, new action to propose.

I believe that there is a distinct turning among many young men and women toward this simple acceptance of Christ's message. They resent the assumption that Christianity is a set of ideas which belong to the religious consciousness, whatever that may be, that it is a thing to be proclaimed and instituted apart from the social life of the community [. . .] If love is the creative force of the universe, the principle which binds men together, and by their interdependence on each other makes them human, just so surely is anger and the spirit of opposition the destructive principle of the universe, that which tears down, thrusts men apart, and makes them isolated and brutal.

I cannot, of course, speak for other Settlements, but it would, I think, be unfair to Hull House not to emphasize the conviction with which the first residents went there, that it would simply be a foolish and an unwarrantable expenditure of force to oppose or to antagonize any individual or set of people in the neighborhood; that whatever of good the House had to offer should be put into positive terms; that its residents should live with opposition to no man, with recognition of the good in every man, even the meanest. I believe that this turning, this renaissance of the early Christian humanitarianism, is going on in America, in Chicago, if you please, without leaders who write or philosophize, without much speaking, belt with a bent to express in social service, in terms of action, the spirit of Christ. Certain it is that spiritual force is found in the Settlement movement, and it is also true that this force must be evoked and must be called into play before the success of any Settlement is assured. There must be the over-mastering belief that all that is noblest in life is common to men as meal, in order to accentuate the likenesses and ignore the differences which are found among the people whom the Settlement constantly brings into juxtaposition. [. . .]

If you have heard a thousand voices singing in the Hallelujah Chorus in Handel's "Messiah," you have found that the leading voices could still be distinguished, but that the differences of training and cultivation between them and the voices of the chorus were lost in the unity of purpose and the fact that they revere all human voices lifted by a high motive. This is a weak illustration of what a Settlement attempts to do. It aims, in a measure, to lead whatever of social life its neighborhood may afford, to focus and give form to that life, to bring to bear upon it the results of cultivation and training; but it receives in exchange for the music of isolated voices the volume and strength of the chorus. It is quite impossible for me to say in what proportion or degree the subjective necessity which led to the opening of Hull House combined the three trends: first the desire to interpret democracy in social terms; secondly, the impulse beating the very source of our lives urging us to aid in the race progress; and, thirdly, the Christian movement toward Humanitarianism. It is difficult to analyze a living thing; the analysis is at best imperfect. Many more motives may blend with the three trends; possibly the desire for a new form of social success due to the nicety of imagination, which refuses worldly pleasures unmixed with the joys of self-sacrifice; possibly a love of approbation, so vast that is it not content with the treble clapping of delicate hands, but wishes also to hear the bass notes from toughened palms, may mingle with these.

The Settlement, then, is an experimental effort to aid in the solution of the social and industrial problems which are engendered by the modern conditions of life in a great city. It insists that these problems are not confined to any one portion of a city. It is an attempt to relieve, at the same time, the over-accumulation at one end of society and the destitution at the other; but it assumes that this over-accumulation and destitution is most sorely felt in the things that pertain to social and educational advantage. From its very nature it can stand for no political or social propaganda [. . .] The one thing to be dreaded in the Settlement is that it loses its flexibility, its power of quick adaptation, its readiness to change its methods as its environment may demand. It must be open to conviction and must have a deep and abiding sense of tolerance. It must be hospitable and ready for experiment. It should demand from its residents a scientific patience in the accumulation of facts and the steady holding of their sympathies as one of the best instruments for that accumulation. It must be grounded in a philosophy whose foundation is on the solidarity of the human race, a philosophy which will not waver when the race happens to be represented by a drunken woman or an idiot boy. Its residents must be emptied of all conceit of opinion and all self-assertion, and ready to arouse and interpret the public opinion of their neighborhood. They must be content to live quietly side by side with their neighbors until they grow into a sense of relationship and mutual interests. Their neighbors are held apart by differences of race and language which the residents can more easily overcome. They are bound to see the needs of their neighborhood as a whole, to furnish data for legislation, and use their influence to secure it. In short, residents are pledged to devote themselves to the duties of good citizenship and to the arousing of the social energies which too largely lie dormant in every neighborhood given over to industrialism. They are bound to regard the entire life of their city as organic, to make an effort to unify it, and to protest against its over-differentiation.

Our philanthropies of all sorts are growing so expensive and institutional that it is to be hoped the Settlement movement will keep itself facile and unencumbered. From its very nature it needs no endowment, no roll of salaried officials. Many residents must always come in the attitude of students, assuming that the best teacher of life is life itself, and regarding the Settlement as a classroom. Hull House from the outside may appear to be a cumbrous plant of manifold industries, with its round of clubs and classes, its day nursery, diet kitchen, library, art exhibits, lectures, statistical walk and polyglot demands for information, a thousand people coming and going in an average week. But viewed as a business enterprise it is not costly, for from this industry are eliminated two great items of expense—the cost of superintendence and the cost of distribution. All the management and teaching are voluntary and unpaid, and the consumers—to continue the commercial phraseology—are at the door and deliver the goods themselves. In the instance of Hull House, rent is also largely eliminated through the courtesy of the owner.

Life is manifold and Hull House attempts to respond to as many sides as possible. It does this fearlessly, feeling sure that among the able people of Chicago are those who will come to do the work when once the outline is indicated. It pursues much the same policy in regard to money. It seems to me an advantage—this obligation to appeal to business men for their judgment and their money, to the educated for their effort and enthusiasm, to the neighborhood for their response and co-operation. It tests the sanity of an idea, and we enter upon a new line of activity with a feeling of support and confidence. We have always been perfectly frank with our neighbors. I have never tried so earnestly to set forth the gist of the Settlement movement, to make clear its reciprocity, as I have to them. At first we were often asked why we came to live there when we could afford to live somewhere else. I remember one man who used to shake his head and say it was "the strangest thing he had met in his experience," but who was finally convinced that it was not strange but natural. I trust that now it seems natural to all of us that the Settlement should be there. If it is natural to feed the hungry and care for the sick, it is certainly natural to give pleasure to the young and to minister to the deep-seated craving for social intercourse that all men feel. Whoever does it is rewarded by something which, if not gratitude, is at least spontaneous and vital and lacks that irksome sense of obligation with which a substantial benefit is too often acknowledged. The man who looks back to the person who first put him in the way of good literature has no alloy in his gratitude.

I remember when the statement seemed to me very radical that the salvation of East London was the destruction of West London, but I believe now that there will be no wretched quarters in our cities at all when the conscience of each man is so touched that he prefers to live with the poorest of his brethren, and not with the richest of them that his income will allow. It is to be hoped that this moving and living will at length be universal and need no name. The Settlement movement is from its nature a provisional one. It is easy in writing a paper to make all philosophy point one particular moral and all history adorn one particular tale; but I hope you forgive me for reminding you that the best speculative philosophy sets forth the solidarity of the human race; that the highest moralists have taught that without the advance and improvement of the whole no man can hope for any lasting improvement in his own moral or material individual condition. The subjective necessity for Social Settlements is identical with that necessity which urges us on toward social and individual salvation.

Questions for Review and Discussion

1. According to Addams, what were the three theories/motives for Hull House?

2. Why does Addams think that political equality is insufficient for democracy? What else is necessary?

3. Describe Hull House and the Settlement House movement. What is the purpose of Settlement Houses? How do they achieve their goals?

4. Evaluate Addams's argument that the privileged should give back to those in the city who are less fortunate. Do you agree or disagree with her?

Late Modern Readings (1900–1969)

Georg Simmel

A native of Berlin, Georg Simmel (1858–1918) was trained in philosophy and spent most of his career as a private lecturer at the University of Berlin, teaching surveys of philosophy as well as the newly emerging field of sociology. Although Max Weber and other German intellectuals immediately recognized his intellectual gifts, Simmel never obtained the official academic recognition that they did within the German academy. Nevertheless, Simmel's social philosophical work on the city very much influenced the Chicago school of sociology and underlies much of contemporary urban studies. Jürgen Habermas called Simmel a "diagnostician of the times."

Simmel was interested in how the individual parts of society interacted with one another, including how persons within cities engage or disengage from one another. In this essay, Simmel argues that urban dwellers develop particular kinds of identities or personality traits. Simmel remains ambivalent about whether these modern developments are good or bad, but he thinks it important for us to understand the characteristics of modernization. This reading brings forth both negative and positive aspects of city life, allowing comparison to other discussions of urban ideals and difficulties and well as issues of urban identity; see for example, Plato, Mumford, Conlon, Young, and Mendieta.

"THE METROPOLIS AND MENTAL LIFE" (1903)

The psychological foundation, upon which the metropolitan individuality is erected, is the intensification of emotional life due to the swift and continuous shift of external and internal stimuli. Man is a creature whose existence is dependent on differences, i.e., his mind is stimulated by the difference between present impressions and those which have preceded. Lasting impressions, the slightness in their differences, the habituated regularity of their course and contrasts between them, consume, so to speak, less mental energy than the rapid telescoping of changing images, pronounced differences within what is grasped at a single glance, and the unexpectedness of violent stimuli. To the extent that the metropolis creates these psychological conditions—with every crossing of the street, with the tempo and multiplicity of economic, occupational and social life—it creates in the sensory foundations of mental life, and in the degree of awareness necessitated by our organization as creatures dependent on differences, a deep contrast with the slower, more habitual, more smoothly flowing rhythm of the sensory-mental phase of small town and rural existence. Thereby the essentially intellectualistic character of the mental life of the metropolis becomes intelligible as over against that of the small town which rests more on feelings and emotional relationships. These latter are rooted in the unconscious levels of the mind and develop most readily in the steady equilibrium of unbroken customs. The locus of reason, on the other hand, is in the lucid, conscious upper strata of the mind and it is the most adaptable of our inner forces. In order to adjust itself to the shifts and contradictions in events, it does not require the disturbances and inner upheavals which are the only means whereby more conservative personalities are able to adapt themselves to the same rhythm of events. Thus the metropolitan type—which naturally takes on a thousand individual modifications—creates a protective organ for itself against the profound disruption with which the fluctuations and discontinuities of the external milieu threaten it. Instead of reacting emotionally, the metropolitan type reacts primarily in a rational manner, thus creating a mental predominance through the intensification of consciousness, which in turn is caused by it. Thus the reaction of the metropolitan person to those events is moved to a sphere of mental activity which is at least sensitive and which is furthest removed from the depths of the personality.

This intellectualistic quality which is thus recognized as a protection of the inner life against the domination of the metropolis, becomes ramified into numerous specific phenomena. The metropolis has always been the seat of money economy because the many-sidedness and concentration of commercial activity have given the medium of exchange an importance which it could not have acquired in the commercial aspects of rural life. But money economy and the domination of the intellect stand in the closest relationship to one another. They have in common a purely matter-of-fact attitude in the treatment of persons and things in which a formal justice is often combined with an unrelenting hardness. The purely intellectualistic person is indifferent to all things personal because, out of them, relationships and reactions develop which are not to be completely understood by purely rational methods—just as the unique element in events never enters into the principle of money. Money is concerned only with what is common to all, i.e., with the exchange value which reduces all quality and individuality to a purely quantitative level. All emotional relationships between persons rest on their individuality, whereas intellectual relationships deal with persons as with numbers, that is, as with elements which, in themselves, are indifferent, but which are of interest only insofar as they offer something objectively perceivable. It is in this very manner that the inhabitant of the metropolis reckons with his merchant, his customer, and with his servant, and frequently with the persons with whom he is thrown into obligatory association. These relationships stand in distinct contrast with the nature of the smaller circle in which the inevitable knowledge of individual characteristics produces, with an equal inevitability, an emotional tone in conduct, a sphere which is beyond the mere objective weighting of tasks performed and payments made. What is essential here as regards the economic-psychological aspect of the problem is that in less advanced cultures production was for the customer who ordered the product so that the producer and the purchaser knew one another. The modern city, however, is supplied almost exclusively by production for the market, that is, for entirely unknown purchasers who never appear in the actual field of vision of the producers themselves. Thereby, the interests of each party acquire a relentless matter-of-factness, and its rationally calculated economic egoism need not fear any divergence from its set path because of the imponderability of personal relationships. This is all the more the case in the money economy which dominates the metropolis in which the last remnants of domestic production and direct barter of goods have been eradicated and in which the amount of production on direct personal order is reduced daily. Furthermore, this psychological intellectualistic attitude and the money economy are in such close integration that no one is able to say whether it was the former that effected the latter or *vice versa*. What is certain is only that the form of life in the metropolis is the soil which nourishes this interaction most fruitfully, a point which I shall attempt to demonstrate only with the statement of the most outstanding English constitutional historian to the effect that through the entire course of English history London has never acted as the heart of England but often as its intellect and always as its money bag. [. . .]

There is perhaps no psychic phenomenon which is so unconditionally reserved to the city as the blasé outlook. It is at first the consequence of those rapidly shifting stimulations of the nerves which are thrown together in all their contrasts and from which it seems to us the intensification of metropolitan intellectuality seems to be derived.

We see that the self-preservation of certain types of personalities is obtained at the cost of devaluing the entire objective world, ending inevitably in dragging the personality downward into a feeling of its own valuelessness.

Whereas the subject of this form of existence must come to terms with it for himself, his self-preservation in the face of the great city requires of him a no less negative type of social conduct. The mental attitude of the people of the metropolis to one another may be designated formally as one of reserve. If the unceasing external contact of numbers of persons in the city should be met by the same number of inner reactions as in the small town, in which one knows almost every person he meets and to each of whom he has a positive relationship, one would be completely atomized internally and would fall into an unthinkable mental condition. [. . .]

This appears to me to be the most profound cause of the fact that the metropolis places emphasis on striving for the most individual forms of personal existence—regardless of whether it is always correct or always successful. The development of modern culture is characterised by the predominance of what one can call the objective spirit over the subjective; that is, in language as well as in law, in the technique of production as well as in art, in science as well as in the objects of domestic environment, there is embodied a sort of spirit [*Geist*], the daily growth of which is followed only imperfectly and with an even greater lag by the intellectual development of the individual. If we survey for instance the vast culture which during the last century has been embodied in things and in knowledge, in institutions and comforts, and if we compare them with the cultural progress of the individual during the same period—at least in the upper classes—we should see a frightful difference in rate of growth between the two which represents, in many points, rather a regression of the culture of the individual with reference to spirituality, delicacy and idealism. This discrepancy is in essence the result of the success of the growing division of labor. For it is this which requires from the individual an ever more one-sided type of achievement which, at its highest point, often permits his personality as a whole to fall into neglect. In any case this overgrowth of objective culture has been less and less satisfactory for the individual. Perhaps less conscious than in practical activity and in the obscure complex of feelings which flow from him, he is reduced to a negligible quantity. He becomes a single cog as over against the vast overwhelming organization of things and forces which gradually take out of his hands everything connected with progress, spirituality and value. The operation of these forces results in the transformation of the latter from a subjective form into one of purely objective existence. It need only be pointed out that the metropolis is the proper arena for this type of culture which has outgrown every personal element. Here in buildings and in educational institutions, in the wonders and comforts of space-conquering technique, in the formations of social life and in the concrete institutions of the State is to be found such a tremendous richness of crystallizing, depersonalized cultural accomplishments that the personality can, so to speak, scarcely maintain itself in the face of it. From one angle life is made infinitely more easy in the sense that stimulations, interests, and the taking up of time and attention, present themselves from all sides and carry it in a stream which scarcely requires any individual efforts for its ongoing. But from another angle, life is composed more and more of these impersonal cultural elements and existing goods and values which seek to suppress peculiar personal interests and incomparabilities. As a result, in order that this most personal element be saved, extremities and peculiarities and individualizations must be produced and they must be over-exaggerated merely to be brought into the awareness even of the individual himself. The atrophy of individual culture through the hypertrophy of objective culture lies at the root of the bitter hatred which the preachers of the most extreme individualism, in the footsteps of Nietzsche, directed against the metropolis. But it is also the explanation of why indeed they are so passionately loved in the metropolis and indeed appear to its residents as the saviors of their unsatisfied yearnings.

When both of these forms of individualism which are nourished by the quantitative relationships of the metropolis, i.e., individual independence and the elaboration of personal peculiarities, are examined with reference to their historical position, the metropolis attains an entirely new value and meaning in the world history of the spirit. The eighteenth century found the individual in the grip of powerful bonds which had become meaningless—bonds of a political, agrarian, guild and religious nature—delimitations which imposed upon the human being at the same time an unnatural form and for a long time an unjust inequality. In this situation arose the cry for freedom and equality—the belief in the full freedom of movement of the individual in all his social and intellectual relationships which would then permit the same noble essence to emerge equally from all individuals as Nature had placed it in them and as it had been distorted by social life and historical development. Alongside of this liberalistic ideal there grew up in the nineteenth century from Goethe and the Romantics, on the one hand, and from the economic division of labor on the other, the further tendency, namely, that individuals who had been liberated from their historical bonds sought now to distinguish themselves from one another. No longer was it the "general human quality" in every individual but rather his qualitative uniqueness and irreplaceability that now became the criteria of his value. In the conflict and shifting interpretations of these two ways of defining the position of the individual within the totality is to be found the external as well as the internal history of our time. It is the function of the metropolis to make a place for the conflict and for the attempts at unification of both of these in the sense that its own peculiar conditions have been revealed to us as the occasion and the stimulus for the development of both. Thereby they attain a quite unique place, fruitful with an inexhaustible richness of meaning in the development of the mental life. They reveal themselves as one of those great historical structures in which conflicting life-embracing currents find themselves with equal legitimacy. Because of this, however, regardless of whether we are sympathetic or antipathetic with their individual expressions, they transcend the sphere in which a judge-like attitude on our part is appropriate. To the extent that such forces have been integrated, with the fleeting existence of a single cell, into the root as well as the crown of the totality of historical life to which we belong—it is our task not to complain or to condone but only to understand.

Questions for Review and Discussion

1. According to Simmel, do urban dwellers have different characteristics than rural dwellers?

2. What features of city life does Simmel argue best suit our human natures?

3. From Simmel's perspective, what are the advantages of city life? What are its disadvantages?

Max Weber

While perhaps best known for his sociological analysis of the *Protestant Ethic and the Spirit of Capitalism*, German intellectual Max Weber also has had a powerful philosophical influence, especially in his analysis of modernity. Weber argues that the modern world is different from previous epochs because of the dominance of instrumental rationality and what he calls increasing "disenchantment." Instrumental rationality is means-ends thinking, where we focus on goals and the means to achieve them. Weber used the term the "disenchantment of the world" to describe the replacement of magic and religious thinking with reason. Weber was interested both in the history of urban development as well as the city as a form of modern life. In this essay, Weber defines the city through different lenses in an effort to explain and clarify the nature of the city. Weber developed a typology of what he thought made modern Western cities unique relative to other world social and political formations. Compare Weber's analysis to the efforts of Aristotle, Simmel, Mumford, Engels, and Mendieta to define and describe cities.

"CONCEPTS AND CATEGORIES OF THE CITY" (1921)

THE ECONOMIC CONCEPT OF THE CITY: THE MARKET SETTLEMENT

The notion of the "city" can be defined in many different ways. The only element which all these definitions have in common is the following: the city is a relatively closed settlement, and not simply a collection of a number of separate dwellings. As a rule the houses in cities—but not only in them—are built very close to each other, today normally wall-to-wall. The common concept further associates with the word "city" a purely quantitative aspect: it is a *large* locality. In itself, this is not imprecise. Sociologically speaking, this would mean: the city is a settlement of closely spaced dwellings which form a colony so extensive that the reciprocal personal acquaintance of the inhabitants, elsewhere characteristic of the neighborhood, is lacking. But on this definition only very large localities would qualify as cities, and the special conditions of various cultures would have to determine at which size the absence of personal acquaintance would be characteristic. Many localities which in the past had the *legal* character of cities were not marked by this feature. Conversely, in present-day Russia there are "villages" which, with many thousands of inhabitants, are much larger than many of the old "cities"—for example, in the Polish settlement area of the German East—with only a few hundred inhabitants. Size alone, certainly, cannot be decisive.

If we were to attempt a definition in purely economic terms, the city would be a settlement whose inhabitants live primarily from commerce and the trades rather than from agriculture. It would not be expedient, however, to call all localities of this type "cities," for this would include the concept settlements of kinship groups practicing a single, practically hereditary trade such as the "craft villages" of Asia and Russia. A further characteristic, hence, might have to be a certain multiplicity of the trades practiced. But even this would, by itself, not appear suitable as a decisive characteristic. Economic diversity can be called forth in two ways: by the presence of a court, or by that of a market. A feudal, and, especially, a princely court constitutes a center whose economic or political needs evoke specialization of craft production and exchange of goods. However, a seigneurial or princely *oikos* with an attached settlement of artisans and small merchants encumbered with tribute and service obligations, even if it be of large size, we would not usually call a "city," though it is true that a large proportion of important cities have their historical origin in such settlements and that the production for a prince's court remained a highly important, if not the chief, source of income for the inhabitants of such "princely towns" for a long time. A further characteristic is required for us to speak of a "city": the existence of a regular, and not only occasional, exchange of goods in the settlement itself, an exchange which constitutes an essential component of the livelihood and the satisfaction of needs of the settlers—in other words: a market. But again: not every "market" converts the locality in which it is conducted into a "city." The periodic fairs and markets for the long-distance trade, at which travelling merchants gathered at fixed times in order to sell their wares in large or small lots to each other or to consumers, very often took place in localities which we would call "villages."

Accordingly, we shall speak of a "city" in the economic sense of the word only if the local population satisfies an economically significant part of its everyday requirements in the local market, and if a significant part of the products bought there were acquired or produced specifically for sale on the market by the local population or that of the immediate hinterland. A city, then, is always a market center. It has a local market which forms the economic center of the settlement and on which both the non-urban population and the townsmen satisfy their wants for craft products or trade articles by means of exchange on the basis of an existing specialization in production. It was originally quite normal for the city, wherever it was structurally differentiated from the countryside, to be both a seigneurial or princely residence *and* a market place and thus to possess economic centers of both types, *oikos* and market. Frequently, in addition to the regular local market, it might also have periodical fairs for the long-distance trade of travelling merchants. But the city, as we use the word here, is essentially a "market settlement."

The existence of the market is often based on concessions and guarantees of protection by the lord or prince. [. . .] As a rule the quantitative expansion of cities which had originated as "princely cities" and the growth of their economic significance went hand in hand with an increase in the market-orientation of the satisfaction of wants by the princely court and the large urban households of vassals and major officials attached to it. [. . .]

THREE TYPES: THE "CONSUMER CITY," THE "PRODUCER CITY," THE "MERCHANT CITY"

The "princely city," that is, one whose inhabitants are directly or indirectly dependent on the purchasing power of the court and the other large households, is similar in type to other cities in which the purchasing power of other large consumers—and that means: of *rentiers*—determines the economic opportunities of the resident artisans and traders. These large consumers can be of very different types, depending upon the kind and sources of their incomes. They may be officials spending their legal or illegal revenues, or manorial lords and political power holders consuming their non-urban ground rents or other more politically determined incomes in the city. In both cases the city is very similar to the type of the "princely city" in that it depends upon patrimonial and political revenues which supply the purchasing power of the larger consumers. An example for a city of officials might be Peking, for a city of land-rent consumers Moscow before the abolition of serfdom.

From these cases we must differentiate the only apparently similar case in which *urban* land-rents, based on the "monopoly of location" of urban land lots, are concentrated in the hands of a city aristocracy. Here the source of the spending power is the urban trade and commerce itself. This city type has been ubiquitous, especially in Antiquity from the beginnings up to the Byzantine period and also in the Middle Ages. The city is in that case economically not of a *rentier* type, but rather, depending upon the circumstances, a merchant or producer city, and those rents are a tribute exacted by the real-estate owners from the economically active population. But the conceptual differentiation of this case from that in which the rents stem from extra-urban sources should not cause us to overlook the historical interrelation of the two forms.

Finally, the large consumers can also be *rentiers* consuming business incomes in the city—today mainly interest on bonds, royalties or dividends on shares; the purchasing power then rests primarily on revenue sources based on the (capitalistic) money economy. An example would be the city of Arnhem. Or is it based on state pensions and interest on government bonds, as in a "pensionopolis" like Wiesbaden. In these and many other similar cases one may speak of a "consumer city," for the residence of these various types of large consumers is of decisive importance for the economic opportunities of the local producers and merchants.

Conversely, the city may be a "producer city." The population expansion and the purchasing power of this population would then depend, as in Essen or Bochum, on the location there of factories, manufactures or putting-out industries which supply outside territories. This is the modern type. In the Asian, ancient, and medieval type, it would depend on the existence of local crafts which ship their goods to outside markets. The large consumers on the local market are the entrepreneurs, if they are locally resident—which is not always the case—, and the mass consumers may be formed by the merchants and local landowners who are indirectly maintained by the city's productive activity.

Besides a "consumer city" and a "producer city," we can also distinguish a "merchant city," a type in which the purchasing power of the large consumers rests on the profits derived either from the retailing of foreign products on the local market (as in the case of the woolen drapers of the Middle Ages), or from the sale abroad of domestic products or at least of products obtained by domestic producers (as the herring of the Hanseatic towns), or finally from the purchase of foreign products and their resale abroad with or without local stapling (*"entrepôt* cities"). Very often all these activities are combined: the essence of the *commenda* and *societas maris* contracts of the Mediterranean countries[1] was that a *tractator* (travelling partner) carried to the Levantine markets domestic products purchased entirely or in part with capital entrusted to him by local capitalists—although often he may have journeyed entirely in ballast—and after the sale of these products returned with Oriental articles for sale on the domestic market; the profits were to be divided between *tractator* and capital-supplier according to a formula set in the contract. Thus the purchasing power and tax yield of the merchant city, like that of the producer city, and in contrast to that of the consumer city, rest on the local economic

---

1. On the medieval forms of partnership, *commenda* and *societas maris*, as well as on the "seal loan," cf. Weber *Handelsgesellschaften*, 324–44; *id., General Economic History*, Trans. Frank H. Knight. New York, Collier Books, 1961, 158f; *Cambridge Economic History of Europe*, III, 49–59.

enterprises. The economic opportunities of the shipping and transport trades and of numerous small and large secondary activities are tied up with those of the merchants, although only in the case of local retail sales do these benefits materialize entirely on the local market, while in long-distance trade a considerable part is realized abroad. A similar state of affairs prevails in a modern city which is the seat of the national or inter-national financiers or of the giant banks (London, Paris, Berlin), or of large joint stock companies and cartels (Düsseldorf). Today, of course, it hap-pens more than ever before that the larger part of the profits of an enter-prise flows to localities other than that in which the producing plant is situated. Moreover, an ever increasing part of the gains is consumed by the recipients not at the metropolitan seat of the business headquarters, but in the suburbs, and increasingly even more in rural summer homes and in-ternational hotels. Parallel to these developments, the town centers tend to atrophy to mere business sections, to "The City."

It is not our intention here to produce the further casuistic distinc-tions and specialization of concepts which would be required for a strictly economic theory of the city. Nor do we need to stress that actual cities almost always represent mixed types and hence can be classified only in terms of their respective predominant economic components.

RELATION OF THE CITY TO AGRICULTURE

Historically, the relation of the city to agriculture has in no way been unambiguous and simple. There were and are "agrarian cities" (*Ackerbürgerstädte*), which as market centers and seats of the typically urban trades are sharply differentiated from the average village, but in which a broad stratum of the burghers produces food for their own consumption and even for the market. Normally, to be sure, it would be true that the larger a city, the less likely it is that its inhabitants would dispose of farmland sufficient for their food needs—nor would they have the pasturage and forest utilization rights typical of the "village." The largest German city of the Middle Ages, Cologne, apparently from the very beginning almost completely lacked the *Allmende* (commons) which at that time was part of every normal village. But other German and foreign medieval cities owned, at the least, considerable pastures and woods which stood at the disposal of their burghers. And the further to the south or back toward Antiquity one turns, the more frequent be-comes the presence of large amounts of farmland within the territory (*Weichbild*) of the towns. If today we are quite correct in regarding the typical "townsman" as a man who does not grow his own food, the contrary was originally true for the majority of typical cities (*poleis*) of

Antiquity. We shall see that the urban "citizen" with full rights was in Antiquity, in contrast to the Middle Ages, identified precisely by the fact that he owned a *kleros* or *fundus* (in Israel: *ḥelek*): a full lot of arable land, which fed him.[2] [. . .] The "citizens" of Antiquity were "agrarian burghers."

THE "URBAN ECONOMY" AS A STAGE OF ECONOMIC DEVELOPMENT

The relation of the city as the carrier of the craft and trading activities to the countryside as the supplier of food forms one aspect of that complex of phenomena which has been called the "urban economy" (*Stadtwirtschaft*), juxtaposed, as a special economic stage, to the "household economy" (*Eigenwirtschaft*), on the one hand and the "national economy" (*Volkswirtschaft*) on the other (or to a multiplicity of similar conceptual "stages").[3] In this concept, however, categories relevant to measures of economic *policy* are fused with purely economic categories. The reason for this is that the mere facts of the crowding together of merchants and tradesmen and of the satisfaction of everyday wants on a regular basis in the market do not by themselves exhaust the concept of the "city." [. . .]

It is not the mere fact of regulation which differentiated the cities of the past from other types of settlements, but the kinds of regulations: the objects of regulatory economic policy, and the range of measures which were characteristic for it. The bulk of the measures of "urban economic policy" (*Stadtwirtschaftspolitik*) were based on the fact that, under the transportation conditions of the past, the majority of all inland cities were dependent upon the agricultural resources of the immediate hinterland (a statement which, of course, does not hold for maritime cities—as shown by the grain policies of Athens and Rome), that the hinterland provided the natural marketing area for the majority of the urban trades, and finally that for this natural local process of exchange the urban market place provided, if not the only, then at least the normal locality, especially in the case of foods. [. . .]

THE POLITICO-ADMINISTRATIVE CONCEPT OF THE CITY

The very fact that in these observations we had to employ categories such as "urban economic policy," "urban territory" and "urban authority"

---

2. Cf. *General Economic History*, Trans. Frank H. Knight. New York, Collier Books, 1961, 243; *Ancient Judaism*, Trans. and ed. Hans H. Gerth and Don Martindale. Glencoe, IL: The Free Press, 1952, 73.

3. Cf. Max Weber, *Economy and Society*, ed. Guenther Roth and Claus Wittich. Berkeley: University of California Press, 1978, Part One, ch. 2, n. 24.

indicates that the concept of the "city" can and must also be analyzed in terms of a series of categories other than the purely economic ones hitherto discussed, namely, in terms of political categories. It is quite true that the initiator of the urban economic policy may be a prince in whose political territory the city and its inhabitants belong. In this case, whenever a specifically urban economic policy exists at all, it is determined *for* the city and its inhabitants and not *by* it. However, this does not have to be the case, and even if it is, the city must still to some extent be a partially autonomous organization, a "community" (*Gemeinde*) with special administrative and political institutions.

The economic concept of the city previously discussed must, at any rate, be clearly differentiated from the political-administrative concept. Only in the latter sense may a special urban *territory* be associated with it. A locality can be thought of as a city in the political-administrative sense even though it could not claim this name in the economic sense. The inhabitants of some medieval settlements with the legal status of "cities" derived nine-tenths or more of their livelihood from agriculture, a far larger fraction than those of many places with the legal status of "villages." Naturally, the dividing lines between such "agrarian cities" and the "consumer," "producer," and "merchant" cities are completely fluid. But in all settlements which are differentiated administratively from the village and are treated as "cities," one point, namely the nature of land ownership, is as a rule quite different from that prevailing in the countryside. Economically speaking, this is due to the specific basis of the earning capacity of urban real estate: house ownership, to which land ownership is merely accessory. But from the administrative point of view, the special position of urban real estate is connected above all with divergent principles of taxation; at the same time, however, it is closely connected with another trait which is decisive for the political-administrative concept of the city and which stands entirely outside the purely economic analysis, namely, the fact that the city in the past, in Antiquity and in the Middle Ages, outside as well as within Europe, was also a special kind of a *fortress* and a *garrison*. At present this feature of the city has been entirely lost, and even in the past it was not universal. [. . .]

THE "COMMUNE" AND THE "BURGHER": A SURVEY

A. Features of the Occidental Commune

Not every "city" in the economic sense, nor every garrison whose inhabitants had a special status in the political-administrative sense, has in the past constituted a "commune" (*Gemeinde*). The city-commune in the full meaning of the word appeared as a mass phenomenon only in the Occident; the Near East (Syria, Phoenicia, and perhaps Mesopotamia) also knew it, but only as a temporary structure. Elsewhere one finds nothing but rudiments. To develop into a city-commune, a settlement had to be of the nonagricultural-commercial type, at least to a relative extent, and to be equipped with the following features: 1. a fortification; 2. a market; 3. its own court of law and, at least in part, autonomous law; 4. an associational structure (*Verbandscharakter*) and, connected therewith, 5. at least partial autonomy and autocephaly, which includes administration by authorities in whose appointment the burghers could in some form participate. In the past, such rights almost always took the form of privileges of an "estate" (*Stand*); hence the characteristic of the city in the political definition was the appearance of a distinct "bourgeois" estate.

Questions for Review and Discussion

1. Why does Weber think definitions of the city based on size or purely economic terms are inadequate?

2. How does Weber distinguish between a "consumer city," a "producer city," and a "merchant city"?

3. How does Weber define cities in terms of political categories?

4. What does Weber think is required if a city is to constitute a full urban "commune" or community?

John Dewey

John Dewey (1859–1952) is one of the major philosophers of his time, an American who shaped the American pragmatist tradition as well as many other areas of philosophy, psychology, education, and democratic theory. While at the University of Chicago, he founded the Chicago school of pragmatism, a group with which Jane Addams was also associated. Michael Weinstein argues that while other American pragmatists imagined philosophy in the wilderness, Dewey remained grounded in the city (*The Wilderness and the City*. Amherst, MA: University of Massachusetts Press, 1982, p. 10). In contrast, commentators Morton and Lucia White (*The Intellectual Versus the City*. New York: Mentor Books, 1962, pp. 159–180) view Dewey as anti-urban insofar as he emphasizes the need to create community and worries about the challenges to the formation of community that urbanization presents.

The essay included here does not address such concerns directly, but rather focuses on Dewey's view of the relationship between philosophy and civilization. If we take urbanization to be the hallmark of civilization, then Dewey's essay raises questions about the task of the philosopher and the relationship between philosophy and urban life. Dewey is critical of philosophical idealism that tries to situate itself in the realm of Truth and apart from everyday practices. Instead, Dewey argues that philosophy and civilization are interdependent and transform one another. Compare to Plato and Conlon.

"PHILOSOPHY AND CIVILIZATION" (1927)

The two views of the history of thought are usually proffered as irreconcilable opposites. According to one, it is the record of the most profound dealings of the reason with ultimate being; according to the other, it is a scene of pretentious claims and ridiculous failures. Nevertheless, there is a point of view from which there is something common to the two notions, and this common denominator is more significant than the oppositions. Meaning is wider in scope as well as more precious in value than is truth, and philosophy is occupied with meaning rather than with truth. Making such a statement is dangerous; it is easily misconceived to signify that truth is of no great importance under any circumstances; while the fact is that truth is so infinitely important when it is important at all, namely, in records of events and descriptions of existences, that we extend its claims to regions where it has no jurisdiction. But even as respects truths, meaning is the wider category; truths are but one class of meanings, namely, those in which a claim to verifiability by their consequences is an intrinsic part of their meaning. Beyond this island of meanings which in their own nature are true or false lies the ocean of meanings to which truth and falsity are irrelevant. We do not inquire whether Greek civilization was true or false, but we are immensely concerned to penetrate its meaning. We may indeed ask for the truth of Shakespeare's *Hamlet* or Shelley's *Skylark*, but by truth we now signify something quite different from that of scientific statement and historical record.

In philosophy we are dealing with something comparable to the meaning of Athenian civilization or of a drama or a lyric. Significant history is lived in the imagination of man, and philosophy is a further excursion of the imagination into its own prior achievements. All that is distinctive of man, marking him off from the clay he walks upon or the potatoes he eats, occurs in his thought and emotions, in what we have agreed to call consciousness. Knowledge of the structure of sticks and stones, an enterprise in which, of course, truth is essential, apart from whatever added control it may yield, marks in the end but an enrichment of consciousness, of the area of meanings. Thus scientific thought itself is finally but a function of the imagination in enriching life with the significance of things; it is of its peculiar essence that it must also submit to certain tests of application and control. Were significance identical with existence, were values the same as events, idealism would be the only possible philosophy.

It is commonplace that physically and existentially man can but make a superficial and transient scratch upon the outermost rind of the world. It has become a cheap intellectual pastime to contrast the infinitesimal pettiness of man with the vastness of the stellar universes. Yet all such comparisons are illicit. We cannot compare existence and meaning; they are disparate. The characteristic life of man is itself the meaning of vast stretches of existences, and without it the latter have no value or significance. There is no common measure of physical existence and conscious experience because the latter is the only measure there is for the former. The significance of being, though not its existence, is the emotion it stirs, the thought it sustains.

It follows that there is no specifiable difference between philosophy and its role in the history of civilization. Discover and define the right characteristic and unique function in civilization, and you have defined philosophy itself. To try to define philosophy in any other way is to search for a will-of-the-wisp; the conceptions which result are of purely private interpretation, for they only exemplify the particular philosophies of their authorship and interpretation. Take the history of philosophy from whatever angle and in whatever cross-section you please, Indian, Chinese, Athenian, the Europe of the twelfth or the twentieth century, and you find a load of traditions proceeding from an immemorial past. You find certain

preoccupying interests that appear hypnotic in their rigid hold upon imagination and you also find certain resistances, certain dawning rebellions,
struggles to escape and to express some fresh value of life. The preoccupations may be political and artistic as in Athens; they may be economic
and scientific as today. But in any case, there is a certain intellectual work
to be done; the dominant interest working throughout the minds of masses
of men as to be clarified, a result which can be accomplished only by
selection, elimination, reduction and formulation; the interest has to be
intellectually forced, exaggerated in order to be focused. Otherwise it is
not intellectually in consciousness, since all clear consciousness by its very
nature marks a wrenching of something from its subordinate place to
confer upon it a centrality which is existentially absurd. Where there is
sufficient depth and range of meanings for consciousness to arise at all,
there is a function of adjustment, of reconciliation of the ruling interest of
the period with preoccupations which had a different origin and an irrelevant meaning. Consider, for example, the uneasy, restless effort of Plato
to adapt his new mathematical insights and his political aspirations to the
traditional habits of Athens; the almost humorously complacent union of
Christian supernaturalism in the middle ages with the naturalism of pagan
Greece; the still fermenting effort of the recent age to unite the new
science of nature with inherited classic and medieval institutions. The life
of all thought is to effect a junction at some point of the new and the old,
of deep-sunk customs and unconscious dispositions, that are brought to
the light of attention by some conflict with newly emerging directions of
activity. Philosophies which emerge at distinctive periods define the larger
patterns of continuity which are woven in effecting the enduring junctions
of a stubborn past and an insistent future.

Philosophy thus sustains the closest connection with the history of
culture, with the succession of changes in civilization. It is fed by the
streams of tradition, traced at critical moments to their sources in order
that the current may receive a new direction; it is fertilized by the fer-
ment of new inventions in industry, new explorations of the globe, new
discoveries in science. But philosophy is not just a passive reflex of civilization that persists through changes, and that changes while persisting.
It is itself a change; the patterns formed in this junction of the new and
the old are prophecies rather than records; they are policies, attempts to
forestall subsequent developments. The intellectual registrations which
constitute a philosophy are generative just because they are selective and
eliminative exaggerations. While purporting to say that such and such is
and always *has* been the purport of the record of nature, in effect they
proclaim that such and such *should* be the significant value to which
mankind should loyally attach itself. Without evidence adduced in its

behalf such a statement may seem groundless. But I invite you to examine for yourselves any philosophical idea which has had for any long period a significant career, and find therein your own evidence. Take, for example, the Platonic patterns of cosmic design and harmony; the Aristotelian perpetually recurrent ends and grooved potentialities; the Kantian fixed forms of intellectual synthesis; the conception of nature itself as it figured in seventeenth and eighteenth century thought. Discuss them as revelations of eternal truth, and something almost childlike or something beyond possibility of decision enters in; discuss them as selections from existing culture by means of which to articulate forces which the author believed should and would dominate the future, and they become preciously significant aspects of human history.

Thus philosophy marks a change of culture. In forming patterns to be conformed to in future thought and action, it is additive and transforming in its role in the history of civilization. Man states anything at his peril; once stated, it occupies a place in a new perspective; it attains a permanence which does not belong to its existence; it enters provokingly into wont and use; it points in a troubling way to need of new endeavors. I do not mean that the creative element in the role of philosophy is necessarily the dominant one; obviously its formulations have been often chiefly conservative, justificatory of selected elements of traditions and received institutions. But even these preservative systems have had a transforming if not exactly a creative effect; they have lent the factors which were selected a power over later human imagination and sentiment which they would otherwise have lacked. And there are other periods, such as those of the seventeenth and eighteenth centuries in Europe, when philosophy is overtly revolutionary in attitude. To their authors, the turn was just from complete error to complete truth; to later generations looking back, the alteration in strictly factual content does not compare with that in desire and direction of effort. [...]

Philosophy, we have been saying, is a conversion of such culture as exists into consciousness, into an imagination which is logically coherent and is not incompatible with what is factually known. But this conversion is itself a further movement of civilization; it is not something performed upon the body of habits and tendencies from without, that is, miraculously. [...]

Please do not imagine that this is a plea in disguise for any particular type of philosophizing. On the contrary, any philosophy which is a sincere outgrowth and expression of our own civilization is better than none, provided it speaks the authentic idiom of an enduring and dominating corporate experience. If we are really, for instance, a materialistic people, we are at least materialistic in a new fashion and on a new scale. I should welcome then a consistent materialistic philosophy, if only it were sufficiently bold. For in the degree in which, despite attendant esthetic repulsiveness, it marked the coming to consciousness of a group of ideas, it would formulate a coming to self-consciousness of our civilization. Thereby it would furnish ideas, supply an intellectual polity, direct further observations and experiments, and organize their results on a grand scale. As long as we worship science and are afraid of philosophy we shall have no great science; we shall have a lagging and halting continuation of what is thought and said elsewhere. As far as any plea is implicit in what has been said, it is, then, a plea for the casting off of that intellectual timidity which hampers the wings of imagination, a plea for speculative audacity, for more faith in ideas, sloughing off a cowardly reliance upon those partial ideas to which we are wont to give the name of facts. I have given to philosophy a more humble function than that which is often assigned it. But modesty as to its final place is not incompatible with boldness in the maintenance of that function, humble as it may be. A combination of such modesty and courage affords the only way I know of in which the philosopher can look his fellowman in the face with frankness and with humanity.

Questions for Review and Discussion

1. What are the two views of the history of thought (philosophy)?

2. Why does Dewey reject the idea that philosophy primarily concerns truth? What does he think it actually concerns?

3. What does Dewey identify as the intellectual work to be done?

4. Does Dewey think that philosophy is merely dependent on culture? Explain.

5. In what sense does Dewey think that philosophy transforms culture?

Walter Benjamin

Walter Benjamin was a German Jewish philosopher and a prominent member of the Frankfurt School. His work primarily focused on political theory and aesthetics. Both of those interests are combined in his unfinished study of Paris's shops or arcades. Written in note or aphoristic form, Benjamin explores how history crystallizes in particular urban elements (something John Dewey also examines). The sections excerpted focus on two issues: a) a critique of the scientization of urban planning, and b) how boundaries for cities are created. Benjamin's analysis of city boundaries has influenced many contemporary urban theorists and planners. He was particularly critical of the massive reconstruction of Paris that occurred in the nineteenth century under the direction of Baron Haussmann. Haussmann ordered that most of the city be dug up so that broad, new boulevards could be built. While many urban planners and theorists greatly admire Haussmann, others such as Benjamin were very critical of what they saw as Haussmann's dehumanized, overly scientific approach. By the twentieth century, social scientists have supplanted philosophers as the urban thinkers par excellence, but some philosophers have offered resistance. Compare with Dewey, Lefebvre, Foucault, and Bickford.

THE ARCADES PROJECT (1935–1939)

E. HAUSSMANN, OR THE BARRICADES

I

I venerate the Beautiful, the Good, and all things great;
Beautiful nature, on which great art rests—
How it enchants the ear and charms the eye!
I love spring in blossom: women and roses.

—Baron Haussmann, *Confession d'un lion devenu vieux*[1]

Haussmann's activity is incorporated into Napoleonic imperialism, which favors investment capital. In Paris, speculation is at its height. Haussmann's expropriations give rise to speculation that borders on

---

1. *Confession d'un lion devenu vieux* [Confession of a Lion Grown Old] (Paris, 1888), 4 pp., was published anonymously, without year or place, by Baron Haussmann. [R.T.]

fraud. The rulings of the Court of Cassation, which are inspired by the bourgeois and Orleanist opposition, increase the financial risks of Haussmannization. Haussmann tries to shore up his dictatorship by placing Paris under an emergency regime. In 1864, in a speech before the National Assembly, he vents his hatred of the rootless urban population. This population grows ever larger as a result of his projects. Rising rents drive the proletariat into the suburbs. The *quartiers* of Paris in this way lose their distinctive physiognomy. The "red belt" forms. Haussmann gave himself the title of "demolition artist." He believed he had a vocation for his work, and emphasizes this in his memoirs. The central marketplace passes for Haussmann's most successful construction—and this is an interesting symptom. It has been said of the Ile de la Cité, the cradle of the city, that in the wake of Haussmann only one church, one public building, and one barracks remained. Hugo and Mérimée suggest how much the transformations made by Haussmann appear to Parisians as a monument of Napoleonic despotism. The inhabitants of the city no longer feel at home there; they start to become conscious of the inhuman character of the metropolis. Maxime Du Camp's monumental work *Paris* owes its existence to this dawning awareness. The etchings of Meryon (around 1850) constitute the death mask of old Paris.

The true goal of Haussmann's projects was to secure the city against civil war. He wanted to make the erection of barricades in the streets of Paris impossible for all time. With the same end in mind, Louis Philippe had already introduced wooden paving. Nevertheless, barricades had played a considerable role in the February Revolution. Engels studied the tactics of barricade fighting. Haussmann seeks to forestall such combat in two ways. Widening the streets will make the erection of barricades impossible, and new streets will connect the barracks in straight lines with the workers' districts. Contemporaries christened the operation "strategic embellishment."

II

The flowery realm of decorations,
The charm of landscape, or architecture,
And all the effects of scenery rest
Solely on the law of perspective.
—Franz Böhle, *Theater-Catechismus* (Munich), p. 74

Haussmann's ideal in city planning consisted of long straight streets opening onto broad perspectives. This ideal corresponds to the tendency—common in the nineteenth century—to ennoble technological necessities through spurious artistic ends. The temples of the bourgeoisie's spiritual and secular power were to find their apotheosis within the framework of these long streets. The perspectives, prior to their inauguration, were screened with canvas draperies and unveiled like monuments; the view would then disclose a church, a train station, an equestrian statue, or some other symbol of civilization. With the Haussmannization of Paris, the phantasmagoria was rendered in stone. Though intended to endure in quasi-perpetuity, it also reveals its brittleness. The Avenue de l'Opéra—which, according to a malicious saying of the day, affords a perspective on the porter's lodge at the Louvre—shows how unrestrained the prefect's megalomania was.

A. [ARCADES, *MAGASINS DE NOUVEAUTÉS*, SALES CLERKS]

The magic columns of these palaces
Show to the amateur on all sides,
In the objects their porticos display,
That industry is the rival of the arts.

—"Chanson nouvelle," cited in *Nouveaux Tableaux de Paris, ou Observations sur les moeurs et usages des Parisiens au commencement du XIXe siècle* (Paris, 1828), vol. 1, p. 27

For sale the bodies, the voices, the tremendous unquestionable wealth, what will never be sold.

—Rimbaud[2]

"In speaking of the inner boulevards," says the *Illustrated Guide to Paris*, a complete picture of the city on the Seine and its environs from the year 1852, "we have made mention again and again of the arcades which open onto them. These arcades, a recent invention of industrial luxury, are glass-roofed, marble-paneled corridors extending through whole blocks of buildings, whose owners have joined together for such enterprises.

Names of *magasins de nouveautés*: La Fille d'Honneur, La Vestale, Le Page Inconstant, Le Masque de Fer <The Iron Mask>, Le Petit chaperon Rouge <Little Red Riding Hood>, Petite Nanette, La Chaumière allemande <The German Cottage>, Au Mamelouk, Le Coin de la Rue <On the Streetcorner>—names that mostly come from successful vaudevilles. ▯ Mythology ▯ A glover: Au Ci-Devant Jeune Homme. A confectioner: Aux Armes de Werther.

2. Arthur Rimbaud, *Complete Works and Selected Letters*, trans. Wallace Fowllie (Chicago: University of Chicago Press, 1966), p. 254 (*Illuminations*, "Sale").

Lining both sides of these corridors, which get their light from above, are the most elegant shops, so that the arcade is a city, a world in miniature ▯ Flâneur ▯, in which customers will find everything they need. During sudden rainshowers, the arcades are a place of refuge for the unprepared, to whom they offer a secure, if restricted, promenade—one from which the merchants also benefit." ▯ Weather ▯

This passage is the locus classicus for the presentation of the arcades; for not only do the divagations on the flâneur and the weather develop out of it, but, also, what there is to be said about the construction of the arcades, in an economic and architectural vein, would have a place here.   [A1,1]

The city is only apparently homogeneous. Even its name takes on a different sound from one district to the next. Nowhere, unless perhaps in dreams, can the phenomenon of the boundary be experienced in a more originary way than in cities. To know them means to understand those lines that, running alongside railroad crossings and across privately owned lots, within the park and along the riverbank, function as limits; it means to know these confines, together with the enclaves of the various districts. As threshold, the boundary stretches across streets; a new precinct begins like a step into the void—as though one had unexpectedly cleared a low step on a flight of stairs.   [C3,3]

Haussmann's predilection for perspectives, for long open vistas, represents an attempt to dictate arts forms to technology (the technology of city planning). This always results in kitsch.   [E2a,7]

Questions for Review and Discussion

1. What does Benjamin think that Haussmann's true motive was in widening the streets?

2. According to Benjamin, what is Haussmann's ideal of city planning? What is Benjamin's assessment of that ideal?

3. What does Benjamin mean by a "boundary"? Why are they important in cities?

Martin Heidegger

Martin Heidegger (1889–1976) was a twentieth-century German philosopher who developed an extensive theory of existential phenomenology. He asks fundamental questions of human existence and our relationship to the world (both nature and the built environment). Although Heidegger did not write about cities per se, his work on the existential concept of dwelling, that is, how we find a sense of place for ourselves in the world, has had a major impact on architectural theorists as well as environmental and urban philosophers. Taken from his famous essay of the same name, this selection introduces Heidegger's concept of dwelling, its connection to building, and how dwelling allows humans to find existential meaning by bringing together earth, and sky, mortality, and spirituality. Compare to Mugerauer and Norberg-Schulz, both of whom are heavily influenced by Heidegger, as well as to Mendieta and Weiss who also work out of the phenomenological tradition.

"BUILDING DWELLING THINKING" (1954)

In what follows we shall try to think about dwelling and building. This thinking about building does not presume to discover architectural ideas, let alone to give rules for building. This venture in thought does not view building as an art or as a technique of construction; rather it traces building back into that domain to which everything that *is* belongs. We ask:

1. What is it to dwell?

2. How does building belong to dwelling?

I

We attain to dwelling, so it seems, only by means of building. The latter, building, has the former, dwelling, as its goal. Still, not every building is a dwelling. Bridges and hangars, stadiums and power stations are buildings but not dwellings; railway stations and highways, dams and market halls are built, but they are not dwelling places. Even so, these buildings are in the domain of our dwelling. That domain extends over these buildings and yet is not limited to the dwelling place. The truck driver is at home on the highway, but he does not have his shelter there; the working woman is at home in the spinning mill, but does not have her dwelling place there; the chief engineer is at home in the power station, but he does not dwell there. These buildings house man. He inhabits them and yet does not dwell in them, when to dwell means merely that we take shelter in them. In today's housing shortage even this much is reassuring and to the good; residential buildings do indeed provide shelter; today's houses may even be well planned, easy to keep, attractively cheap, open to air, light, and sun, but—do the houses in themselves hold any guarantee that *dwelling* occurs in them? Yet those buildings that are not dwelling places remain in turn determined by dwelling insofar as they serve man's dwelling. Thus dwelling would in any case be the end that presides over all building. Dwelling and building are related as end and means. However, as long as this is all we have in mind, we take dwelling and building as two separate activities, an idea that has something correct in it. Yet at the same time by the means-end schema we block our view of the essential relations. For building is not merely a means and a way toward dwelling—to build is in itself already to dwell. Who tells us this? Who gives us a standard at all by which we can take the measure of the nature of dwelling and building?

It is language that tells us about the nature of a thing, provided that we respect language's own nature. In the meantime, to be sure, there rages round the earth an unbridled yet clever talking, writing, and broadcasting of spoken words. Man acts as though *he* were the shaper and master of language, while in fact *language* remains the master of man. Perhaps it is before all else man's subversion of *this* relation of dominance that drives his nature into alienation. That we retain a concern for care in speaking is all to the good, but it is of no help to us as long as language still serves us even then only as a means of expression. Among all the appeals that we human beings, on our part, can help to be voiced, language is the highest and everywhere the first.

What, then, does *Bauen*, building, *mean*? The Old English and High German word for building, *buan*, means to dwell. This signifies: to remain, to stay in a place. The real meaning of the verb *bauen*, namely, to dwell, has been lost to us. But a covert trace of it has been preserved in the German word *Nachbar*, neighbor. The neighbor is in Old English the *neahgebur; neah*, near, and *gebur*, dweller. The *Nachbar* is the *Nachgebur*, the *Nachgebauer*, the near-dweller, he who dwells nearby. The verbs *buri, büren, beuren, beuron*, all signify dwelling, the abode, the place of dwelling. Now to be sure the old word *buan* not only tells us that *bauen*, to build, is really to dwell; it also gives us a clue as to how we have to think about the dwelling it signifies. When we speak of dwelling we usually think of an activity that man performs alongside many other activities. We work here and dwell there. We do not merely dwell—that would be virtual inactivity—we practice a profession, we do business, we travel and lodge on the way, now here, now there. *Bauen* originally means to dwell. Where the word *bauen* still speaks in its original sense it also says *how far* the nature of dwelling reaches. That is, *bauen, buan, bhu, beo* are our word *bin* in the versions: *ich bin*, I am, *du bist*, you are, the imperative form *bis*, be. What then does *ich bin* mean? The old word *bauen*, to which the *bin* belongs, answers: *ich bin, du bist* meaning: I dwell, you dwell. The way in which you are and I am, the manner in which we humans *are* on the earth, is *Buan*, dwelling. To be a human being means to be on the earth as a mortal. It means to dwell. The old word *bauen*, which says that man *is* insofar as he *dwells*, this word *bauen* however *also* means at the same time to cherish and protect, to preserve and care for, specifically to till the soil, to cultivate the vine. Such building only takes care—it tends the growth that ripens into its fruit of its own accord. Building in the sense of preserving and nurturing is not making anything. Shipbuilding and temple-building, on the other hand, do in a certain way make their own works. Here building, in contrast with cultivating, is a constructing. Both modes of building—building as cultivating, Latin *colere, cultura*, and building as the raising up of edifices, *aedificare*—are comprised within genuine building, that is, dwelling. Building as dwelling, that is, as being on the earth, however, remains for man's everyday experience that which is from the outset "habitual"—we inhabit it, as our language says so beautifully: it is the *Gewohnte*. For this reason it recedes behind the manifold ways in which dwelling is accomplished, the activities of cultivation and construction. These activities later claim the nature of *bauen*, building, and with it the fact of building, exclusively for themselves. The real sense of *bauen*, namely dwelling, falls into oblivion.

At first sight this event looks as though it were no more than a change of meaning of mere terms. In truth, however, something decisive is concealed in it, namely, dwelling is not experienced as man's being; dwelling is never thought of as the basic character of human being.

That language in a way retracts the real meaning of the word *bauen*, which is dwelling, is evidence of the primal nature of these meanings; for with the essential words of language, their true meaning easily falls into oblivion in favor of foreground meanings. Man has hardly yet pondered the mystery of this process. Language withdraws from man its simple and high speech. But its primal call does not thereby become incapable of speech; it merely falls silent. Man, though, fails to heed this silence.

But if we listen to what language says in the word *bauen* we hear three things:

1. Building is really dwelling.

2. Dwelling is the manner in which mortals are on the earth.

3. Building as dwelling unfolds into the building that cultivates growing things and the building that erects buildings.

If we give thought to this threefold fact, we obtain a clue and note the following: as long as we do not bear in mind that all building is in itself a dwelling, we cannot even adequately *ask*, let alone properly decide, what the building of buildings might be in its nature. We do not dwell because we have built, but we build and have built because we dwell, that is, because we are *dwellers*. But in what does the nature of dwelling consist? Let us listen once more to what language says to us. The Old Saxon *wuon*, the Gothic *wunian*, like the old word *bauen*, mean to remain, to stay in a place. But the Gothic *wunian* says more distinctly how this remaining is experienced. *Wunian* means: to be at peace, to be brought to peace, to remain in peace. The word for peace, *Friede*, means the free, *das Frye*, and *fry* means: preserved from harm and danger, preserved from something, safeguarded. To free really means to spare. The sparing itself consists not only in the fact that we do not harm the one whom we spare. Real sparing is something *positive* and takes place when we leave something beforehand in its own nature, when we return it specifically to its being, when we "free" it in the real sense of the word into a preserve of peace. To dwell, to be set at peace, means to remain at peace within the free, the preserve, the free sphere that safeguards each thing in its nature. *The fundamental character of dwelling is this sparing and preserving.* It pervades dwelling in its whole range. That range reveals itself to us as soon as we reflect that human being consists in dwelling and, indeed, dwelling in the sense of the stay of mortals on the earth.

But "on the earth" already means "under the sky." Both of these *also* mean "remaining before the divinities" and include a "belonging to men's being with one another." By a *primal* oneness the four—earth and sky, divinities and mortals—belong together in one.

Earth is the serving bearer, blossoming and fruiting, spreading out in rock and water, rising up into plant and animal. When we say earth, we are already thinking of the other three along with it, but we give no thought to the simple oneness of the four.

The sky is the vaulting path of the sun, the course of the changing moon, the wandering glitter of the stars, the year's seasons and their changes, the light and dusk of day, the gloom and glow of night, the clemency and inclemency of the weather, the drifting clouds and blue depth of the ether. When we say sky, we are already thinking of the other three along with it, but we give no thought to the simple oneness of the four.

The divinities are the beckoning messengers of the godhead. Out of the holy sway of the godhead, the god appears in his presence or withdraws into his concealment. When we speak of the divinities, we are already thinking of the other three along with them, but we give no thought to the simple oneness of the four.

The mortals are the human beings. They are called mortals because they can die. To die means to be capable of death *as* death. Only man dies, and indeed continually, as long as he remains on earth, under the sky, before the divinities. When we speak of mortals, we are already thinking of the other three along with them, but we give no thought to the simple oneness of the four.

This simple oneness of the four we call *the fourfold*. Mortals *are* in the fourfold by *dwelling*. But the basic character of dwelling is to spare, to preserve. Mortals dwell in the way they preserve the fourfold in its essential being, its presencing. Accordingly, the preserving that dwells is fourfold.

Mortals dwell in that they save the earth—taking the word in the old sense still known to Lessing. Saving does not only snatch something from a danger. To save really means to set something free into its own presencing. To save the earth is more than to exploit it or even wear it out. Saving the earth does not master the earth and does not subjugate it, which is merely one step from spoliation.

Mortals dwell in that they receive the sky as sky. They leave to the sun and the moon their journey, to the stars their courses, to the seasons their blessing and their inclemency; they do not turn night into day nor day into a harassed unrest.

Mortals dwell in that they await the divinities as divinities. In hope they hold up to the divinities what is unhoped for. They wait for intimations of their coming and do not mistake the signs of their absence. They do not make their gods for themselves and do not worship idols. In the very depth of misfortune they wait for the weal that has been withdrawn.

Mortals dwell in that they initiate their own nature—their being capable of death as death—into the use and practice of this capacity, so that there may be a good death. To initiate mortals into the nature of death in no way means to make death, as empty Nothing, the goal. Nor does it mean to darken dwelling by blindly staring toward the end.

In saving the earth, in receiving the sky, in awaiting the divinities, in initiating mortals, dwelling occurs as the fourfold preservation of the fourfold. To spare and preserve means: to take under our care, to look after the fourfold in its presencing. What we take under our care must be kept safe. But if dwelling preserves the fourfold, where does it keep the fourfold's nature? How do mortals make their dwelling such a preserving? Mortals would never be capable of it if dwelling were merely a staying on earth under the sky, before the divinities, among mortals. Rather, dwelling itself is always a staying with things. Dwelling, as preserving, keeps the fourfold in that with which mortals stay: in things.

Staying with things, however, is not merely something attached to this fourfold preserving as a fifth something. On the contrary; staying with things is the only way in which the fourfold stay within the fourfold is accomplished at any time in simple unity. Dwelling preserves the fourfold by bringing the presencing of the fourfold into things. But things themselves secure the fourfold *only when* they themselves *as* things are let be in their presencing. How is this done? In this way, that mortals nurse and nurture the things that grow, and specially construct things that do not grow. Cultivating and construction are building in the narrower sense. *Dwelling*, insofar as it keeps or secures the fourfold in things, is, as this keeping, *a building*. With this, we are on our way to the second question. [...]

Questions for Review and Discussion

1. What does Heidegger mean by "gathering the fourfold"? What are the four elements that are gathered? How is this concept connected to dwelling?

2. What is it to dwell?

3. How does building belong to dwelling?

Lewis Mumford

Lewis Mumford (1895–1990) was an American public intellectual who wrote in the areas of social philosophy, American literary and cultural history, the history of technology, and the history of cities and urban planning practice. The selection here is from the last chapter of his major opus, *The City in History*. Mumford sums up the history of Western cities, arguing that the prospects for great cities lie in recovering the human drama and interaction at the heart of urban life in the ancient Greek city (polis). This requires the development of new institutions so that cities fulfill their ultimate function, namely, to further humanity's conscious participation in the cosmos and history. Mumford takes a clear position on the question, "what is a city?" Note the metaphor he uses in his definition. He draws his ideal in part from his understanding of the ancient Athenian polis. Compare to Plato, Aristotle, Augustine, Weber, Conlon, and Mendieta on the definition of cities. His views are best contrasted with Lefebvre, who explicitly criticizes this view of the city as ideology.

"RETROSPECT AND PROSPECT" (1961)

In taking form, the ancient city brought together many scattered organs of the common life, and within its walls promoted their interaction and fusion. The common functions that the city served were important; but the common purposes that emerged through quickened methods of communication and co-operation were even more significant. The city mediated between the cosmic order, revealed by the astronomer priests, and the unifying enterprises of kingship. The first took form within the temple and its sacred compound, the second within the citadel and the bounding city wall. By polarizing hitherto untapped human aspirations and drawing them together in a central political and religious nucleus, the city was able to cope with the immense generative abundance of neolithic culture.

By means of the order so established, large bodies of men were for the first time brought into effective co-operation. Organized in disciplined work groups, deployed by central command, the original urban populations in Mesopotamia, Egypt, and the Indus Valley controlled flood, repaired storm damage, stored water, remodelled the landscape, built up a great water network for communication and transportation, and filled the urban reservoirs with human energy available for other collective enterprises. In time, the rulers of the city created an internal fabric of order and justice that gave to the mixed populations of cities, by conscious effort, some of the moral stability and mutual aid of the village. Within the theater of the city new dramas of life were enacted.

But against these improvements we must set the darker contributions of urban civilization: war, slavery, vocational over-specialization, and in many places, a persistent orientation toward death. These institutions and activities, forming a 'negative symbiosis,' have accompanied the city through most of its history, and remain today in markedly brutal form, without their original religious sanctions, as the greatest threat to further human development. Both the positive and the negative aspects of the ancient city have been handed on, in some degree, to every later urban structure.

Through its concentration of physical and cultural power, the city heightened the tempo of human intercourse and translated its products into forms that could be stored and reproduced. Through its monuments, written records, and orderly habits of association, the city enlarged the scope of all human activities, extending them backwards and forwards in time. By means of its storage facilities (buildings, vaults, archives, monuments, tablets, books), the city became capable of transmitting a complex culture from generation to generation, for it marshalled together not only the physical means but the human agents needed to pass on and enlarge this heritage. That remains the greatest of the city's gifts. As compared with the complex human order of the city, our present ingenious electronic mechanisms for storing and transmitting information are crude and limited.

From the original urban integration of shrine, citadel, village, workshop, and market, all later forms of the city have, in some measure, taken their physical structure and their institutional patterns. Many parts of this fabric are still essential to effective human association, not least those that sprang originally from the shrine and the village. Without the active participation of the primary group, in family and neighborhood, it is doubtful if the elementary moral loyalties—respect for the neighbor and reverence for life—can be handed on, without savage lapses, from the old to the young.

At the other extreme, it is doubtful, too, whether those multifarious co-operations that do not lend themselves to abstraction and symbolization can continue to flourish without the city, for only a small part of the contents of life can be put on the record. Without the superposition of many different human activities, many levels of experience, within a limited urban area, where they are constantly on tap, too large a portion of life would be restricted to record-keeping. The wider the area of communication and the greater the number of participants, the more need there is for providing numerous accessible permanent centers for face-to-face intercourse and frequent meetings at every human level.

The recovery of the essential activities and values that first were incorporated in the ancient cities, above all those of Greece, is accordingly a primary condition for the further development of the city in our time. Our elaborate rituals of mechanization cannot take the place of the human dialogue, the drama, the living circle of mates and associates, the society of friends. These sustain the growth and reproduction of human culture, and without them the whole elaborate structure becomes meaningless—indeed actively hostile to the purposes of life.

Today the physical dimensions and the human scope of the city have changed; and most of the city's internal functions and structures must be recast to promote effectively the larger purposes that shall be served: the unification of man's inner and outer life, and the progressive unification of mankind itself. The city's active role in the future is to bring to the highest pitch of development the variety and individuality of regions, cultures, personalities. These are complementary purposes: their alternative is the current mechanical grinding down of both the landscape and the human personality. Without the city modern man would have no effective defenses against those mechanical collectives that, even now, are ready to make all veritably human life superfluous, except to perform a few subservient functions that the machine has not yet mastered.

Ours is an age in which the increasingly automatic processes of production and urban expansion have displaced the human goals they are supposed to serve. Quantitative production has become, for our mass-minded contemporaries, the only imperative goal: they value quantification without qualification. In physical energy, in industrial productivity, in invention, in knowledge, in population the same vacuous expansions and explosions prevail. As these activities increase in volume and in tempo, they move further and further away from any humanly desirable objectives. As a result, mankind is threatened with far more formidable inundations than ancient man learned to cope with. To save himself he must turn his attention to the means of controlling, directing, organizing, and subordinating to his own biological functions and cultural purposes the insensate forces that would, by their very superabundance, undermine his life. He must curb them and even eliminate them completely when, as in the case of nuclear and bacterial weapons, they threaten his very existence.

Now it is not a river valley, but the whole planet, that must be brought under human control: not an unmanageable flood of water, but even more alarming and malign explosions of energy that might disrupt the entire ecological system on which man's own life and welfare depends. The prime need of our age is to contrive channels for excessive energies and impetuous vitalities that have departed from organic norms and limits: cultural flood control in every field calls for the erection of embankments, dams, reservoirs, to even out the flow and spread it into the final receptacles, the cities and regions, the groups, the families, and personalities, who will be able to utilize this energy for their own growth and development. If we were prepared to restore the habitability of the earth and cultivate the empty spaces in the human soul, we should not be so preoccupied with sterile escapist projects for exploring inter-planetary space, or with even more rigorously dehumanized policies based on the strategy of wholesale collective extermination. It is time to come back to earth and confront life in all its organic fecundity, diversity, and creativity, instead of taking refuge in the under-dimensioned world of Post-historic Man.

Modern man, unfortunately, has still to conquer the dangerous aberrations that took institutional form in the cities of the Bronze Age and gave a destructive destination to our highest achievements. Like the rulers of the Bronze Age, we still regard power as the chief manifestation of divinity, or if not that, the main agent of human development. But 'absolute power,' like 'absolute weapons,' belongs to the same magico-religious scheme as ritual human sacrifice. Such power destroys the symbiotic co-operation of man with all other aspects of nature, and of men with other men. Living organisms can use only limited amounts of energy. 'Too much' or 'too little' is equally fatal to organic existence. Organisms, societies, human persons, not least, cities, are delicate devices for regulating energy and putting it to the service of life.

The chief function of the city is to convert power into form, energy into culture, dead matter into the living symbols of art, biological reproduction into social creativity. The positive functions of the city cannot be performed without creating new institutional arrangements, capable of coping with the vast energies modern man now commands: arrangements just as bold as those that originally transformed the overgrown village and its stronghold into the nucleated, highly organized city.

These necessary changes could hardly be envisaged, were it not for the fact that the negative institutions that accompanied the rise of the city have for the last four centuries been falling into decay, and seemed until recently to be ready to drop into limbo. Kingship by divine right has all but disappeared, even as a moribund idea; and the political functions that were once exercised solely by the palace and the temple, with the coercive aid of the bureaucracy and the army, were during the nineteenth century assumed by a multitude of organizations, corporations, parties, associations, and committees. So, too, the conditions laid down by Aristotle for the abolition of slave labor have now been largely met, through the harnessing of inorganic sources of energy and the invention of automatic machines and utilities. Thus slavery, forced labor, legalized expropriation, class monopoly of knowledge, have been giving way to free labor, social security, universal literacy, free education, open access to knowledge, and the beginnings of universal leisure, such as is necessary for wide participation in political duties. If vast masses of people in Asia, Africa, and South America still live under primitive conditions and depressing poverty, even the ruthless colonialism of the nineteenth century brought to these peoples the ideas that would release them. 'The heart of darkness,' from Livingstone on to Schweitzer, was pierced by a shaft of light.

In short, the oppressive conditions that limited the development of cities throughout history have begun to disappear. Property, caste, even vocational specialization have—through the graded income tax and the 'managerial revolution'—lost most of their hereditary fixations. What Alexis de Tocqueville observed a century ago is now more true than ever: the history of the last eight hundred years is the history of the progressive equalization of classes. This change holds equally of capitalist and communist systems, in a fashion that might have shocked Karl Marx, but would not have surprised John Stuart Mill. For the latter foresaw the conditions of dynamic equilibrium under which the advances of the machine economy might at last be turned to positive human advantage. Until but yesterday, then, it seemed that the negative symbiosis that accompanied the rise of the city was doomed. The task of the emerging city was to give an ideal form to these radically superior conditions of life.

Unfortunately, the evil institutions that accompanied the rise of the ancient city have been resurrected and magnified in our own time: so the ultimate issue is in doubt. Totalitarian rulers have reappeared, sometimes elevated, like Hitler, into deities, or mummified in Pharaoh-fashion after death, for worship, like Lenin and Stalin. Their methods of coercion and terrorism surpass the vilest records of ancient rulers, and the hoary practice of exterminating whole urban populations has even been exercised by the elected leaders of democratic states, wielding powers of instantaneous destruction once reserved to the gods. Everywhere secret knowledge has put an end to effective criticism and democratic control; and the emancipation from manual labor has brought about a new kind of enslavement: abject dependence upon the machine. The monstrous gods of the ancient world have all reappeared, hugely magnified, demanding total human sacrifice. To appease their super-Moloch in the Nuclear Temples, whole nations stand ready, supinely, to throw their children into his fiery furnace.

If these demoralizing tendencies continue, the forces that are now at work will prove uncontrollable and deadly; for the powers man now commands must, unless they are detached from their ancient ties to the citadel, and devoted to human ends, lead from their present state of paranoid suspicion and hatred to a final frenzy of destruction. On the other hand, if the main negative institutions of civilization continue to crumble—that is, if the passing convulsions of totalitarianism mark in fact the death-throes of the old order—is it likely that war will escape the same fate? War was one of the 'lethal genes' transmitted by the city from century to century, always doing damage but never yet widely enough to bring civilization itself to an end. That period of tolerance is now over. If civilization does not eliminate war as an open possibility, our nuclear agents will destroy civilization—and possibly exterminate mankind. The vast village populations that were once reservoirs of life will eventually perish with those of the cities.

Should the forces of life, on the other hand, rally together, we shall stand on the verge of a new urban implosion. When cities were first founded, an old Egyptian scribe tells us, the mission of the founder was to "put the gods in their shrines." The task of the coming city is not essentially different: its mission is to put the highest concerns of man at the center of all his activities: to unite the scattered fragments of the human personality, turning artificially dismembered men—bureaucrats, specialists, 'experts,' depersonalized agents—into complete human beings, repairing the damage that has been done by vocational separation, by social segregation, by the over-cultivation of a favored function, by tribalisms and nationalisms, by the absence of organic partnerships and ideal purposes.

Before modern man can gain control over the forces that now threaten his very existence, he must resume possession of himself. This sets the chief mission for the city of the future: that of creating a visible regional and civic structure, designed to make man at home with his deeper self and his larger world, attached to images of human nurture and love.

We must now conceive the city, accordingly, not primarily as a place of business or government, but as an essential organ for expressing and actualizing the new human personality—that of 'One World Man.' The old separation of man and nature, of townsman and countryman, of Greek and barbarian, of citizen and foreigner, can no longer be maintained: for communication, the entire planet is becoming a village; and as a result, the smallest neighborhood or precinct must be planned as a working model of the larger world. Now it is not the will of a single deified ruler, but the individual and corporate will of its citizens, aiming at self-knowledge, self-government, and self-actualization, that must be embodied in the city. Not industry but education will be the center of their activities; and every process and function will be evaluated and approved just to the extent that it furthers human development, whilst the city itself provides a vivid theater for the spontaneous encounters and challenges and embraces of daily life.

Apparently, the inertia of current civilization still moves toward a worldwide nuclear catastrophe; and even if that fatal event is postponed, it may be a century or more before the possibility can be written off. But happily life has one predictable attribute: it is full of surprises. At the last moment—and our generation may in fact be close to the last moment— the purposes and projects that will redeem our present aimless dynamism may gain the upper hand. When that happens, obstacles that now seem insuperable will melt away; and the vast sums of money and energy, the massive efforts of science and technics, which now go into the building of nuclear bombs, space rockets, and a hundred other cunning devices directly or indirectly attached to dehumanized and de-moralized goals, will be released for the recultivation of the earth and the rebuilding of cities: above all, for the replenishment of the human personality. If once the sterile dreams and sadistic nightmares that obsess the ruling élite are banished, there will be such a release of human vitality as will make the Renascence seem almost a stillbirth.

It would be foolish to predict when or how such a change may come about; and yet it would be even more unrealistic to dismiss it as a possibility, perhaps even an imminent possibility, despite the grip that the myth of the machine still holds on the Western World. Fortunately, the preparations for the change from a power economy to a life economy have been long in the making; and once the reorientation of basic ideas and purposes takes place, the necessary political and physical transformations may swiftly follow. Many of the same forces that are now oriented toward death will then be polarized toward life.

In discussing the apparent stabilization of the birthrate, as manifested throughout Western civilization before 1940, the writer of 'The Culture of Cities' then observed: "One can easily imagine a new cult of family life, growing up in the face of some decimating catastrophe, which would necessitate a swift revision in plans for housing and city development: a generous urge toward procreation might clash in policy with the views of the prudent, bent on preserving a barely achieved equilibrium."

To many professional sociologists, captivated by the smooth curves of their population graphs, that seemed a far-fetched, indeed quite unimaginable possibility before the Second World War. But such a spontaneous reaction actually took place shortly after the war broke out, and has continued, despite various 'expert' prediction to the contrary, for the last twenty years. Many people who should be vigilantly concerned over the annihilation of mankind through nuclear explosions have concealed that dire possibility from themselves by excessive anxiety over the 'population explosion'—without the faintest suspicion, apparently, that the threat of de-population and that of over-population might in fact be connected.

As of today, this resurgence of reproductive activity might be partly explained as a deep instinctual answer to the premature death of scores of millions of people throughout the planet. But even more possibly, it may be the unconscious reaction to the likelihood of an annihilating outburst of nuclear genocide on a planetary scale. As such, every new baby is a blind desperate vote for survival: people who find themselves unable to register an effective political protest against extermination do so by a biological act. In countries where state aid is lacking, young parents often accept a severe privation of goods and an absence of leisure, rather than accept privation of life by foregoing children. The automatic response of every species threatened with extirpation takes the form of excessive reproduction. This is a fundamental observation of ecology.

No profit-oriented, pleasure-dominated economy can cope with such demands: no power-dominated economy can permanently suppress them. Should the same attitude spread toward the organs of education, art, and culture, man's super-biological means of reproduction, it would alter the entire human prospect: for public service would take precedence over private profit, and public funds would be available for the building and rebuilding of villages, neighborhoods, cities, and regions, on more generous lines than the aristocracies of the past were ever able to afford for themselves. Such a change would restore the discipline and the delight of the garden to every aspect of life; and it might do more to balance the birthrate, by its concern with the quality of life, than any other collective measure.

As we have seen, the city has undergone many changes during the last five thousand years; and further changes are doubtless in store. But the innovations that beckon urgently are not in the extension and perfection of physical equipment: still less in multiplying automatic electronic devices for dispersing into formless sub-urban dust the remaining organs of culture. Just the contrary: significant improvements will come only through supplying art and thought to the city's central human concerns, with a fresh dedication to the cosmic and ecological processes that enfold all being. We must restore to the city the material, life-nurturing functions, the autonomous activities, the symbiotic associations that have long been neglected or suppressed. For the city should be an organ of love; and the best economy of cities is the care and culture of men.

The city first took form as the home of a god: a place where eternal values were represented and divine possibilities revealed. Though the symbols have changed the realities behind them remain. We know now, as never before, that the undisclosed potentialities of life reach far beyond the proud algebraics of contemporary science; and their promises for the further transformations of man are as enchanting as they are inexhaustible. Without the religious perspectives fostered by the city, it is doubtful if more than a small part of man's capacities for living and learning could have developed. Man grows in the image of his gods, and up to the measure they have set. The mixture of divinity, power, and personality that brought the ancient city into existence must be weighed out anew in terms of the ideology and the culture of our own time, and poured into fresh civic, regional, and planetary molds. In order to defeat the insensate forces that now threaten civilization from within, we must transcend the original frustrations and negations that have dogged the city throughout its history. Otherwise the sterile gods of power, unrestrained by organic limits or human goals, will remake man in their own faceless image and bring human history to an end.

The final mission of the city is to further man's conscious participation in the cosmic and the historic process. Through its own complex and enduring structure, the city vastly augments man's ability to interpret these processes and take an active, formative part in them, so that every phase of the drama it stages shall have, to the highest degree possible, the illumination of consciousness, the stamp of purpose, the color of love. That magnification of all the dimensions of life, through emotional communion, rational communication, technological mastery, and above all, dramatic representation, has been the supreme office of the city in history. And it remains the chief reason for the city's continued existence.

Questions for Review and Discussion

1. What does Mumford think is the chief accomplishment and purpose of cities?

2. Discuss Mumford's metaphor of the city as theater.

3. What does Mumford think must be restored if cities of the future are to flourish?

4. What earlier negative elements of city life have modern cities, according to Mumford, come close to successfully eliminating?

Contemporary Readings (1970–present)

Henri Lefebvre

Henri Lefebvre, French philosopher (1900–1991), was influenced by Marx, Nietzsche, and phenomenology. Although Lefebvre was not part of the movement itself, he influenced Guy DeBord and others who founded situationism. Situationism was an avant-garde movement inspired by Marxism, anarchism, and surrealism to stage artistic interventions in urban streets as a way of recapturing what Lefebvre called the "right to the city," which is an effort to find renewed human meaning in urban spaces. Although his writings were first received in the Anglo world by geographers interested in his work on cities and concepts of space, his political philosophy and sociological theory is now being discovered by philosophers working on a wide range of urban issues.

Critical of Heidegger's emphasis on dwelling as being too focused on nostalgia for home, Lefebvre argues that the city (rather than the home) expresses and symbolizes a person's being and consciousness. He is critical of philosophical efforts to totalize the city, that is, to view the city from a bird's eye perspective without grounding it in the realities of everyday urban life. Lefebvre also is critical of urban ideals that are still based on the ancient Athenian polis. In the passage here, a chapter from his book *Right to the City*, Lefebvre reflects on the history of the relationship between philosophy and the city. He argues that philosophical ideals of city play ideological roles, but he is even more critical of attempts to make urban planning scientific. Contrast Lefebvre's work with Heidegger and Mumford, but also compare him to Engels and Benjamin.

"PHILOSOPHY OF THE CITY
AND PLANNING IDEOLOGY" (1965–1968)

In order to formulate the problematic of the city (to articulate problems by linking them), the following must be clearly distinguished:

1. The philosophers and philosophies of the city who define it speculatively as whole by defining the 'homo urbanicus' as man in general, the world or the cosmos, society, history.

2. Partial knowledge concerning the city (its elements, functions, structures).

3. The technical application of this knowledge (in a particular context defined by strategic and political decision).

136

4. Planning as doctrine, that is, as ideology, interpreting partial knowledge, justifying its application and raising these (by extrapolation) to a poorly based or legitimated totality.

The aspects or elements which this analysis distinguishes do not appear separately in various works; they interest, reinforcing or neutralizing each other. Plato proposes a concept of the city and ideal town in *Critias*. In *The Republic* and *The Laws*, Platonic utopia is tempered by very concrete analyses. It is the same for Aristotle's political writings which study the constitution of Athens and other Greek cities.

Today, Lewis Mumford and G. Bardet among others still imagine a city made up not of townspeople, but of free citizens, free from the division of labour, social classes and class struggles, making up a community, freely associated for the management of this community. As philosophers, they make up a model of the ideal city. They conceive freedom in the twentieth century according to the freedom of the Greek city (this is an ideological travesty: only the city as such possessed freedom and not individuals and groups). Thus they think of the modern city according to a model of the antique city, which is at the same time identified with the ideal and rational city. The agora, place and symbol of a democracy limited to its citizens, and excluding women, slaves and foreigners, remains for a particular philosophy of the city the symbol or urban society in general. This is a typically ideological extrapolation. To this ideology these philosophers add partial knowledge, this purely ideological operation consisting in a passage (a leap), from the partial to the whole, from the elementary to the total, from the relative to the absolute. As for Le Corbusier, as philosopher of the city he describes the relationship between the urban dweller and dwelling with nature, air, sun, and trees, with cyclical time and the rhythms of the cosmos. To this metaphysical vision, he adds an unquestionable knowledge of the real problems of the modern city, a knowledge which gives rise to a planning practice and an ideology, a functionalism which reduces urban society to the achievement of a few predictable and prescribed functions laid out on the ground by the architecture. Such an architect sees himself as a 'man of synthesis,' thinker and practitioner. He believes in and wants to create human relations by defining them, by creating their environment and décor. Within this well-worn perspective, the architect perceives and imagines himself as architect of the world, human image of God the Creator.

Philosophy of the city (or if one wants, urban ideology), was born as a superstructure of society into which structures entered a certain type of city. This philosophy, precious heritage of the past, extends itself into speculations which often are travesties of science just because they integrate a few bits of real knowledge.

Planning as ideology has acquired more and more precise definitions. To study the problems of circulation, of the conveying of orders and information in the great modern city, leads to real knowledge and to technical applications. To claim that the city is defined as a network of circulation and communication, as a centre of information and decision-making, is an absolute ideology; this ideology proceeding from a particularly arbitrary and dangerous reduction-extrapolation and using terrorist means, sees itself as total truth and dogma. It leads to a planning of pipes, of roadworks and accounting, which one claims to impose in the name of science and scientific rigour. Or even worse!

This ideology has two interdependent aspects, mental and social. Mentally, it implies a theory of rationality and organization whose expression date from around 1910, a transformation in contemporary society (characterized by the beginning of a deep crisis and attempts to resolve it by organizational methods, firstly the scale of the firm, and then on a global scale). It is then that socially the notion of space comes to the fore, relegating into shadow time and becoming. Planning as ideology formulates all the problems of society into questions of space and transposes all that comes from history and consciousness into spatial terms. It is an ideology which immediately divides up. Since society does not function in a satisfactory manner, could there not be a pathology of space? Within this perspective, the virtually official recognition of the priority of space over time is not conceived of as indication of social pathology, as symptom among others of a reality which engenders social disease. On the contrary, what are represented are healthy and diseased spaces. The planner should be able to distinguish between sick spaces and spaces linked to mental and social health which are generators of this health. As physician of space, he should have the capacity to conceive of an harmonious social space, normal and normalizing. Its function would then be to grant to this space (perchance identical to geometrical space, that of abstract topologies) preexisting social realities.

The radical critique of philosophies of the city as well as of ideology is vital, as much on the theoretical as on the practical level. It can be made in the name of public health. However, it cannot be carried out without extensive research, rigorous analyses and the patient study of texts and contexts.

Questions for Review and Discussion

1. What does Lefebvre mean by planning as ideology?

2. What is Lefebvre's critique of most philosophies of the city?

3. Why is Lefebvre critical of twentieth-century thinkers who still draw on the ancient Athenian polis as the source for the ideal city?

4. According to Lefebvre, what is the problem with the scientization of urban planning?

5. Why does Lefebvre argue that "a radical critique of philosophies of the city as well as ideology is vital"?

William J. Gavin

William J. Gavin, a living American philosopher, continues the American pragmatist interest in philosophy and its role in public life. The article included is one of his earliest writings; his most recent work focuses on John Dewey [*In Dewey's Wake: Unfinished Work of Pragmatic Reconstruction* (ed. 2003)]. In the article here, Gavin worries about the lack of a role for philosophy in the city. Like Benjamin and Lefebvre, Gavin criticizes social scientific approaches to cities that focus only on their problems. Gavin's essay also helps us think about issues concerning the built environment raised by Heidegger and Norberg-Schulz as well as questions regarding citizenship and human engagement with the city.

"THE URBAN AND THE AESTHETIC" (1971)

It is obvious by now that something is drastically wrong with our cities. The plethora of sociological analyses dealing with urban plights is an endless one. In addition, the problem has mushroomed to the stage where the danger is not simply one city vis-à-vis another, or one part or section of a city versus a counterpart; rather has something gone askew with the whole notion of "city" in general.

The basic problem, and perhaps a hint at a possible answer, lies in the basic metaphors which we use to describe our cities. We speak of "a place to work" and mean by it a "pit" we have to "descend into" five days a week. Cities have become urban mine shafts so to speak, and like mine shafts we appraise cities in terms of security and safety. The city, like the shaft, is now something to be stoically endured, not something to be transformed, and certainly not something to be aesthetically appreciated. Our mentality toward cities is nowadays one wherein we do not consider the city part of ourselves.

It has been said that man is an organism going through a self-realization process in response to a context. That context exists as an invitation or a confrontation—not as a neutral object. Furthermore, in responding to the invitation man not only creates himself but also changes the context with which he finds himself involved. By considering the city "impartially" as a problem or an object, or in other words, by looking at the city as a spectator rather than as a participator involved with a context, man basically "accomplishes" two things. First, he alienates himself from the city, and in so doing cuts himself off from a significant portion of his context and therefore of his possibilities for self-realization. Secondly, in setting up the dichotomy wherein he portrays himself as a neutral spectator looking at a disinterested amorphous object (a place to work) he tacitly admits that the city as object is a given, i.e., is in a fixed, certain condition or state. The fact that we plead again and again for security and safety simply highlights this.

Man, at various critical stages of his cultural development has found himself in an age of crisis. Usually he has responded to this situation by looking for objectivity and certainty, or in other words, by seeking out absolutes. To do so entails weeding out any subjective attitudes which might prejudice the issue. So man sets up a subject/object dichotomy in which he, as a neutral spectator, looks at impartial objects in an uninvolved manner.

This procedure allows man to withdraw—to remain uncommitted. "You can't fight city hall," the saying goes. I no longer consider myself part of the city because I have allowed the subject/object dichotomy to be set up. I have done this to avoid dealing with issues and problems. But in doing this, I have radically alienated myself from my context as a self-developing organism and this, quite frankly, is agonizing and ultimately dehumanizing.

This is, by no means, to say that the problems of the city are easy or even that they are capable of solution. But, it is to say that we cannot have our cake and eat it. Man's context is important; it should be viewed as analogous to an artist's material. With his material, the artist might indeed create a great painting; but without it, he will certainly do nothing. The artist's material then, is by no means something totally divorced from him—it is not a group of neutral objects lying before him. Rather, it is the case that only insofar as he responds to the "invitation" of these "contexts" that he has the possibility of becoming an artist.

The city constitutes the material of the artist (or at least some of it). And like it or not, we are all condemned to be artists. The very fact that we are organisms going through a process of self-realization forces us to be creative creatures. But man has stopped looking at the city as an inviting context and started looking at it "objectively" as "a place to work." He no longer judges his city in aesthetic terms. This, we submit, is disastrous because man is basically an aesthetic animal.

Let us end with an example. The most obvious aesthetic category is "harmony" which has been defined in several different ways. Simply for illustrative purposes, we list three: harmony is the greatest amount of diversity with the fewest assumptions for unity; harmony is maximum feasible participation; harmony is a creative tension of opposites. The notion of harmony, however, is not a static one—the idea is not to set up a single equilibrium of opposites once and for all—but to have a "continuously changing" equilibrium, thereby allowing for new individuality and yet preserving unity. The city in this sense would not be a group of buildings, but a continuously changing pattern, a cultural matrix in and through which man undergoes the process of self-realization. Unfortunately, we have stopped associating the aesthetic notion of harmony in any of the above senses with that of the city. Precisely because we have alienated ourselves from urban contexts, we no longer consider them in terms of possible aesthetic metamorphosis, but rather look at them as apodictic givens.

Our metaphors for the city nowadays are almost entirely quantitative; we prefer to substitute blueprints for contexts and to give technological answers to human dilemmas. In our desire to be impartial and uninvolved, we have arrived at the curious stage of "letting the forest get in the way of the tree." A return to considering the city in aesthetic categories will certainly not give answers to the pressing issues. But, it will at least make us aware that man is an artist involved with his context, be it urban or pastoral, and furthermore, that he is responsible for what he does (or doesn't) create from it.

Questions for Review and Discussion

1. According to Gavin, what metaphors do we use about cities? Why does Gavin think that the metaphors we use about the city are important?

2. What does Gavin think that problems are with impartial or objective looks at the city?

3. What does he think would be a more productive way to approach the city?

Jürgen Habermas

Jürgen Habermas is a living German philosopher who has continued the Frankfurt school (of which Walter Benjamin was an earlier member). Habermas has focused on legal, social, and political theory, developing a theory of communicative action that explains how both ethics and politics can be rationally legitimated. His most recent work focuses on the challenges of citizenship in the age of globalization. Although the selected passage is not explicitly about cities, his discussion of the public sphere as the space of citizenship and political participation has been highly influential in urban studies. Habermas's analysis may be compared to discussions of Heidegger, Lefebvre, and Foucault and the links between the physical spaces of cities and their political meanings as well as to Greek (Pericles, Plato, Aristotle) and later (Mumford, Kemmis) discussions of citizenship.

"THE PUBLIC SPHERE" (1973)

CONCEPT

By "public sphere" we mean first of all a domain of our social life in which such a thing as public opinion can be formed. Access to the public sphere is open in principle to all citizens. A portion of the public sphere is constituted in every conversation in which private persons come together to form a public. They are then acting neither as business or professional people conducting their private affairs, nor as legal consociates subject to the legal regulations of a state bureaucracy and obligated to obedience. Citizens act as a public when they deal with matters of general interest without being subject to coercion; thus with the guarantee that they may assemble and unite freely, and express and publicize their opinions freely. When the public is large, this kind of communication requires certain means of dissemination and influence; today, newspapers and periodicals, radio and television are the media of the public sphere. We speak of a political public sphere (as distinguished from a literary one, for instance) when the public discussions concern objects connected with the practice of the state. The coercive power of the state is the counterpart, as it were, of the political public sphere, but it is not a part of it. State power is, to be sure, considered "public" power, but it owes the attribute of publicness to its task of caring for the public, that is, providing for the common good of all legal consociates. Only when the exercise of public authority has actually been subordinated to the requirement of democratic publicness does the political public sphere acquire

143

an institutionalized influence on the government, by way of the legislative body. The term "public opinion" refers to the functions of criticism and control of organized state authority that the public exercises informally, as well as formally during periodic elections. Regulations concerning the publicness (or publicity [*Publizität*] in its original meaning) of state-related activities, as, for instance, the public accessibility required of legal proceedings, are also connected with this function of public opinion. To the public sphere as a sphere mediating between state and society, a sphere in which the public as the vehicle of public opinion is formed, there corresponds the principle of publicness—the publicness that once had to win out against the secret politics of monarchs and that since then has permitted democratic control of state activity.

It is no accident that these concepts of the public sphere and public opinion were not formed until the eighteenth century. They derive their specific meaning from a concrete historical situation. It was then that one learned to distinguish between opinion and public opinion, or *opinion publique*. Whereas mere opinions (things taken for granted as part of a culture, normative convictions, collective prejudices and judgments) seem to persist unchanged in their quasi-natural structure as a kind of sediment of history, public opinion, in terms of its very idea, can be formed only if a public that engages in rational discussion exists. Public discussions that are institutionally protected and that take, with critical intent, the exercise of political authority as their theme have not existed since time immemorial—they developed only in a specific phase of bourgeois society, and only by virtue of a specific constellation of interests could they be incorporated into the order of the bourgeois constitutional state. [...]

The political public sphere in the welfare state is characterized by a singular weakening of its critical functions. Whereas at one time publicness was intended to subject persons or things to the public use of reason and to make political decisions susceptible to revision before the tribunal of public opinion, today it has often enough already been enlisted in the aid of the secret policies of interest groups; in the form of "publicity" it now acquires public prestige for persons or things and renders them capable of acclamation in a climate of nonpublic opinion. The term "public relations" itself indicates how a public sphere that formerly emerged from the structure of society must now be produced circumstantially on a case-by-case basis. The central relationship of the public, political parties, and parliament is also affected by this change in function.

This existing trend toward the weakening of the public sphere, as a principle, is opposed, however, by a welfare-state transformation of the functioning of basic rights: the requirement of publicness is extended by state organs to all organizations acting in relation to the state. To the extent to which this becomes a reality, a no longer intact public of private persons acting as individuals would be replaced by a public of organized private persons. Under current circumstances, only the latter could participate effectively in a process of public communication using the channels of intra-party and intra-organizational public spheres, on the basis of a publicness enforced for the dealings of organizations with the state. It is in this process of public communication that the formation of political compromises would have to achieve legitimation. The idea of the public sphere itself, which signified a rationalization of authority in the medium of public discussions among private persons, and which has been preserved in mass welfare-state democracy, threatens to disintegrate with the structural transformation of the public sphere. Today it could be realized only on a different basis, as a rationalization of the exercise of social and political power under the mutual control of rival organizations committed to publicness on their internal structure as well as in their dealings with the state and with one another.

Questions for Review and Discussion

1. What does Habermas mean by "the public sphere"?

2. What does he mean by "public opinion"?

3. How does the public sphere mediate between state and society?

4. Why does Habermas argue that the concepts of public sphere and public opinion could not have developed until the eighteenth century?

5. How does Habermas characterize the public sphere in the welfare state?

Michel Foucault

Michel Foucault (1926–1984) was a French philosopher who focused on political power and analysis of the modern condition. Influenced by Heidegger, he developed his own philosophical method called "geneology" in which he traces the roots of concepts to shed light on our present situation. Although Foucault did not write much on cities specifically, his analysis of the Panopticon has been applied to analyses of a wide range of urban phenomena. Designed by eighteenth-century philosopher Jeremy Bentham, the Panopticon was a prison designed for maximum surveillance by placing the cells in a circle, all facing a guard tower. The prison isolated prisoners and organized their cells in such a way that prisoners never knew when they were being observed. The result is that prisoners always acted as if they were being observed, and internalized the disciplinary gaze. While few prisons were actually built according to Bentham's design because it was found that the arrangement often caused prisoners to go mad, Foucault argues that the concept of the panopticon can be understood as the quintessential realization of modern discipline and power. In modernity, we eschew public displays of punishment in favor of internalized, self-discipline. The references to Bentham that appear in the text are made to Bentham's *Works*, ed. Bowring, IV, 1843. Young and Bickford are both indebted to Foucault in their analyses of contemporary American urban public spaces.

"PANOPTICISM" (1975)

Bentham's Preface to *Panopticon* opens with a list of the benefits to be obtained from his 'inspection-house': '*Morals reformed—health preserved—industry invigorated—instruction diffused—public burthens lightened—*Economy seated, as it were, upon a rock—the gordian knot of the Poor-Laws not cut, but untied—all by a simple idea in architecture!' (Bentham, 39).

Bentham's *Panopticon* is the architectural figure of this composition. We know the principle on which it was based; at the periphery, an annular building; at the centre, a tower; this tower is pierced with wide windows that open onto the inner side of the ring; the peripheric building is divided into cells, each of which extends the whole width of the building; they have two windows, one on the inside, corresponding to the windows of the tower; the other, on the outside, allows the light to cross the cell from one end to the other. All that is needed, then, is to

146

place a supervisor in a central tower and to shut up in each cell a madman, a patient, a condemned man, a worker or a schoolboy. By the effect of backlighting, one can observe from the tower, standing out precisely against the light, the small captive shadows in the cells of the periphery. They are like so many cages, so many small theatres, in which each actor is alone, perfectly individualized and constantly visible. The panoptic mechanism arranges spatial unities that make it possible to see constantly and to recognize immediately. In short, it reverses the principle of the dungeon; or rather of its three functions—to enclose, to deprive of light and to hide—it preserves only the first and eliminates the other two. Full lighting and the eye of a supervisor capture better than darkness, which ultimately protected. Visibility is a trap. [. . .]

Each individual, in his place, is securely confined to a cell from which he is seen from the front by the supervisor; but the side walls prevent him from coming into contact with his companions. He is seen, but he does not see; he is the object of information, never a subject in communication. The arrangement of his room, opposite the central tower, imposes on him an axial visibility; but the divisions of the ring, those separated cells, imply a lateral invisibility. And this invisibility is a guarantee of order. If the inmates are convicts, there is no danger of a plot, an attempt at collective escape, the planning of new crimes for the future, bad reciprocal influences; if they are patients, there is no danger of contagion; if they are madmen there is no risk of their committing violence upon one another; if they are schoolchildren, there is no copying, no noise, no chatter, no waste of time; if they are workers, there are no disorders, no theft, no coalitions, none of those distractions that slow down the rate of work, make it less perfect or cause accidents. The crowd, a compact mass, a locus of multiple exchanges, individualities merging together, a collective effect, is abolished and replaced by a collection of separated individualities. From the point of view of the guardian, it is replaced by a multiplicity that can be numbered and supervised; from the point of view of the inmates, by a sequestered and observed solitude (Bentham, 60–64).

Hence the major effect of the Panopticon: to induce in the inmate a state of conscious and permanent visibility that assures the automatic functioning of power. So to arrange things that the surveillance is permanent in its effects, even if it is discontinuous in its action; that the perfection of power should tend to render its actual exercise unnecessary; that this architectural apparatus should be a machine for creating and sustaining a power relation independent of the person who exercises it; in short, that the inmates should be caught up in a power situation of which they are themselves the bearers. To achieve this, it is at once too much and too little that the prisoner should be constantly observed by an inspector; too little, for what matters is that he knows himself to be observed; too much, because he has no need in fact of being so. In view of this, Bentham laid down the principle that power should be visible and unverifiable. Visible: the inmate will constantly have before his eyes the tall outline of the central tower from which he is spied upon. Unverifiable: the inmate must never know whether he is being looked at at any one moment; but he must be sure that he may always be so. In order to make the presence or absence of the inspector unverifiable, so that the prisoners, in their cells, cannot even see a shadow, Bentham envisaged not only venetian blinds on the windows of the central obser- vation hall, but, on the inside, partitions that intersected the hall at right angles and, in order to pass from one quarter to the other, not doors but zig-zag openings; for the slightest noise, a gleam of light, a brightness in a half-opened door would betray the presence of the guardian.[1] The Panopticon is a machine for dissociating the see/being seen dyad: in the peripheric ring, one is totally seen, without ever seeing; in the central tower, one sees everything without ever being seen.[2]

It is an important mechanism, for it automatizes and disindividualizes power. Power has its principle not so much in a person as in a certain concerted distribution of bodies, surfaces, lights, gazes; in an arrangement whose internal mechanisms produce the relation in which individuals are caught up. The ceremonies, the rituals, the marks by which the sovereign's surplus power was manifested are useless. There is a machinery that assures dissymmetry, disequilibrium, difference. Consequently, it does not matter who exercises power. Any individual, taken almost at random, can operate the machine: in the absence of the director, his family, his friends, his visitors, even his servants (Bentham, 45). Similarly, it does not matter what motive animates him: the curiosity of the indiscreet, the malice of a child, the thirst for knowledge of a philosopher who wishes to visit this museum of human nature, or the perversity of those who take pleasure in spying and punishing. The more numerous those anonymous and temporary observers are, the greater the risk for the inmate of being surprised and the

---

1. In the *Postscript to the Panopticon*, 1791, Bentham adds dark inspection galleries painted in black around the inspector's lodge, each making it possible to observe two storeys of cells.

2. In his first version of the *Panopticon*, Bentham had also imagined an acoustic surveil- lance, operated by means of pipes leading from the cells to the central tower. In the *Postscript* he abandoned the idea, perhaps because he could not introduce into it the principle of dissymetry and prevent the prisoners from hearing the inspector as well as the inspector hearing them. Julius tried to develop a system of dissymetrical listening (Julius, N.H., *Leçons sure les prisons*, I, 1831, p. 18).

greater his anxious awareness of being observed. The Panopticon is a marvellous machine which, whatever use one may wish to put it to, produces homogeneous effects of power.

A real subjection is born mechanically from a fictitious relation. So it is not necessary to use force to constrain the convict to good behaviour, the madman to calm, the worker to work, the schoolboy to application, the patient to the observation of the regulations. Bentham was surprised that panoptic institutions could be so light: there were no more bars, no more chains, no more heavy locks; all that was needed was that the separations should be clear and the openings well arranged. The heaviness of the old 'houses of security,' with their fortress-like architecture, could be replaced by the simple, economic geometry of a 'house of certainty.' The efficiency of power, its constraining force have, in a sense, passed over to the other side—to the side of its surface of application. He who is subjected to a field of visibility, and who knows it, assumes responsibility for the constraints of power; he makes them play spontaneously upon himself; he inscribes in himself the power relation in which he simultaneously plays both roles; he becomes the principle of his own subjection.

Questions for Review and Discussion

1. What does Bentham think the benefits of the Panopticon will be?

2. Describe the architecture of the Panopticon?

3. According to Foucault, what is the effect of the Panopticon in terms of power?

4. Why would the physical layout of the Panopticon encourage prisoners to become their own wardens?

Christian Norberg-Schulz

Christian Norberg-Schulz (1926–2000) was a Norwegian architect and philosopher of architecture and urban planning. This essay is an application of Heidegger's essay "Building Dwelling Thinking" to urban architecture. Norberg-Schulz engages in a phenomenological analysis of both natural places and urban built environments, arguing that there are varying ways that humans can create built environments that connect to natural place and therefore provide existential meaning to humans. Conversely, humans can create built environments that cause a loss of place and meaning. Norberg-Schulz draws on Heidegger's understanding of "dwelling" as gaining an existential foothold in a place. He introduces a new term, *genius loci*, by which he means the "spirit of the place," to help us understand how we might read places to better connect to that spirit. This reading connects to those by Heidegger, Gavin, and Mugerauer most particularly, in that it urges us to think about the urban built environment as a potentially meaning-giving place. It can also be fruitfully used in discussion with the work of bell hooks, who connects sense of place and feeling at home to the importance of political identity formation.

"THE LOSS AND RECOVERY OF PLACE" (1979–1980)

1. THE LOSS OF PLACE

After the second world war most places have been subjected to profound changes. The qualities which traditionally distinguished human settlements have been corrupted or have got irreparably lost. Reconstructed or new towns also look very different from the places of the past. Before we consider the reasons for this fundamental change, it is necessary to give it a more precise definition in structural terms. Again it is useful to employ our concepts of "space" and "character," and relate them to the more general categories of natural and manmade place.

Spatially the new settlements do not anymore possess enclosure and density. They usually consist of buildings "freely" placed within a park-like space. Streets and squares in the traditional sense are no longer found, and the general result is a scattered assembly of units. This implies that a distinct figure-ground relationship no more exists; the continuity of the landscape is interrupted and the buildings do not form clusters or groups. Although a general order may be present, particularly when the settlement is seen from an airplane, it usually does not bring about any

150

sense of place. The changes done to already existing towns have analogous effects. The urban tissue is "opened up," the continuity of the urban "walls" is interrupted, and the coherence of the urban spaces damaged. As a consequence, nodes, paths and districts lose their identity, and the town as a whole its imageability. Together with the loss of the traditional urban structure, the landscape is deprived of its meaning as comprehensive extension, and reduced to rests within the complex network of man-made elements.

The *character* of the present day environment is usually distinguished by monotony. If any variety is found, it is usually due to elements left over from the past. The "presence" of the majority of new buildings is very weak. Very often "curtain-walls" are used which have an unsubstantial and abstract character, or rather, a lack of character. Lack of character implies poverty of stimuli. The modern environment in fact offers very little of the surprises and discoveries which make the experience of old towns so fascinating. When attempts to break the general monotony are made, they mostly appear as arbitrary fancies.

In general, the symptoms indicate a *loss of place*. Lost is the settlement as a place in nature, lost are the urban foci as places for common living, lost is the building as a meaningful sub-place where man may simultaneously experience individuality and belonging. Lost is also the relationship to earth and sky. Most modern buildings exist in a "nowhere"; they are not related to a landscape and not to a coherent, urban whole, but live their abstract life in a kind of mathematical-technological space which hardly distinguishes between up and down. The same feeling of "nowhere" is also encountered in the interiors of the dwellings. A neutral, flat surface has substituted the articulate ceilings of the past, and the window is reduced to a standard device which lets in a measurable quantity of air and light. In most modern rooms it is meaningless to ask: "What slice of sun does your building have?", that is: "what range of moods does the light offer from morning to night, from day to day, from season to season, and all through the years?"[1] In general, all *qualities* are lost, and we may indeed talk about an "environmental crisis."

It has often been pointed out that the modern environment makes human orientation difficult. The work of Kevin Lynch evidently took this deficiency as its point of departure, and he implies that poor imageability may cause emotional insecurity and fear.[2] The effects of scarce possibilities of identification, however, have hardly been the subject of direct study.

1. Kahn, *Credo*, in *Architectural Digest* 5/1974, p. 280.
2. Kevin Lynch, "The Image of the City," Cambridge, MA: 1960, pp. 4–5.

From psychological literature we know that a general poverty of stimuli may cause passivity and reduced intellectual capacity,[3] and we may also infer that human identity in general depends on growing up in a "characteristic" environment.[4] The environmental crisis therefore implies a *human* crisis. Evidently the environmental problem has to be met with intelligence and efficiency. In our opinion this can only be done on the basis of an understanding of the concept of place. "Planning" does not help much as long as the concrete, qualitative nature of places is ignored. How, then, may a theory of place help us to solve our actual problems? Before we give some suggestions for the answers to this question, we have, however, to say a few words about the reasons for the environmental crisis.

Paradoxically, the present situation is a result of a wish for making man's environment better. The open, "green city" thus represented a reaction against the inhuman conditions in the industrial cities of nineteenth century Europe, and modern architecture in general took the need for better dwellings as its point of departure.[5] Le Corbusier wrote: "Man dwells badly, that is the deep and real reason for the upheavals of our time,"[6] and at the Exposition Internationale des Arts Décoratifs in Paris 1925, he showed a prototype apartment which he called the *Pavillon de l'esprit nouveau.* To demonstrate the "spirit" of the modern age, he thus made a dwelling for the common man. Le Corbusier's point of view is clearly indicated in *Vers une Architecture* (1923). Here he tells us that "we are to be pitied for living in unworthy houses, since they ruin our health and our morale."[7] The new spirit therefore aimed at something more than the satisfaction of mere physical needs. Evidently it implied a new way of life which should make man "normal" again, in the sense of allowing him to follow "the organic development of his existence."[8] At the root of the modern movement, as defined by Le Corbusier, was the wish to help alienated modern man to regain a true and meaningful existence. To achieve this he needed "freedom" as well as "identity." "Freedom" meant primarily liberation from the absolutist systems of the Baroque age

---

3. A. Rapoport, R. E. Kantor, "Complexity and Ambiguity in Environmental Design," in *American Institute of Planners Journal,* July 1967.

4. See Chapter 1 of *Genius Loci: Towards a Phenomenology of Architecture.* New York: Rizzoli, 1980.

5. Norberg-Schulz, "The Dwelling and the Modern Movement," in *LOTUS International,* no. 9, Milan 1975.

6. Le Corbusier, *La maison des hommes.* Paris 1942, p. 5.

7. Le Corbusier, *Vers une Architecture,* Paris 1923, English edition, pp. 17ff.

8. Le Corbusier, *Vers . . .* , p. 268.

and their successors, that is, a new right to choose and participate. "Identity" meant to bring man back to what is original and essential. The modern movement in fact used the slogan *Neue Sachlichkeit*, which ought to be translated "back to things" rather than "new rationalism."

The work of the first of modern pioneers, Frank Lloyd Wright, was from the very beginning conditioned by a concrete "hunger for reality," and at 11 he was sent to a Wisconsin farm "to learn how to really work."[9] As a result, his approach to the natural phenomena did not consist in the abstract observation and analysis common in Europe, but in the direct experience of archetypal, meaningful "forces." Thus he said: "It comforted me to see the fire burning deep in the solid masonry of the house itself,"[10] and accordingly he developed his plans around a large chimney-stack, to make the fire-place the expressive core of the dwelling. His use of natural materials must also be understood as the manifestations of a wish for a return to the concrete phenomena, that is, for a "deeper sense of reality."[11] Wright was also the first to give an answer to the demand for "freedom." Traditionally the human dwelling had been a refuge for the individual and the family. Wright wanted rootedness *and* freedom, and thus he destroyed the traditional "box" and created a new interaction between inside and outside by means of continuous walls which direct and unify space. The concept of inside is thereby changed from a refuge to a fixed point in space, from which man could experience a new sense of freedom and participation. This point is marked by the great fireplace with its vertical chimney. Hence man no longer places himself at the centre of the world as was the case in Versailles. Rather we find at the centre an element which symbolizes the forces and order of nature. A reminder evidently, that the modern world should not negate the basic meanings of existence.

The work of Wright made a profound impression on the European pioneers after its publication in Germany in 1910. Evidently they recognized that Wright had managed to define the concrete means which were needed to give man a new dwelling. It is important in this context also to mention his idea of an "architecture of democracy." Before, architecture was determined from "above," and the dwelling only reflected the meaningful forms developed in connection with church and palace. Modern architecture, on the contrary, takes the dwelling as its point of departure, and all other building tasks are considered "extensions" of the

---

9. F. L. Wright, *The Natural House*, New York, 1955, p. 15.

10. Wright, op. cit. p. 37.

11. Wright, op. cit. p. 51.

dwelling, to use the term of Le Corbusier.[12] The traditional order of building tasks is thereby reversed. This means that architecture is no longer based on dogma and authority, but ought to grow out of daily life, as an expression of man's understanding of nature, of other men and of himself. The "higher" building tasks thus become a result rather than a condition, and they represent something man must conquer in his own life. The *esprit nouveau* therefore should free man from the "systems," and conquer the split of thought and feeling which was a characteristic product of bourgeois society.[13] Why, then, did the modern movement lead to the loss of place rather than a reconquest? As far as we can see, the main reasons are two, and both imply an insufficient understanding of the concept of place. They are moreover related to the dimensions of "space" and "character" and thus confirm the validity of our approach. The first reason has to do with the crisis as an *urban* problem. The loss of place is first of all felt on the urban level, and is, as we have seen, connected with a loss of the spatial structures which secure the identity of a settlement. Instead of being an urban place, the modern settlement is conceived as a "blown-up house," of the type developed by the pioneers of modern architecture: Frank Lloyd Wright, Le Corbusier, and Mies van der Rohe. The plan of the modern house was defined as "open," and the space as a "flowing" continuum which hardly distinguished between outside and inside. Such a space may be appropriate for a sub-urban one-family house (as was the ideal of Wright), but it is questionable whether it suits an urban situation. In the city a clear distinction between private and public domains is necessary, and space cannot "flow" freely. This problem was, however, partly understood by the pioneers; the urban houses of Le Corbusier constitute true "insides" and Mies van der Rohe already in 1934 suggested the use of enclosed "court houses" for the city.[14] When we talk about the modern settlement as a "blown-up house," we rather have in mind the fact that *quarters* and *cities* are conceived as large open plans. In the urban projects of the twenties and thirties, and in many neighborhoods which are built today, true urban "insides" are lacking; the space is freely flowing between slab-like buildings which resemble the freestanding walls of an "open" plan, such as the plan of the Barcelona-pavilion by Mies van der Rohe (1929). Spatially, the modern city is therefore based on a *confusion of scales*, a pattern which might be valid on one level is blindly transferred to another. This unfortunate "solution" to the

---

12. *Logement prolongé.*

13. Giedion, *architecture you and me*, Cambridge, MA, 1958, passim.

14. P. Johnson, *Mies van der Rohe*. New York 1947.

problem of the settlement became possible because the concept of "mileu" was at the outset of the modern movement only understood in physical terms, that is, as a mere need for "air, light and green."[15]

The second reason has to do with the idea of an *international style*.[16] In the twenties it was maintained that modern architecture should not be local or regional, but follow the same principles everywhere. It is characteristic that the first volume in the series of *Bauhausbücher* was called *Internationale Architektur*. Although Gropius reacted against the world "style," he thus embraced the idea of internationalism. Thus he said: . . . "The forms of the New Architecture differ fundamentally . . . from those of the old, they are . . . simply the inevitable, logical product of the intellectual, social and technical conditions of our age."[17] This does not mean, however, that modern architecture was conceived as a mere practical product; it also ought to give "aesthetic satisfaction to the human soul."[18] This satisfaction ought to be achieved by substituting a "welter of ornament" with simple, mass-produced forms. The result was what Venturi appropriately has called an "architecture of exclusion." This does not mean, however, that the buildings of the European pioneers were aesthetically poor, or "characterless," in an absolute sense. On the contrary, some of them, such as Le Corbusier's Villa Savoye (1928–31) and Mies van der Rohe's Tugendhat House (1930), are true masterpieces which in a convincing way concretize a new way of life. Although they lack the "substance" and presence of many old buildings, their volumetric composition and structural integrity fully satisfy modern man's demand for freedom and identity. Moreover they undoubtedly represent a reconquest of essential meanings and means, and hence a new *Sachlichkeit*, in the true sense of the word. But something strange happens when the ascetic character of early modernism is transferred to the *urban* level. What was a subtle interplay of forms, which (almost) confirms Mies' thesis that "less is more," becomes sterile monotony.[19] The essence of settlement consists in *gathering*, and gathering means that different meanings are brought together. The architecture of exclusion mainly told us that the modern world is "open"; a statement which in a certain sense is anti-urban. Openness cannot be gathered. Openness means departure, gathering means return.

---

15. Which, according to Le Corbusier are the *joies essentielles*.

16. H. R. Hitchcock, P. Johnson, *The International Style*. New York 1932.

17. W. Gropius, *The New Architecture and the Bauhaus*. London 1935, p. 18.

18. Gropius, op. cit p. 20.

19. See for instance Lafayette Park in Detroit by Mies van der Rohe, 1955–63.

It is somewhat unfair, however, to blame the modern movement for shortcomings which only belonged to a certain phase of its development. The modern movement did not come to an end with the images of a green city and an international architecture. Already in 1944 the spokesman of the movement, S. Giedion, put forward the demand for a "new monumentality" and said: "Monumentality springs from the eternal need of people to create symbols for their activities and for their fate or destiny, for their religious belief and for their social convictions."[20] And in 1951 a CIAM conference discussed the *Core of the City*, that is, the problem of introducing in the open tissue of the modern settlement a gathering focus. Again we may refer to Giedion: "Contemporary interest in the core is part of a general humanizing process; of a return to the human scale and the assertion of the rights of the individual. . . ."[21] Finally, in 1954, Giedion wrote an essay with the title "On the New Regionalism" where he asked for a new respect for the "way of life," which ought to be studied with "reverence" before designing a project. "The new regionalism has as its motivating force a respect for individuality and a desire to satisfy the emotional and material needs of each area."[22] We understand thus, that the leaders of the modern movement already 20–30 years ago foresaw some of the most important problems we are facing now. Those who got stuck with the early images of a green city and standardized form, were the epigones and vulgarizers of modern architecture.

2. THE RECOVERY OF PLACE

The critics of the modern movement usually take the general discontent with our present environment as their point of departure, and maintain that modern architecture has not been able to solve the problem. Furthermore they often criticize the architects for carrying out any commission without taking into consideration the consequences of their actions for society and the anonymous "user." Thus the social psychologist Alfred Lorenzer writes: "The architect as a mere technical aid to the dominant powers, corresponds to the ideal of consequent functionalists. The

20. In P. Zucker, *New Architecture and City Planning*. New York 1944. Also in Giedion, *architecture you and me*, p. 28.

21. Giedion, op. cit. p. 127.

22. In *Architectural Record*, January 1954, "The State of Contemporary Architecture, the Regional Approach." Also in Giedion, op. cit. p. 145.

sacrificium intellectus of these architects is architecture."[23] Whereas we have taken the general criticism very seriously, and asked whether the modern movement really failed in giving man a new dwelling, the statement of Lorenzer sounds rather surprising to those who have participated actively in the propagation of modern architecture. It is certainly possible to find cases when protagonists of the modern movement served as "aids" to the dominant powers, but the fact that many of them had to leave their countries or withdraw from active professional life because of their artistic creed, is certainly more significant. Thus Giedion could write: "Architecture has long ceased to be the concern of passive and businesslike specialists who built precisely what their clients demanded. It has gained the courage to deal with life. . . ."[24] The criticism of Lorenzer therefore only holds true for the work of certain imitators who did not really understand the aims of the modern movement, and his criticism obviously stems from an insufficient comprehension of the concept of "functionalism." We have demonstrated that the point of departure of the modern movement was profoundly meaningful and that its development showed an ever more complete understanding of the environmental problem. A *constructive* criticism on this basis is given by Robert Venturi in his remarkable book *Complexity and Contradiction in Architecture*, which advocates a "both-and" rather than an "either-or" approach.[25]

The basic aim of the second phase of modern architecture is to give buildings and places individuality, with regard to space and character. This means to take the circumstantial conditions of locality and building task into consideration, rather than basing the design upon general types and principles. The new approach became manifest in the works of Alvar Aalto already before the second world war. In general Aalto wants to adapt the spatial structure of his buildings as well as the surrounding space, and thus he reintroduces topological forms which were hardly admitted by early functionalism. His approach was shown in a programmatic way in the Finnish pavilion at the World's Fair in New York 1939, and found a convincing realization in his MIT Senior Dormitory in Cambridge, Mass. (1947–48). The undulating wall of this building concretizes the general modern idea of "freedom," at the same time as it represents an adaptation to the spatial circumstances. Aalto also aimed at giving his architecture an outspoken local character. In works such as

23. H. Berndt, A. Lorenzer, K. Horn, *Architektur als Ideologie*. Frankfurt a.M. 1968, p. 51.

24. Giedion, *Space, Time and Architecture*, Cambridge, MA, 1967, p. 708.

25. Venturi, *Complexity and Contradiction in Architecture*. New York, 1966.

Villa Mairea (1938–39) and the town-hall in Säynätsalo (1945–52), the Finnish *genius loci* is strongly present.[26] Mairea may in fact be considered the first manifestation of the new "regional" approach. Again, thus, the development of modern architecture took the dwelling as its point of departure. The works of Aalto are eminently "romantic," and illustrate how this attitude was able to free modern architecture from the "cosmic" abstractions of early European modernism. Thus Aalto satisfies Wright's "hunger for reality."

A hunger for reality was also felt by Le Corbusier, although he, as a child of European civilization, did not have that direct contact with the concrete phenomena which was normal in the "new world" of America, or in countries such as Finland, where popular traditions and a more "natural" way of life had survived. Le Corbusier therefore needed a long and "patient search" (to use his own words), before he could give buildings true presence and character. In his *Unité d'Habitation* in Marseilles (1947–52), however, a new plastic force becomes manifest. The slender *pilotis* of the thirties have become massive and powerful, and the abstract outer skin has been replaced by a *brise-soleil* which characterizes the building as a sculptural body. "A new, mid-twentieth-century image of the embattled human presence in the world"[27] is thus concretized. The great turning point, however, came with the church of Ronchamp (1953–55). Here the psychological dimension of architecture returns with full force. Le Corbusier himself said that he wanted to create "a vessel of intense concentration and meditation."[28] In fact the building has become a true centre of meaning and a "gathering force," as Vincent Scully said with fine intuitive understanding.[29] Le Corbusier recognized also at an early date the gathering nature of the urban settlement, and indicated the idea of a "core" which comprises the important institutions of the community (St. Dié 1945). His search in this direction culminated with the Capitol of Chandigarh in India (1951–56).

A third decisive contribution to the recovery of architecture as the making of places must be mentioned. The work of Louis Kahn appeared as something of a revelation at a moment of crisis when many architects were losing their self-confidence and faith in architecture. Kahn's approach is defined in his dictum: "What does the building want to be?" In his projects he gives answers to this question in terms of space and

26. Giedion, *Space*... p. 620, pp. 645ff.

27. V. Scully, *Modern Architecture*. New York 1961, p. 45.

28. Le Corbusier, *Oeuvre complète 1946–52*. Zürich 1961, p. 72.

29. Scully, op. cit. p. 46. For an analysis see Norberg-Schulz, *Meaning in Western Architecture*. London and New York 1975, pp. 407ff.

character. Suddenly everything is there again: open and closed spaces, clusters and groups, symmetry and asymmetry, node and path; and above all: the wall as a "threshold" between interior and exterior. In the walls of Kahn, past and present are united, and thus he said: "I thought of wrapping ruins around buildings."[30] First of all, however, the walls of Kahn are there to receive light, "the giver of all presences."[31] No wonder that Vincent Scully wrote: "The impression becomes inescapable that in Kahn, as once in Wright, architecture began anew."[32]

What then is the message of Louis Kahn?

In numerous talks he defined his position, using a very personal, poetical way of expression. At a closer scrutiny, however, a coherent philosophy of architecture emerges. First of all Kahn understood architecture in terms of place. A "room" is for him a place with its particular character, its "spiritual aura," and a building is a "society of rooms." The street is "a room of agreement," and the city "an assembly of places vested with the care to uphold the sense of a way of life."[33] The character of places is both determined by their spatial properties and by the way they receive light. Thus he said: "The sun was not aware of its wonder before it struck the side of a building," and: "Of the elements of a room the window is the most marvelous."[34] Here he comes very close to Heidegger, who describes a Greek temple saying: "The luster and gleam of the stone, though itself apparently glowing only by the grace of the sun, yet first brings to light the light of the day, the breadth of the sky, the darkness of the night."[35] And Kahn even understands the concept of "setting-into-work" when he says that places "are *put into being* by inspired technology."[36] Of particular importance in the work of Kahn is in fact the conception of architecture as *built order*. "Form is not simply function, but a conceived order; thus a being. . . ."[37] In the late works of Le Corbusier form became presence, but it is still conceived in "sculptural" terms. Kahn, instead, returned to "building" and thereby recovered a sense of truth which had for long been forgotten. His works are real things which make us aware of our existence between earth and sky.

30. Scully, *Louis I. Kahn*. New York 1962, p. 36.

31. Louis I. Kahn, *L'architecture d'aujourd'hui 142*, Feb. 1969, p. 13.

32. Kahn, op. cit., p. 25.

33. Kahn, *Credo*.

34. Kahn, op. cit.

35. Heidegger, *Poetry, Language, Thought*. Ed. Albert Hofstadter. New York, 1971, p. 42.

36. Kahn, op. cit.

37. Scully, *Louis I. Kahn*, p. 33.

Common to Le Corbusier and Kahn is a "classical" attitude. Both understand architecture as an embodiment of characters which are simultaneously human and natural, and their buildings give these characters material presence. Although Kahn's works are rooted in concrete phenomena, they tend towards a certain "formalism." The spatial layout starts to live its own life, and the articulation becomes a function of symmetry rather than "light." This danger is however counteracted most efficiently by the built substance.

In various ways the "third generation" of modern architects have taken up and developed the intentions of the pioneers.[38] During the last two decades a series of significant works have been made which promise a more complete recovery of place. This does not mean, however, that the present situation is clear. The development of modern architecture makes many choices possible, and the tendency to understand things in a formalistic rather than an existential sense is always present. In the Nordic countries, thus, the "romantic" approach of Aalto may easily degenerate into a superficial sentimental play with "anti-classical" forms. This tendency is in fact strongly felt, especially in Sweden where contact with nature has been reduced to nostalgia. In the "classical" South, on the contrary, the danger of mistaking "order" for concrete reality is most typical. The architecture of the Fascist epoch was based on this mistake, and it reappears in the strangely abstract works of Aldo Rossi and his followers which "stand frozen in surreal timelessness."[39] Rossi calls his architecture "rational," a term which may be appropriate if it means a complete absence of live character. Rossi's conception of "typology" is certainly important, but it remains sterile as long as the local circumstances are left out. Another characteristic danger consists in mistaking character for empty "rhetoric" gestures. This tendency has been particularly strong in the United States, where architecture has become a means to demonstrate the "power" of firms and institutions. A modern "historicism" results, where those forms which were created to give man a sense of freedom and identity, are reduced to mere clichés. Whereas nineteenth century historicism should give man a "cultural alibi," modern historicism aims at proving that he is "up to date."[40]

Where then, do we find a creative interpretation of the actual situation? Where do we find an architecture which avoids the dangers men-

---

38. The term stems from S. Giedion.

39. A. Colquhoun, "Rational Architecture," in *Architectural Design*, June 1975.

40. We have in mind certain works by Rudolph, Yamasaki, Stone, Johnson, Kallmann etc. Cf. Giedion, *Napoleon and the Devaluation of Symbols*, in "Architectural Review," no. 11, 1947.

tioned above, and represents a true contribution to the solution of the environmental crisis? One of the first architects who approached the problem in a simple and human way was the Dane Jörn Utzon, who was immediately recognized by Giedion as a protagonist of the new phase of modern architecture.[41] In his residential projects, Kingo (1956), Birkehöj (1960), and Fredensborg (1962), Utzon created unified settlements which possess figural character in relation to the landscape, and a strong sense of place as a meaningful, social "inside." Moreover they have an outspoken local character and recover the traditional Danish value of cultivated intimacy. Utzon has also proved himself capable of creative adaptation to other environmental characters in his projects for the Sydney Opera House (1957) and the Theatre in Zurich (1964). His works are always "built," and possess the quality of true "things." In connection with the residential projects of Utzon, it is natural to mention the widely published Siedlung Halen near Berne by the Swiss group of architects, Atelier 5 (1961). Here we also find a strong figural character, and a most convincing identity of place. Siedlung Halen demonstrates that it is still possible to house people in dense settlements which conserve the integrity of the landscape, even in a country where land is very scarce.

Among the works of the third generation, there is one which treats the problems of place and local character in a particularly interesting way. We refer to the Finnish Students' Union Building at Otaniemi by Reima Pietilä (1965–67). With his "Dipoli" Pietilä wanted to express "the dream of the people of the forest."[42] To gain his end he used a new kind of topological space which visualizes the structure of the Finnish landscape, and the choice of materials and forms gives the intention a most convincing presence. In general, Dipoli represents a culmination of the "romantic" approach to architecture, and it is certainly not a "model" to be imitated everywhere. The approach of Pietilä however is universally valid, and makes us eager to see other analogous but circumstantially different solutions. Such works actually exist. The metal-and-glass buildings of James Stirling are for instance eminently English and seem to embody "the dream of the people of the factory." In the houses of MLTW (Moore, Lyndon, Thurnbull, Whitaker), the American *genius* has found a new convincing concretization. The four architects have defined their approach with these words: "The dreams which accompany all human actions should be nurtured by the places in which people live."[43] We may

41. Giedion, *Space* . . . pp. 668ff.

42. Norberg-Schulz, *Meaning* . . . pp. 420ff.

43. C. Moore, D. Lyndon, *The Place of Houses*. New York 1975.

in this context also mention a more particular work, Ricardo Bofill's pyramid-monument on the border between Catalonia and France. Here the pointed shapes of the surrounding mountains are "gathered" and condensed by man-made geometry, whereas the crowning "temple" recalls a decisive moment in the history of Catalonia. A most convincing synthesis of general, local and temporal factors is thus created.

Our brief survey of the aims of Aalto, Kahn, the later Le Corbusier, and some exponents of the third generation, shows that the means for a solution of the environment crisis exist. [. . .]

Questions for Review and Discussion

1. What, according to Norberg-Schulz, is lost after World War II? What are the symptoms or signs of the loss?

2. Why does Norberg-Schulz claim that the environmental crisis implies a human crisis? What is the nature of the crisis?

3. Why is Norberg-Schulz critical of Le Corbusier?

4. Compare and contrast architects Le Corbusier, Frank Lloyd Wright, Alvar Aalto, and Louis Kahn. Which architects do Norberg-Schulz think cause loss of place? Which contribute to the recovery of place?

5. What are signs of the recovery of place?

Iris Marion Young

Iris Marion Young (1949–2006) was an influential philosopher who taught in the University of Chicago's department of political science, the University of Pittsburgh's school of public policy, and elsewhere. She has written widely on political and feminist theory. With her pathbreaking work in phenomenology in which she analyzed both body issues and political phenomenon from a feminist perspective, Young made a major impact on contemporary continental and political philosophy. Urban planners and geographers frequently cite this essay, which appeared as a chapter in her book *Justice and the Politics of Difference*. The essay also encouraged other contemporary philosophers to think more about cities. Young argues that city life can serve as a "normative ideal," that is, it allows for us to imagine what life ought to be like. This reading connects to those concerned with urban identity and diversity (e.g., Simmel, Conlon, and hooks) and can be fruitfully compared to those raising social justice issues and concepts of citizenship (e.g., West). Contrast Young with Mumford, Kemmis, and others who retain the polis as the ideal city, as well as with Lefebvre who rejects it.

"CITY LIFE AS A NORMATIVE IDEAL" (1990)

Appeals to community are usually antiurban. Much sociological literature diagnoses modern history as a movement to the dangerous bureaucratized *Gesellschaft* from the manageable and safe *Gemeinschaft*, nostalgically reconstructed as a world of lost origins (Stein, 1960; Nisbet, 1953). Many others follow Rousseau in romanticizing the ancient *polis* and the medieval Swiss *Bürger*, deploring the commerce, disorder, and unmanageable mass character of the modern city (Ellison, 1985; cf. Sennett, 1974, chaps. 7–10). Throughout the modern period, the city has often been decried as embodying immortality, artificiality, disorder, and danger—as the site of treasonous conspiracies, illicit sex, crime, deviance, and disease (Mosse, 1985, pp. 32–33, 137–38; Gilman, 1985, p. 214). The typical image of the modern city finds it expressing all the disvalues that a reinstantiation of community would eliminate.

Yet urbanity is the horizon of the modern, not to mention the postmodern, condition. Contemporary political theory must accept urbanity as a material given for those who live in advanced industrial societies. Urban relations define the lives not only of those who live in the huge metropolises, but also of those who live in suburbs and large towns. Our social life is structured by vast networks of temporal and spatial mediation among persons, so that nearly everyone depends on the activities of seen and unseen strangers who mediate between oneself and one's associates, between oneself and one's objects of desire. Urbanites find themselves relating geographically to increasingly large regions, thinking little of traveling seventy miles to work or an hour's drive for an evening's entertainment. Most people frequently and casually encounter strangers in their daily activities. The material surroundings and structures available to us define and presuppose urban relationships. The very size of populations in our society and most other nations of the world, coupled with a continuing sense of national or ethnic identity with millions of other people, supports the conclusion that a vision of dismantling the city is hopelessly utopian.

Starting from the given of modern urban life is not simply necessary, moreover; it is desirable. Even for many of those who decry the alienation, bureaucratization, and mass character of capitalist patriarchal society, city life exerts a powerful attraction. Modern literature, art, and film have celebrated city life, its energy, cultural diversity, technological complexity, and the multiplicity of its activities. Even many of the most staunch proponents of decentralized community love to show visiting friends around the Boston or San Francisco or New York in or near which they live, climbing up towers to see the glitter of lights and sampling the fare at the best ethnic restaurants.

I propose to construct a normative ideal of city life as an alternative to both the ideal of community and the liberal individualism it criticizes as asocial. By "city life" I mean a form of social relations which I define as the being together of strangers. In the city persons and groups interact within spaces and institutions they all experience themselves as belonging to, but without those interactions dissolving into unity or commonness. City life is composed of clusters of people with affinities—families, social group networks, voluntary associations, neighborhood networks, a vast array of small "communities." City dwellers frequently venture beyond such familiar enclaves, however, to the more open public of politics, commerce, and festival, where strangers meet and interact (cf. Lofland, 1973). City dwelling situates one's own identity and activity in relation to a horizon of a vast variety of other activity, and the awareness that this unknown, unfamiliar activity affects the conditions of one's own.

City life is a vast, even infinite, economic network of production, distribution, transportation, exchange, communication, service provision, and amusement. City dwellers depend on the mediation of thousands of other people and vast organizational resources in order to accomplish their individual ends. City dwellers are thus together, bound to one another, in what should be and sometimes is a single polity. Their being together entails some common problems and common interests, but they do not create a community of shared final ends, of mutual identification and reciprocity.

A normative ideal of city life must begin with our given experience of cities, and look there for the virtues of this form of social relations. Defining an ideal as unrealized possibilities of the actual, I extrapolate from that experience four such virtues.

(1) *Social differentiation without exclusion.* City life in urban mass society is not inconsistent with supportive social networks and subcultural communities. Indeed, for many it is their necessary condition. In the city social group differences flourish. Modernization theory predicted a decline in local, ethnic, and other group affiliations as universalist state institutions touch people's lives more directly and as people encounter many others with identifications and life styles different from their own. There is considerable evidence, however, that group differences are often reinforced by city life, and that the city even encourages the formation of new social group affinities (Fischer, 1982, pp. 206–30; Rothschild, 1981). Deviant or minority groups find in the city both a cover of anonymity and a critical mass unavailable in the smaller town. It is hard to imagine the formation of gay or lesbian group affinities, for example, without the conditions of the modern city (D'Emilio, 1983). While city dwelling as opposite to rural life has changed the lives and self-concepts of Chicanos, to take another example, city life encourages group identification and a desire for cultural nationalism at the same time that it may dissolve some traditional practices or promote assimilation to Anglo language and values (Jankowski, 1986). In actual cities many people express violent aversions to members of groups with which they do not identify. More than those who live in small towns, however, they tend to recognize social group difference as a given, something they must live with (Fischer, 1982, pp. 206–40).

In the ideal of city life freedom leads to group differentiation, to the formation of affinity groups, but this social and spatial differentiation of groups is without exclusion. The urban ideal expresses differences as I defined it in chapter 6 [of *Justice and the Politics of Difference*], a side-by-side particularity neither reducible to identity nor completely other. In this ideal groups do not stand in relations of inclusion and exclusion, but overlap and intermingle without becoming homogeneous. Though city life as we now experience it has many borders and exclusions, even our actual experience of the city also gives hints of what differentiation without exclusion can be. Many city neighborhoods have a distinct ethnic identity, but members of other groups also dwell in them. In the good city one crosses from one distinct neighborhood to another without knowing precisely where one ended and the other began. In the normative ideal of city life, borders are open and undecidable.

(2) *Variety.* The interfusion of groups in the city occurs partly because of the multiuse differentiation of social space. What makes urban spaces interesting, draws people out in public to them, gives people pleasure and excitement, is the diversity of activities they support. When stores, restaurants, bars, clubs, parks, and offices are sprinkled among residences, people have a neighborly feeling about their neighborhood, they go out and encounter one another on the streets and chat. They have a sense of their neighborhood as a "spot" or "place," because of that bar's distinctive clientele, or the citywide reputation of the pizza at that restaurant. Both business people and residents tend to have more commitment to and care for such neighborhoods than they do for single-use neighborhoods. Multifunctional streets, parks, and neighborhoods are also much safer than single-use functionalized spaces because people are out on the streets during most hours, and have commitment to the place (Jacobs, 1961, chap. 8; Sennett, 1970, chap 4; cf. Whyte, 1988, chaps. 9, 22–25).

(3) *Eroticism.* City life also instantiates difference as the erotic, in the wide sense of an attraction to the other, the pleasure and excitement of being drawn out of one's secure routine to encounter the novel, strange, and surprising (cf. Barthes, 1986). The erotic dimension of the city has always been an aspect of its fearfulness, for it holds out the possibility that one will lose one's identity, will fall. But we also take pleasure in being open to and interested in people we experience as different. We spend a Sunday afternoon walking through Chinatown, or checking out this week's eccentric players in the park. We look for restaurants, stores, and clubs with something new for us, a new ethnic food, a different atmosphere, a different crowd of people. We walk through sections of the city that we experience as having unique characters which are not ours, where people from diverse places mingle and then go home.

The erotic attraction here is precisely the obverse of community. In the ideal of community people feel affirmed because those with whom they share experiences, perceptions, and goals recognize and are recognized by them; one sees oneself reflected in the others. There is another kind of pleasure, however, in coming to encounter a subjectivity, a set of meanings, that is different, unfamiliar. One takes pleasure in being drawn out of oneself to understand that there are other meanings, practices, perspectives on the city, and that one could learn or experience something more and different by interacting with them.

The city's eroticism also derives from the aesthetics of its material being: the bright and colored lights, the grandeur of its buildings, the juxtaposition of architecture of different times, styles, and purposes. City space offers delights and surprises. Walk around the corner, or over a few blocks, and you encounter a different spatial mood, a new play of sight and sound, and new interactive movement. The erotic meaning of the city arises from its social and spatial inexhaustibility. A place of many places, the city folds over on itself in so many layers and relationships that it is incomprehensible. One cannot "take it in," one never feels as though there is nothing new and interesting to explore, no new and interesting people to meet.

(4) *Publicity.* Political theorists who extol the value of community often construe the public as a realm of unity and mutual understanding, but this does not cohere with our actual experience of public spaces. Because by definition a public space is a place accessible to anyone, where anyone can participate and witness, in entering the public one always risks encounter with those who are different, those who identify with different groups and have different opinions or different forms of life. The group diversity of the city is most often apparent in public spaces. This helps account for their vitality and excitement. Cities provide important public spaces—streets, parks, and plazas—where people stand and sit together, interact and mingle, or simply witness one another, without becoming unified in a community of "shared final ends."

Politics, the critical activity of raising issues and deciding how institutional and social relations should be organized, crucially depends on the existence of spaces and forums to which everyone has access. In such public spaces people encounter other people, meanings, expressions, issues, which they may not understand or with which they do not identify. The force of public demonstrations, for example, often consists in bringing to people who pass through public spaces those issues, demands, and people they might otherwise avoid. As a normative ideal city life provides public places and forums where anyone can speak and anyone can listen.

Because city life is a being together of strangers, diverse and overlapping neighbors, social justice cannot issue from the institution of an Enlightenment universal public. On the contrary, social justice in the city requires the realization of a politics of difference. This politics lays down institutional and ideological means for recognizing and affirming diverse social groups by giving political representation to these groups, and celebrating their distinctive characteristics and cultures. In the unoppressive city people open to unassimilated otherness. We all have our familiar relations and affinities, the people to whom we feel close and with whom we share daily life. These familial and social groups open onto a public in which all participate, and that public must be open and accessible to all. Contrary to the communitarian tradition, however, that public cannot be conceived as a unity transcending group differences, nor as entailing complete mutual understanding. In public life the differences remain unassimilated, but each participating group acknowledges and is open to listening to the others. The public is heterogeneous, plural, and playful, a place where people witness and appreciate diverse cultural expressions that they do not share and do not fully understand.

CITIES AND SOCIAL INJUSTICE

An ideal can inspire action for social change only if it arises from possibilities suggested by actual experience. The ideals of city life I have proposed are realized incidentally and intermittently in some cities today. There is no doubt, however, that many large cities in the United States today are sites of decay, poverty, and crime. There is just as little doubt that the smaller towns and suburbs to which many people escape from these ills are strung along congested highways, are homogeneous, segregated, and privatized. In either case, an ideal of city life as eroticized public vitality where differences are affirmed in openness might seem laughably utopian. For on city streets today the depth of social injustice is apparent: homeless people lying in doorways, rape in parks, and cold-blooded racist murder are the realities of city life.

In chapter 1 I argued that a critical theory of social justice must consider not only distributive patterns, but also the processes and relationships that produce and reproduce those patterns. While issues of the distribution of goods and resources are central to reflections on social justice, issues of decisionmaking power and processes, the division of labor, and culture are just as important. Nowhere is this argument better illustrated than in the context of social injustice in the city. Inequalities of distribution can be read on the face of buildings, neighborhoods, and towns. Most cities have too many places where everyone would agree no one should have to live. These may be a stone's throw from opulent corporate headquarters or luxury condominiums. The correct principles and methods of distribution may be a subject of controversy, but as they wander through American city streets few would deny that something is wrong with existing distributions.

The social structures, processes, and relationships that produce and reproduce these distributions, however, are not so visible on the surface of our cities. Yet normative theory must identify and evaluate them as well as their outcomes. In this section I shall discuss three aspects of these processes that contribute to domination and oppression: (a) centralized corporate and bureaucratic domination of cities; (b) decisionmaking structures in municipalities and their hidden mechanisms of redistribution; and (c) processes of segregation and exclusion, both within cities and between cities and suburbs.

(a) Corporate and city power once coincided. Firms started in a city and exploited the labor the city's population, and the city grew and prospered with the success of its major firms. Industrial magnates ruled the cities, either directly as city officials, or more indirectly as behind-the-scenes framers of city policy. Having a self-serving paternal attitude toward these cities, the ruling families engaged in philanthropic projects, building museums, libraries, parks, plazas, and statues as gifts to the public and monuments to their wealth and entrepreneurial ingenuity. The captains of industry often ruled ruthlessly, keeping the majority of people in squalor and ignorance, but they had a sense of place, were tied economically, socially, and politically to one or a few cities.

Today corporate capital is homeless. [. . .]

The domination of centralized bureaucracies, whether public or private, over municipal economies tends to dissociate lived or experienced space from the commodified space of abstract planning and calculation (Gottdinger, 1985, pp. 290–97; Castells, 1983, chap. 31). Capitalist bureaucratic rationality fosters bird's-eye planning which encompasses vast regions including huge metropolitan areas, or even several states together. From this skytop vision, investors and planning bureaucrats determine the placement and design of highways, factories, shopping facilities, offices, and parks. They decide the most rational and efficient investment from the point of view of their portfolio and their centralized office operations, but not necessarily from the point of view of the locales in which they invest. Too often this bureaucratic rationality and efficiency results in a deadening separation of functions, with oppressive consequences that I will discuss shortly. It also often results in abrupt disinvestment in one region and massive disruptive speculation in another, each with significant consequences for the welfare of people in those locales.

(b) Though city and town governments are seriously constrained by the domination of state and corporate imperatives, they nevertheless do make decisions, especially about land use and zoning. Decisionmaking structures and processes at the local level, however, often tend to create and exacerbate injustice. [. . .]

With the basic resources and institutional structure already given, interest groups in the city vie for and bargain over the distributive effects of city projects. Because some interests are better able to organize than others, have easier access to the major decisionmakers and their information, and so on, this political process usually either reproduces initial distributions or increases inequalities (Harvey, 1973, pp. 73–79; Elkin, 1987, pp. 93–102).

The framework of privatized land use decisionmaking according to unquestioned routines, coupled with interest-group bargaining over the consequences of applying the framework, illustrates one of several "hidden mechanisms" that David Harvey (1973, esp. chap. 3) argues produce and reproduce social inequalities and oppression in cities. Policies to improve the lives and opportunities of the poor, the marginalized, or those otherwise disadvantaged will have little effect unless these hidden mechanisms are understood and restructured. Two other such mechanisms that Harvey cites are location and adaptability.

The location of land use projects often has serious redistributional impact on residents of a city. Some, usually the poor and unorganized, are displaced by projects. The location of production facilities, public services, transportation facilities, housing, and shopping areas affects different sectors of the population differently. Proximity to one facility may benefit some, by giving them easier or less costly access to a good or activity. Proximity to another kind of facility, on the other hand, may disadvantage some by imposing inconveniences such as dirt, noise, or environmental danger. Although a person's own material situation may remain constant, his or her life opportunities may nevertheless change significantly because of surrounding changes (Harvey, 1973, pp. 56–63). The losses caused by urban changes may involve not only monetary burdens, inconvenience, and loss of access to resources and services, but also the loss of the very environment that helps define a person's sense of self or a group's space and culture (Elkin, 1987, p. 90).

Another hidden mechanism of redistribution, according to Harvey, is the different adaptability of groups: some groups are better able than others to adjust to change in the urban environment. Thus one group's adjustment often lags behind another's, usually increasing inequality between them. Sometimes the disparity is caused by differences in initial levels of material resources. Just as often, however, the differences in ability to adjust have their sources in culture or life style (Harvey, 1973, pp. 62–64). Poverty, exploitation, marginalization, and cultural imperialism often determine that those less able to adapt to urban changes are more often required to do so (Elkin, 1987, p. 86).

(c) I have already noted how bureaucratic rationality imposes an abstract space of order and function over the lived space of multiuse interaction. The twentieth century has seen a steady increase in the functionalization and segregation of urban space. The earliest separation was the creation of residential districts spatially separated from manufacturing, retail, entertainment, commerce, and government. Recent decades, however, have seen a rapid increase in the spatial segregation of each of these other functions from one another. Each sort of activity occurs in its own walled enclaves, distinctly cut off from the others.

The separation of functions in urban space reduces the vitality of cities, making city life more boring, meaningless, and dangerous. Downtown districts bustling with people in the day hours become eerily deserted at night, when people swarm to the indoor shopping mall, which, despite the best efforts of designers, is boring and frenetic. Residential neighborhoods find few people on the streets either day or night, because there is nowhere to go and not much to look at without appearing to encroach on the privacy of others.

This separation of functions augments oppression and domination in several ways. The territorial separation of workplaces from residential communities divides the interest of working people between the shop floor, on the one hand, and consumer and neighborhood concerns, on the other. While corporate and state bureaucrats construct their bird's-eye view of cities and regions, citizens are unable to engage in significant collective action on the same scale, because the separation of home and work prevents them from constructing a larger pattern.

Territorial separation of residences from shopping centers, manufacturing, public plazas, and so on has specific damaging consequences for the lives of women, especially mothers. A full-time homemaker and mother who lives in a central city apartment within walking distance of stores, restaurants, offices, parks, and social services has a life very different from that of the woman who spends her day in a suburban house surrounded for miles by only houses and schools. The separation of urban functions forces homemaking women into isolation and boredom. It also makes their work—shopping, occupying children, taking them to activities, going to doctors, dentists, insurance agents, and so on—more difficult and time consuming. To the degree that they retain primary responsibility for children and other dependent family members, working women too suffer from the spatial separation of urban functions, which often limits their work opportunities to the few usually low-paying clerical and service jobs close to residential locations, or else forces them to traverse large spans of city space each day in a triangle or square, from home to child care to work to grocery store to child care to home (Hayden, 1983, pp. 49–59). The separation of functions and the consequent need for transportation to get to jobs and services also contributes directly to the increased marginality of old people, poor people, disabled people, and others who because of life situation as well as limited access to resources are less able to move independently in wide areas.

One aspect of the normative ideal of city life, I have said, is a social differentiation without exclusion. Groups will differentiate by affinities, but the borders will be undecidable, and there will be much overlap and intermingling. One of the most disturbing aspects of contemporary urban life is the depth and frequency of aversive behavior which occurs within it. Group segregation is produced by aversive perceptions that deprecate some groups, defining them as entirely other, to be shunned and avoided. Banks, real estate firms, city officials, newspapers, and residents all promote an image of neighborhoods as places where only certain kinds of people belong and others do not, deeply reinforcing aversive racism and the mechanism by which some groups are constructed as the despised Others. Zoning regulation enforces class segregation, and to a large degree racial segregation as well, by, for example, excluding multifamily dwellings from prosperous neighborhoods and even from entire municipalities. These group exclusions produce the conditions for harassment of or violence against any persons found where they do not "belong." The myth of neighborhood community, of common values and life style, I have argued, fuels such exclusions.

The separation perhaps most far reaching in its effect on social justice is the legal separation of municipalities themselves. While social and economic processes have nearly obliterated any distinction between urban and rural life, and corporate and bureaucratic planning encompasses huge metropolitan regions, these same regions include scores of legally distinct municipalities, with their own local governments, ordinances, and public services. To avoid the ugliness, complexity, and dangers of contemporary city life, and often to avoid having to interact with certain kinds of people, many people seek community in the suburbs and small towns outside the city. The town's smallness and the fact that it is legally autonomous to make its own ordinances within the limits of state and federal regulation produce the illusion of local control. In fact the separation of towns renders them powerless against corporate and bureaucratic domination.

The legal and social separation of city and suburbs, moreover, contributes to social injustice. A direct relation of exploitation exists between most large American cities and their suburbs. Residents of the suburbs work in the city, use the city's services, and enjoy its life but, except in those rare cases where there is a city income or sales tax, pay no taxes to the city. Suburban municipalities usually benefit from their proximity to the city, but their legal autonomy ensures that they pay little or nothing for these benefits (Lowi, 1969, p. 197; Harvey, 1973, p. 94).

By means of their legal autonomy, some municipalities exclude certain kinds of people and certain kinds of activities from their borders. Because local governments generate funds to pay for local services by taxing residents, some towns and cities have far better schools and services than others. Because each municipality runs its own schools, police, fire department, and other public services, there is often an unjust and inefficient imbalance in the density and quality of services among different areas.

In the context of a large-scale and interdependent economic system under the control of private capital, "autonomy becomes a lead weight for the majority of cities, with only the most affluent towns able to create privilege from their formal independence. The political autonomy of places, as well as the planning power this entails, reproduces and exaggerates the inequalities between places rather than leveling them" (Logan and Molotch, 1987, p. 152).

These injustices have their primary source in the structural organization of decisionmaking. While all of the problems of city life I have discussed in this section involve distributive issues, the full extent of oppression and domination they involve can be understood only by considering culture and decisionmaking structures as they affect city geography, activities, and distributions. [. . .]

REFERENCES

Barthes, Roland. 1986. "Semiology and the Urban." In M. Gottdiener and Alexandros P. Lagopoulos, eds. *The City and the Sign: An Introduction to Urban Semiotics.* New York: Columbia University Press.

Castells, Manuel. 1983. *The City and the Grass Roots.* Berkeley and Los Angeles: University of California Press.

D'Emilio, Joseph. 1983. *Sexual Politics, Sexual Communities.* Chicago: University of Chicago Press.

Elkin, Stephen L. 1987. *City Regime in the American Republic.* Chicago: University of Chicago Press.

Ellison, Charles. 1985. "Rousseau and the Modern City: The Politics of Speech and Dress." *Political Theory* 13 (November):497–534.

Fischer, Claude. 1982. *To Dwell among Friends: Personal Networks in Town and City.* Chicago: University of Chicago Press.

Gilman, Sander. 1985. *Difference and Pathology: Stereotypes of Sexuality, Race and Madness.* Ithaca: Cornell University Press.

Gottdiener, Mark. 1985. *The Social Production of Urban Space.* Austin: University of Texas Press.

Jacobs, Jane. 1961. *The Death and Life of Great American Cities.* New York: Random House.

Jankowski, Martin Sanchez. 1986. *City Bound: Urban Life and Political Attitudes among Chicano Youth.* Albuquerque: University of New Mexico Press.

Lofland, Lyn, H. 1973. *A World of Strangers: Order and Action in Urban Public Space*. New York: Basic.

Logan, John R. and Harvey L. Molotch. 1987. *Urban Fortunes: The Political Economy of Place*. Berkeley and Los Angeles: University of California Press.

Lowi, Theodore. 1969. *The End of Liberalism*. New York: Norton.

Mosse, George. 1985. *Nationalism and Sexuality*. New York: Fertig.

Nisbet, Robert A. 1953. *The Quest for Community*. New York: Oxford University Press.

Rothschild, Joseph. 1981. *Ethnopolitics*. New York: Columbia University Press.

Sennett, Richard. 1974. *The Fall of Public Man*. New York: Random House.

Sennett, Richard, and Jonathan Cobb, 1972. *The Hidden Injuries of Class*. New York: Vintage.

Stein, Maurice. 1960. *The Eclipse of Community*. Princeton: Princeton University Press.

Whyte, William. 1988. *City: Rediscovering the Center*. New York: Doubleday.

Questions for Review and Discussion

1. Why does Young argue that we should think about the city rather than community as a way of generating political ideals?

2. Why does Young reject the idea of returning to the polis as the source of our ideal?

3. What, according to Young, are the four features implicit in city life from which we can draw a normative ideal?

4. What are the causes of social injustice in cities? How might Young's city ideal inform a theory of social justice?

bell hooks

bell hooks is a contemporary American philosopher and cultural theorist. Born Gloria Jean Watkins, bell hooks took the nom de plume after one of her great grandmothers in an effort to honor her female legacy, and does not capitalize it as a matter of humility. Growing up in the 1950s and '60s in Kentucky, hooks learned the hard lessons of racism, class bias, and sexism early in life, and they have shaped her intellectual work on literature, feminist theory, and cultural and political criticism. hooks discusses the importance of a place to call "home" for a sense of self, personhood, and identity, and the way in which both formal and informal segregation policies have worked to deprive black people of a "homeplace." She argues that black women have engaged in important and effective measures intended to counter these effects of racism by creating homes where black people could restore their sense of subjectivity and dignity.

The reading connects with several others, especially Young, who discuss urban place and identity. In addition, connections can be made to the readings on the urban built environment that argue that place is more than just a built space, but a meaning-giving (or meaning-taking) phenomenon (see especially Heidegger, Norberg-Schulz, and Mugerauer in this connection). For social class and race issues, compare to Addams, West, and Mendieta.

"HOMEPLACE: A SITE OF RESISTANCE" (1990)

When I was a young girl the journey across town to my grandmother's house was one of the most intriguing experiences. Mama did not like to stay there long. She did not care for all that loud talk, the talk that was usually about the old days, the way life happened then—who married whom, how and when somebody died, but also how we lived and survived as black people, how the white folks treated us. I remember this journey not just because of the stories I would hear. It was a movement away from the segregated blackness of our community into a poor white neighborhood. I remember the fear, being scared to walk to Baba's (our grandmother's house) because we would have to pass that terrifying whiteness—those white faces on the porches staring us down with hate. Even when empty or vacant, those porches seemed to say "danger," "you do not belong here," "you are not safe."

Oh! that feeling of safety, of arrival, of homecoming when we finally reached the edges of her yard, when we could see the soot black face of our grandfather, Daddy Gus, sitting in his chair on the porch, smell his cigar, and rest on his lap. Such a contrast, that feeling of arrival, of homecoming, this sweetness and the bitterness of that journey, that constant reminder of white power and control.

I speak of this journey as leading to my grandmother's house, even though our grandfather lived there too. In our young minds houses belonged to women, were their special domain, not as property, but as places where all that truly mattered in life took place—the warmth and comfort of shelter, the feeding of our bodies, the nurturing of our souls. There we learned dignity, integrity of being; there we learned to have faith. The folks who make this life possible, who were our primary guides and teachers, were black women.

Their lives were not easy. Their lives were hard. They were black women who for the most part worked outside the home serving white folks, cleaning their houses, washing their clothes, tending their children—black women who worked in the fields or in the streets, whatever they could do to make ends meet, whatever was necessary. Then they returned to their homes to make life happen there. This tension between service outside one's home, family, and kin network, service provided to white folks which took time and energy, and the effort of black women to conserve enough of themselves to provide service (care and nurturance) within their own families and communities is one of the many factors that has historically distinguished the lot of black women in patriarchal white supremacist society from that of black men. Contemporary black struggle must honor this history of service just as it must critique the sexist definition of service as women's "natural" role.

Since sexism delegates to females the task of creating and sustaining a home environment, it has been primarily the responsibility of black women to construct domestic households as spaces of care and nurturance in the face of the brutal harsh reality of racist oppression, of sexist domination. Historically, African-American people believed that the construction of a homeplace, however fragile and tenuous (the slave hut, the wooden shack), had a radical political dimension. Despite the brutal reality of racial apartheid, of domination, one's homeplace was the one site where one could freely confront the issue of humanization, where one could resist. Black women resisted by making homes where all black people could strive to be subjects, not objects, where we could be affirmed in our minds and hearts despite poverty, hardship, and deprivation, where we could restore to ourselves the dignity denied us on the outside in the public world.

This task of making homeplace was not simply a matter of black women providing service; it was about the construction of a safe place where black people could affirm one another and by so doing heal many of the wounds inflicted by racist domination. We could not learn to love or respect ourselves in the culture of white supremacy, on the outside; it was there on the inside, in that "homeplace," most often created and kept by black women, that we had the opportunity to grow and develop, to nurture our spirits. This task of making a homeplace, of making home a community of resistance, has been shared by black women globally, especially black women in white supremacist societies.

I shall never forget the sense of shared history, of common anguish, I felt when first reading about the plight of black women domestic servants in South Africa, black women laboring in white homes. Their stories evoked vivid memories of our African-American past. I remember that one of the black women giving testimony complained that after traveling in the wee hours of the morning to the white folks' house, after working there all day, giving her time and energy, she had "none left for her own." I knew this story. I had read it in the slave narratives of African-American women who, like Sojourner Truth, could say, "When I cried out with a mother's grief none but Jesus heard." I knew this story. I had grown to womanhood hearing about black women who nurtured and cared for white families when they longed to have time and energy to give to their own.

I want to remember these black women today. The act of remembrance is a conscious gesture honoring their struggle, their effort to keep something for their own. I want us to respect and understand that this effort has been and continues to be a radically subversive political gesture. For those who dominate and oppress us benefit most when we have nothing to give our own, when they have so taken from us our dignity, our humanness that we have nothing left, no "homeplace" where we can recover ourselves. I want us to remember these black women today, both past and present. Even as I speak there are black women in the midst of racial apartheid in South Africa, struggling to provide something for their own. "We . . . know how our sisters suffer" (Quoted in the petition for the repeal of the pass laws, August 9, 1956). I want us to honor them, not because they suffer but because they continue to struggle in the midst of suffering, because they continue to resist. I want to speak about the importance of homeplace in the midst of oppression and domination, of homeplace as a site of resistance and liberation struggle. Writing about "resistance," particularly resistance to the Vietnam war, Vietnamese Buddhist monk Thich Nhat Hahn says:

> . . . resistance, at root, must mean more than resistance against war. It is a resistance against all kinds of things that are like

war . . . So perhaps, resistance means opposition to being in-
vaded, occupied, assaulted and destroyed by the system. The
purpose of resistance, here, is to seek the healing of yourself
in order to be able to see clearly . . . I think that communities
of resistance should be places where people can return to
themselves more easily, where the conditions are such that
they can heal themselves and recover their wholeness.

Historically, black women have resisted white supremacist domination by working to establish homeplace. It does not matter that sexism
assigned them this role. It is more important that they took this conventional role and expanded it to include caring for one another, for children, for black men, in ways that elevated our spirits, that kept us from
despair, that taught some of us to be revolutionaries able to struggle for
freedom. In his famous 1845 slave narrative, Frederick Douglass tells the
story of his birth, of his enslaved black mother who was hired out a
considerable distance from his place of residence. Describing their relationship, he writes:

I never saw my mother, to know her as such more than four
or five times in my life; and each of these times was very short
in duration, and at night. She was hired by Mr. Stewart, who
lived about twelve miles from my house. She made her journeys to see me in the night, traveling the whole distance on
foot, after the performance of her day's work. She was a field
hand, and a whipping is the penalty of not being in the field
at sunrise . . . I do not recollect of ever seeing my mother by
the light of day. She was with me in the night. She would lie
down with me and get me to sleep, but long before I waked
she was gone.

After sharing this information, Douglass later says that he never
enjoyed a mother's "soothing presence, her tender and watchful care" so
that he received the "tidings of her death with much the same emotions
I should have probably felt at the death of a stranger." Douglass surely
intended to impress upon the consciousness of white readers the cruelty
of that system of racial domination which separated black families, black
mothers from their children. Yet he does so by devaluing black womanhood, by not even registering the quality of care that made his black
mother travel those twelve miles to hold him in her arms. In the midst
of a brutal racist system, which did not value black life, she valued the
life of her child enough to resist that system, to come to him in the
night, just to hold him.

Now I cannot agree with Douglass that he never knew a mother's care. I want to suggest that this mother, who dared to hold him in the night, gave him at birth a sense of value that provided a groundwork, however fragile, for the person he later became. If anyone doubts the power and significance of this maternal gesture, they would do well to read psychoanalyst Alice Miller's book, *The Untouched Key: Tracing Childhood Trauma in Creativity and Destructiveness*. Holding him in her arms, Douglass's mother provided, if only for a short time, a space where this black child was not the subject of dehumanizing scorn and devaluation but was the recipient of a quality of care that should have enabled the adult Douglass to look back and reflect on the political choices of this black mother who resisted slave codes, risking her life, to care for her son. I want to suggest that devaluation of the role his mother played in his life is a dangerous oversight. Though Douglass is only one example, we are currently in danger of forgetting the powerful role black women have played in constructing for us homeplaces that are the site for resistance. This forgetfulness undermines our solidarity and the future of black liberation struggle.

Douglass's work is important, for he is historically identified as sympathetic to the struggle for women's rights. All too often his critique of male domination, such as it was, did not include recognition of the particular circumstances of black women in relation to black men and families. To me one of the most important chapters in my first book, *Ain't I A Woman: Black Women and Feminism*, is one that calls attention to "Continued Devaluation of Black Womanhood." Overall devaluation of the role black women have played in constructing for us homeplaces that are the site for resistance undermines our efforts to resist racism and the colonizing mentality which promotes internalized self-hated. Sexist thinking about the nature of domesticity has determined the way black women's experience in the home is perceived. In African-American culture there is a long tradition of "mother worship." Black autobiographies, fiction, and poetry praise the virtues of the self-sacrificing black mother. Unfortunately, though positively motivated, black mother worship extols the virtues of self-sacrifice while simultaneously implying that such a gesture is not reflective of choice and will, rather the perfect embodiment of a woman's "natural" role. The assumption then is that the black woman who works hard to be a responsible caretaker is only doing what she should be doing. Failure to recognize the realm of choice, and the remarkable re-visioning of both woman's role and the idea of "home" that black women consciously exercised in practice, obscures the political commitment to racial uplift, to eradicating racism, which was the philosophical core of dedication to community and home.

Though black women did not self-consciously articulate in written discourse the theoretical principles of decolonization, this does not detract from the importance of their actions. They understood intellectually and intuitively the meaning of homeplace in the midst of an oppressive and dominating social reality, of homeplace as site of resistance and liberation struggle. I know of what I speak. I would not be writing this essay if my mother, Rosa Bell, daughter to Sarah Oldham, granddaughter to Bell Hooks, had not created homeplace in just this liberatory way, despite the contradictions of poverty and sexism.

In our family, I remember the immense anxiety we felt as children when mama would leave our house, our segregated community, to work as a maid in the homes of white folks. I believe that she sensed our fear, our concern that she might not return to us safe, that we could not find her (even though she always left phone numbers, they did not ease our worry). When she returned home after working long hours, she did not complain. She made an effort to rejoice with us that her work was done, that she was home, making it seem as though there was nothing about the experience of working as a maid in a white household, in that space of Otherness, which stripped her of dignity and personal power.

Looking back as an adult woman, I think of the effort it must have taken for her to transcend her own tiredness (and who knows what assaults or wounds to her spirit had to be put aside so that she could give something to her own). Given the contemporary notions of "good parenting" this may seem like a small gesture, yet in many post-slavery black families, it was a gesture parents were often too weary, too beaten down to make. Those of us who were fortunate enough to receive such care understood its value. Politically, our young mother, Rosa Bell, did not allow the white supremacist culture of domination to completely shape and control her psyche and her familial relationships. Working to create a homeplace that affirmed our beings, our blackness, our love for one another was necessary resistance. We learned degrees of critical consciousness from her. Our lives were not without contradictions, so it is not my intent to create a romanticized portrait. Yet any attempts to critically assess the role of black women in liberation struggle must examine the way political concern about the impact of racism shaped black women's thinking, their sense of home, and their modes of parenting.

An effective means of white subjugation of black people globally has been the perpetual construction of economic and social structures that deprive many folks of the means to make homeplace. Remembering this should enable us to understand the political value of black women's resistance in the home. It should provide a framework where we can discuss the development of black female political consciousness, acknowledging the political importance of resistance effort that took place in homes. It is no accident that the South African apartheid regime systematically attacks and destroys black efforts to construct homeplace, however tenuous, that small private reality where black women and men can renew their spirits and recover themselves. It is no accident that this homeplace, as fragile and as transitional as it may be, a makeshift shed, a small bit of earth where one rests, is always subject to violation and destruction. For when a people no longer have the space to construct homeplace, we cannot build a meaningful community of resistance.

Throughout our history, African-Americans have recognized the subversive value of homeplace, of having access to private space where we do not directly encounter white racist aggression. Whatever the shape and direction of black liberation struggle (civil rights reform or black power movement), domestic space has been a crucial site for organizing, for forming political solidarity. Homeplace has been a site of resistance. Its structure was defined less by whether or not black women and men were conforming to sexist behavior norms and more by our struggle to uplift ourselves as a people, our struggle to resist racist domination and oppression.

That liberatory struggle has been seriously undermined by contemporary efforts to change that subversive homeplace into a site of patriarchal domination of black women by black men, where we abuse one another for not conforming to sexist norms. This shift in perspective, where homeplace is not viewed as a political site, has had negative impact on the construction of black female identity and political consciousness. Masses of black women, many of whom were not formally educated, had in the past been able to play a vital role in black liberation struggle. In the contemporary situation, as the paradigms for domesticity in black life mirrored white bourgeois norms (where home is conceptualized as politically neutral space), black people began to overlook and devalue the importance of black female labor in teaching critical consciousness in domestic space. Many black women, irrespective of class status, have responded to this crisis of meaning by imitating leisure-class sexist notions of women's role, focusing their lives on meaningless compulsive consumerism.

Identifying this syndrome as "the crisis of black womanhood" in her essay "Considering Feminism as a Model for Social Change," Sheila Radford-Hill points to the mid-sixties as that historical moment when the primacy of black woman's role in liberation struggle began to be questioned as a threat to black manhood and was deemed unimportant. Radford-Hill asserts:

Without the power to influence the purpose and the direction of our collective experience, without the power to influence our culture from within, we are increasingly immobilized, unable to integrate self and role identities, unable to resist the cultural imperialism of the dominant culture which assures our continued oppression by destroying us from within. Thus, the crisis manifests itself as social dysfunction in the black community—as genocide, fratricide, homicide, and suicide. It is also manifested by the abdication of personal responsibility by black women for themselves and for each other . . . The crisis of black womanhood is a form of cultural aggression: a form of exploitation so vicious, so insidious that it is currently destroying an entire generation of black women and their families.

This contemporary crisis of black womanhood might have been avoided had black women collectively sustained attempts to develop the latent feminism expressed by their willingness to work equally alongside black men in black liberation struggle. Contemporary equation of black liberation struggle with the subordination of black women has damaged collective black solidarity. It has served the interests of white supremacy to promote the assumption that the wounds of racist domination would be less severe were black women conforming to sexist role patterns.

We are daily witnessing the disintegration of African-American family life that is grounded in a recognition of the political value of constructing homeplace as a site of resistance; black people daily perpetuate sexist norms that threaten our survival as a people. We can no longer act as though sexism in black communities does not threaten our solidarity; any force which estranges and alienates us from one another serves the interests of racist domination.

Black women and men must create a revolutionary vision of black liberation that has a feminist dimension, one which is formed in consideration of our specific needs and concerns. Drawing on past legacies, contemporary black women can begin to reconceptualize ideas of homeplace, once again considering the primacy of domesticity as a site for subversion and resistance. When we renew our concern with homeplace, we can address political issues that most affect our daily lives. Calling attention to the skills and resources of black women who may have begun to feel that they have no meaningful contribution to make, women who may or may not be formally educated but who have essential wisdom to share, who have practical experience that is the breeding ground for all useful theory, we may begin to bond with one another in ways that renew our solidarity.

When black women renew our political commitment to homeplace, we can address the needs and concerns of young black women who are groping for structures of meaning that will further their growth, young women who are struggling for self-definition. Together, black women can renew our commitment to black liberation struggle, sharing insights and awareness, sharing feminist thinking and feminist vision, building solidarity.

With this foundation, we can regain lost perspective, give life new meaning. We can make homeplace that space where we return for renewal and self-recovery, where we can heal our wounds and become whole.

Questions for Review and Discussion

1. Describe the neighborhoods in hooks's childhood town.

2. How is hooks's journey to her grandmother's house a "reminder of white power and control"?

3. What is the tension that black women who worked outside the home felt?

4. How did black women resist?

5. How does hooks define "homeplace"? Why is it so important? How is it undermined by oppressor groups?

Elizabeth A. Grosz

Elizabeth A. Grosz is a native Australian philosopher who now teaches at Rutgers University. She has written numerous books on philosophy, cultural studies, psychoanalysis, and feminist theory. In her full essay, Grosz demonstrates how feminist philosophers have furthered new understandings of cities and our relationship to them through their critiques of earlier philosophical models. In this excerpt, she explores two common models for thinking about the relationship between bodies and cities, and then develops a third alternative from her critique of them. Compare Grosz's understanding of a city to that of Pericles, Plato, Hobbes, Mumford, Conlon, Young, and Weiss.

"BODY POLITIC AND POLITICAL BODIES" (1992)

I will look at two pervasive models of the interrelation of bodies and cities, and, in outlining their problems, I hope to suggest alternatives that may account for future urban developments and their corporeal consequences.

In the first model, the body and the city have merely a de facto or external, contingent rather than constitutive relation. The city is a reflection, projection, or product of bodies. Bodies are conceived in naturalistic terms, predating the city, the cause and motivation for their design and construction. This model often assumes an ethnological and historical character: the city develops according to human needs and design, developing from nomadism to sedentary agrarianism to the structure of the localized village, the form of the polis through industrialization to the technological modern city and beyond. More recently, we have heard an inverted form of this presumed relation: cities have become (or may have always been) alienating environments, environments which do not allow the body a "natural," "healthy," or "conducive" context.

Underlying this view of the city as a product or projection of the body (in all its variations) is a form of humanism: the human subject is conceived as a sovereign and self-given agent which, individually or collectively, is responsible for all social and historical production. Humans *make* cities. Moreover, in such formulations the body is usually subordinated to and seen merely as a "tool" of subjectivity, of self-given consciousness. The city is a product not simply of the muscles and energy of the body, but the conceptual and reflective possibilities of consciousness itself: the capacity to design, to plan ahead, to function as an intentionality and thereby be transformed in the process. This view is reflected in the separation or binarism of design, on the one hand, and construction, on the other, the

184

division of mind from hand (or art from craft). Both Enlightenment humanism and marxism share this view, the distinction being whether the relation is conceived as a one-way relation (from subjectivity to the environment), or a dialectic (from subjectivity to environment and back again). Nonetheless, both positions consider the active agent in social production (whether the production of commodities or in the production of cities) to be the subject, a rational or potentially rational consciousness clothed in a body, the "captain of the ship," the "ghost in the machine."

In my opinion, this view has at least two serious problems. First, it subordinates the body to the mind while retaining a structure of binary opposites. Body is merely a tool or bridge linking a nonspatial (i.e., Cartesian) consciousness to the materiality and coordinates of the built environment, a kind of mediating term between mind on the one hand and inorganic matter on the other, a term that has no agency or productivity of its own. It is presumed to be a machine, animated by a consciousness. Second, at best, such a view only posits a one-way relation between the body or the subject and the city, linking them through a causal relation in which body or subjectivity is conceived as the cause, and the city its effect. In more sophisticated versions of this view, the city can have a negative feedback relation with the bodies that produce it, thereby alienating them. Implicit in this position is the active causal power of the subject in the design and construction of cities.

Another equally popular formulation proposes a kind of parallelism or isomorphism between the body and the city. The two are understood as analogues, congruent counterparts, in which the features, organization, and characteristics of one are reflected in the other. This notion of the parallelism between the body and social order (usually identified with the state) finds its clearest formulations in the seventeenth century, when liberal political philosophers justified their various allegiances (the divine right of kings, for Hobbes; parliamentary representation, for Locke; direct representation, for Rousseau, etc.) through the metaphor of the body-politic. The state parallels the body; artifice mirrors nature. The correspondence between the body and the body-politic is more or less exact and codified: the King usually represented as the head of the body-politic,[1] the populace as the body. The law has been compared to the body's nerves, the military to its arms, commerce to its legs or stomach, and so on. The exact correspondences vary from text to text, and from one political regime to another. However, if there is a morphological correspondence or parallelism

---

1. The king may also represent the heart. See Michel Feher, ed., *Fragments of a History of the Human Body*, vol. 1 (New York: Zone, 1989).

between the artificial commonwealth (the "Leviathan") and the human body in this pervasive metaphor of the body-politic, the body is rarely attributed a sex. If one presses this metaphor just a little, we must ask: if the state or the structure of the polis/city mirrors the body, what takes on the metaphoric function of the genitals in the body-politic? What kind of genitals are they? In other words, does the body-politic have a sex?

Here once again, I have serious reservations. The first regards the implicitly phallocentric coding of the body-politic, which, while claiming it models itself on the *human* body, uses the male to represent the human. Phallocentrism is, in my understanding, not so much the dominance of the phallus as the pervasive unacknowledged use of the male or masculine to represent the human. The problem, then, is not so much to eliminate as to reveal the masculinity inherent in the notion of the universal, the generic human, or the unspecified subject. The second reservation concerns the political function of this analogy: it serves to provide a justification for various forms of "ideal" government and social organization through a process of "naturalization": the human body is a natural form of organization which functions not only for the good of each organ but primarily for the good of the whole. Similarly, the body politic, whatever form it may take,[2] justifies and naturalizes itself with reference to some form of hierarchical organization modeled on the (presumed and projected) structure of the body. A third problem: this conception of the body-politic relies on a fundamental opposition between nature and culture, in which nature dictates the ideal forms of culture. Culture is a supercession and perfection of nature. The body-politic is an artificial construct which replaces the primacy of the natural body. Culture is molded according to the dictates of nature, but trans-

---

2. There is a slippage from conceptions of the state (which necessarily raise questions of legal sovereignty) and conceptions of the city as a commercial and cultural entity:

> The town is the correlate of the road. The town exists only as a function of a circulation and of circuits; it is a singular point on the circuits which create it and which it creates. It is defined by entries and exits; something must enter it and exit from it. It imposes a frequency. It effects a polarization of matter, inert, living or human . . . It is a phenomenon of transconsistency, a network, because it is fundamentally in contact with other towns. . . .

> The State proceeds otherwise: it is a phenomenon of ultraconsistency. It makes points resonate together, points . . . very diverse points of order—geographic, ethnic, linguistic, moral, economic, technological particulars. The State makes the town resonate with the countryside . . . the central power of the State is hierarchical and constitutes a civil-service sector; the center is not in the middle but on top because [it is] the only way it can recombine what it isolates . . . through subordiantion (Gilles Deleuze and Félix Guattari, "City/State," *Zone* 1/2 [1986]: 195–197).

forms nature's limits. In this sense, nature is a passivity on which culture works as male (cultural) productivity supercedes and overtakes female (natural) reproduction.

But if the relation between bodies and cities is neither causal (the first view) nor representational (the second view), then what kind of relation exists between them? These two models are inadequate insofar as they give precedence to one term or the other in the body/city pair. A more appropriate model combines elements from each. Like the causal view, the body (and not simply a disembodied consciousness) must be considered active in the production and transformation of the city. But bodies and cities are not causally linked. Every cause must be logically distinct from its effect. The body, however, is not distinct, does not have an existence separate from the city, for they are mutually defining. Like the representational model, there may be an isomorphism between the body and the city. But it is not a mirroring of nature in artifice. Rather, there is a two-way linkage which could be defined as an *interface*, perhaps even a cobuilding. What I am suggesting is a model of the relations between bodies and cities which sees them, not as megalithic total entities, distinct identities, but as assemblages or collections of parts, capable of crossing the thresholds between substances to form linkages, machines, provisional and often temporary sub- or microgroupings. This model is a practical one, based on the practical productivity bodies and cities have in defining and establishing each other. It is not a holistic view, one that stresses the unity and integration of city and body, their "ecological balance." Instead, I am suggesting a fundamentally disunified series of systems and interconnections, a series of disparate flows, energies, events or entities, and spaces, brought together or drawn apart in more or less temporary alignments.

The city in its particular geographical, architectural, spatializing, municipal arrangements is one particular ingredient in the social constitution of the body. It is by no means the most significant. The structure and particularity of, say, the family is more directly and visibly influential, although this in itself is to some extent a function of the social geography of cities. But nonetheless, the form, structure, and norms of the city seep into and effect all the other elements that go into the constitution of corporeality and/as subjectivity. It effects the way the subject sees others (domestic architecture and the division of the home into the conjugal bedroom, separated off from other living and sleeping spaces, and the specialization of rooms are as significant in this regard as smaller family size[3]), as well as the subject's understanding of, alignment with, and

---

3. See Jacques Donzelot, *The Policing of Families* (New York: Pantheon, 1979).

positioning in space. Different forms of lived spatiality (the verticality of the city, as opposed to the horizontality of the landscape—at least our own) effect the ways we live space, and thus our comportment and corporeal orientations and the subject's forms of corporeal exertion—the kind of terrain it must negotiate day by day, the effect this has on its muscular structure, its nutritional context, providing the most elementary forms of material support and sustenance for the body. Moreover, the city is, of course, also the site for the body's cultural saturation, its takeover and transformation by images, representational systems, the mass media, and the arts—the place where the body is representationally reexplored, transformed, contested, reinscribed. In turn, the body (as cultural product) transforms, reinscribes the urban landscape according to its changing (demographic, economic, and psychological) needs, extending the limits of the city, of the sub-urban, ever towards the countryside which borders it. As a hinge between the population and the individual, the body, its distribution, habits, alignments, pleasures, norms, and ideals are the ostensible object of governmental regulation, and the city is a key tool.[4]

Questions for Review and Discussion

1. Grosz identifies two common models by which we understand the relationship of bodies and cities. What are they?

2. What does Grosz think are the problems or deficits of each model?

3. Does Grosz think that we can overcome these problems? If so, how?

---

4. See Foucault's discussion of the notion of biopower in the final sections of *The History of Sexuality*.

Cornel West

Cornel West, a living American philosopher trained in the American pragmatist tradition, also works in the areas of African American studies, critical theory, and religious studies. He wrote this essay in response to the riots following the Rodney King verdicts in which two police officers were acquitted of beating Rodney King despite the fact that their actions were caught on videotape. In this essay, West argues that both the left and the right have difficulty talking about race. Narrow discussions of race ignore the flaws of American society that cause both inequalities and racial stereotypes. West calls for a more inclusive understanding of citizenship. He argues that the solutions to the problems that black people experience are best approached by appeal to a common democratic history and attention to the public good, especially in city life. West's essay raises questions of democracy and social justice, and may be read in connection with the ancient Greek essays, as well as those by Addams, Kemmis, and Young. Its treatment of racism might be compared to that of bell hooks. He provides a response to Hayek's claims.

INTRODUCTION TO *RACE MATTERS* (1993)

Since the beginning of the nation, white Americans have suffered from a deep inner uncertainty as to who they really are. One of the ways that has been used to simplify the answer has been to seize upon the presence of black Americans and use them as a marker, a symbol of limits, a metaphor for the "outsider." Many whites could look at the social position of blacks and feel that color formed an easy and reliable gauge for determining to what extent one was or was not American. Perhaps that is why one of the first epithets that many European immigrants learned when they got off the boat was the term "nigger"—it made them feel instantly American. But this is tricky magic. Despite his racial difference and social status, something indisputably American about Negroes not only raised doubts about the white man's value system but aroused the troubling suspicion that whatever else the true American is, he is also somehow black.

—Ralph Ellison, "What America Would Be
Like without Blacks" (1970)

What happened in Los Angeles in April of 1992 was neither a race riot nor a class rebellion. Rather, this monumental upheaval was a multiracial, trans-class, and largely male display of justified social rage. For all its ugly, xenophobic resentment, its air of adolescent carnival, and its downright barbaric behavior, it signified the sense of powerlessness in American society. Glib attempts to reduce its meaning to the pathologies of the black underclass, the criminal actions of hoodlums, or the political revolt of the oppressed urban masses miss the mark. Of those arrested, only 36 percent were black, more than a third had full-time jobs, and most claimed to shun political affiliation. What we witnessed in Los Angeles was the consequence of a lethal linkage of economic decline, cultural decay, and political lethargy in American life. Race was the visible catalyst, not the underlying cause.

The meaning of the earthshaking events in Los Angeles is difficult to grasp because most of us remain trapped in the narrow framework of the dominant liberal and conservative views of race in America, which with its worn-out vocabulary leaves us intellectually debilitated, morally disempowered, and personally depressed. The astonishing disappearance of the event from public dialogue is testimony to just how painful and distressing a serious engagement with race is. Our truncated public discussions of race suppress the best of who and what we are as a people because they fail to confront the complexity of the issue in a candid and critical manner. The predictable pitting of liberals against conservatives, Great Society Democrats against self-help Republicans, reinforces intellectual parochialism and political paralysis.

The liberal notion that more government programs can solve racial problems is simplistic—precisely because it focuses *solely* on the economic dimension. And the conservative idea that what is needed is a change in the moral behavior of poor black urban dwellers (especially poor black men, who, they say, should stay married, support their children, and stop committing so much crime) highlights immoral actions while ignoring public responsibility for the immoral circumstances that haunt our fellow citizens.

The common denominator of these views of race is that each still sees black people as a "problem people," in the words of Dorothy I. Height, president of the National Council of Negro Women, rather than as fellow American citizens with problems. Her words echo the poignant "unasked question" of W. E. B. Du Bois, who, in *The Souls of Black Folk* (1903), wrote:

> They approach me in a half-hesitant sort of way, eye me curiously or compassionately, and then instead of saying directly, How does it feel to be a problem? they say, I know an excellent colored man in my town. . . . Do not these Southern outrages make your blood boil? At these I smile, or am inter-

ested, or reduce the boiling to a simmer, as the occasion may require. To the real question, How does it feel to be a problem? I answer seldom a word.

Nearly a century later, we confine discussions about race in America to the "problems" black people pose for whites rather than consider what this way of viewing black people reveals about us as a nation.

This paralyzing framework encourages liberals to relieve their guilty consciences by supporting public funds directed at "the problems"; but at the same time, reluctant to exercise principled criticism of black people, liberals deny them the freedom to err. Similarly, conservatives blame the "problems" on black people themselves—and thereby render black social misery invisible or unworthy of public attention.

Hence, for liberals, black people are to be "included" and "integrated" into "our" society and culture, while for conservatives they are to be "well behaved" and "worthy of acceptance" by "our" way of life. Both fail to see that the presence and predicaments of black people are neither additions to nor defections from American life, but rather *constitutive elements of that life.*

To engage in a serious discussion of race in America, we must begin not with the problems of black people but with the flaws of American society—flaws rooted in historic inequalities and longstanding cultural stereotypes. How we set up the terms for discussing racial issues shapes our perception and response to these issues. As long as black people are viewed as a "them," the burden falls on blacks to do all the "cultural" and "moral" work necessary for healthy race relations. The implication is that only certain Americans can define what it means to be American—and the rest must simply "fit in."

The emergence of strong black-nationalist sentiments among blacks, especially among young people, is a revolt against this sense of having to "fit in." The variety of black-nationalist ideologies, from the moderate views of Supreme Court Justice Clarence Thomas in his youth to those of Louis Farrakhan today, rest upon a fundamental truth: white America has been historically weak-willed in ensuring racial justice and has continued to resist fully accepting the humanity of blacks. As long as double standards and differential treatment abound—as long as the rap performer Ice-T is harshly condemned while former Los Angeles Police Chief Daryl F. Gates's antiblack comments are received in polite silence, as long as Dr. Leonard Jeffries's anti-Semitic statements are met with vitriolic outrage while presidential candidate Patrick J. Buchanan's anti-Semitism receives a genteel response—black nationalisms will thrive.

Afrocentrism, a contemporary species of black nationalism, is a gallant yet misguided attempt to define an African identity in a white society perceived to be hostile. It is gallant because it puts black doings and sufferings, not white anxieties and fears, at the center of discussion. It is misguided because—out of fear of cultural hybridization and through silence on the issue of class, retrograde views on black women, gay men, and lesbians, and a reluctance to link race to the common good—it reinforces the narrow discussions about race.

To establish a new framework, we need to begin with a frank acknowledgment of the basic humanness and Americanness of each of us. And we must acknowledge that as a people—*E Pluribus Unum*—we are on a slippery slope toward economic strife, social turmoil, and cultural chaos. If we go down, we go down together. The Los Angeles upheaval forced us to see not only that we are not connected in ways we would like to be but also, in a more profound sense, that this failure to connect binds us even more tightly together. The paradox of race in America is that our common destiny is more pronounced and imperiled precisely when our divisions are deeper. The Civil War and its legacy speak loudly here. And our divisions are growing deeper. Today, 86 percent of white suburban Americans live in neighborhoods that are less than 1 percent black, meaning that the prospects for the country depend largely on how its cities fare in the hands of a suburban electorate. There is no escape from our interracial interdependence, yet enforced racial hierarchy dooms us as a nation to collective paranoia and hysteria—the unmaking of any democratic order.

The verdict in the Rodney King case which sparked the incidents in Los Angeles was perceived to be wrong by the vast majority of Americans. But whites have often failed to acknowledge the widespread mistreatment of black people, especially black men, by law enforcement agencies, which helped ignite the spark. The verdict was merely the occasion for deep-seated rage to come to the surface. This rage is fed by the "silent" depression ravaging the country—in which real weekly wages of all American workers since 1973 have declined nearly 20 percent, while at the same time wealth has been upwardly distributed.

The exodus of stable industrial jobs from urban centers to cheaper labor markets here and abroad, housing policies that have created "chocolate cities and vanilla suburbs" (to use the popular musical artist George Clinton's memorable phrase), white fear of black crime, and the urban influx of poor Spanish-speaking and Asian immigrants—all have helped erode the tax base of American cities just as the federal government has cut its supports and programs. The result is unemployment, hunger, homelessness, and sickness for millions.

And a pervasive spiritual impoverishment grows. The collapse of meaning in life—the eclipse of hope and absence of love of self and others, the breakdown of family and neighborhood bonds—leads to the social deracination and cultural denudement of urban dwellers, especially children. We have created rootless, dangling people with little link to the supportive networks—family, friends, school—that sustain some sense of purpose in life. We have witnessed the collapse of the spiritual communities that in the past helped Americans face despair, disease, and death and that transmit through the generations dignity and decency, excellence and elegance.

The result is lives of what we might call "random nows," of fortuitous and fleeting moments preoccupied with "getting over"—with acquiring pleasure, property, and power by any means necessary. (This is not what Malcolm X meant by this famous phrase.) Post-modern culture is more and more a market culture dominated by gangster mentalities and self-destructive wantonness. This culture engulfs all of us—yet its impact on the disadvantaged is devastating, resulting in extreme violence in everyday life. Sexual violence against women and homicidal assaults by young black men on one another are only the most obvious signs of this empty quest for pleasure, property, and power.

Last, this rage if fueled by a political atmosphere in which images, not ideas, dominate, where politicians spend more time raising money than debating issues. The functions of parties have been displaced by public polls, and politicians behave less as thermostats that determine the climate of opinion than as thermometers registering the public mood. American politics has been rocked by an unleashing of greed among opportunistic public officials—who have followed the lead of their counterparts in the private sphere, where, as of 1989, 1 percent of the population owned 37 percent of the wealth and 10 percent of the population owned 86 percent of the wealth—leading to a profound cynicism and pessimism among the citizenry.

And given the way in which the Republican Party since 1968 has appealed to popular xenophobic images—playing the black, female, and homophobic cards to realign the electorate along race, sex, and sexual-orientation lines—it is no surprise that the notion that we are all part of one garment of destiny is discredited. Appeals to special interests rather than to public interests reinforce this polarization. The Los Angeles upheaval was an expression of utter fragmentation by a powerless citizenry that includes not just the poor but all of us.

What is to be done? How do we capture a new spirit and vision to meet the challenges of the post-industrial city, post-modern culture, and post-party politics?

First, we must admit that the most valuable sources for help, hope, and power consist of ourselves and our common history. As in the ages of Lincoln, Roosevelt, and King, we must look to new frameworks and languages to understand our multilayered crisis and overcome our deep malaise.

Second, we must focus our attention on the public square—the common good that undergirds our national and global destinies. The vitality of any public square ultimately depends on how much we *care* about the quality of our lives together. The neglect of our public infrastructure, for example—our water and sewage systems, bridges, tunnels, highways, subways, and streets—reflects not only our myopic economic politics, which impede productivity, but also the low priority we place on our common life.

The tragic plight of our children clearly reveals our deep disregard for public well-being. About one out of every five children in this country lives in poverty, including one out of every two black children and two out of every five Hispanic children. Most of our children—neglected by overburdened parents and bombarded by the market values of profit-hungry corporations—are ill-equipped to live lives of spiritual and cultural quality. Faced with these facts, how do we expect ever to constitute a vibrant society?

One essential step is some form of large-scale public intervention to ensure access to basic social goods—housing, food, health care, education, child care, and jobs. We must invigorate the common good with a mixture of government, business, and labor that does not follow any existing blueprint. After a period in which the private sphere has been sacralized and the public square gutted, the temptation is to make a fetish of the public square. We need to resist such dogmatic swings.

Last, the major challenge is to meet the need to generate new leadership. The paucity of courageous leaders—so apparent in the response to the events in Los Angeles—requires that we look beyond the same elites and voices that recycle the older frameworks. We need leaders—neither saints nor sparkling television personalities—who can situate themselves within a larger historical narrative of this country and our world, who can grasp the complex dynamics of our peoplehood and imagine a future grounded in the best of our past, yet who are attuned to the frightening obstacles that now perplex us. Our ideals of freedom, democracy, and quality must be invoked to invigorate all of us, especially the landless, propertyless, and luckless. Only a visionary leadership that can motivate "the better angels of our nature," as Lincoln said, and activate possibilities for a freer, more efficient, and stable America—only that leadership deserves cultivation and support.

This new leadership must be grounded in grass-roots organizing that highlights democratic accountability. Whoever *our* leaders will be as we approach the twenty-first century, their challenge will be to help Americans determine whether a genuine multiracial democracy can be created and sustained in an era of global economy and a moment of xenophobic frenzy.

Let us hope and pray that the vast intelligence, imagination, humor, and courage of Americans will not fail us. Either we learn a new language of empathy and compassion, or the fire this time will consume us all.

Questions for Review and Discussion

1. According to West, what was the real cause of the Rodney King uprising?

2. What does West argue is common to both liberal and conservative approaches to race issues that is troublesome?

3. What do white persons fail to understand about the black American experience?

4. Does West think that Afrocentricism or black nationalism is the answer? Why or why not?

5. How have race perceptions affected our cities?

6. What does West think that we should do to heal our racial divisions and our cities?

Joseph Grange

Joseph Grange is Professor of Philosophy at the University of Southern Maine. His work spans the American pragmatist and process philosophy traditions as well as continental theory. This essay comes from the last chapter of his book *The City: An Urban Cosmology*. Like Mumford, Conlon, and others, Grange views the city as the pinnacle of human meaning and experience. In the essay included here, Conlon argues that the role of the philosopher in the city is important now more than ever, and that the American pragmatist tradition provides the best resources for us to understand that role. Grange argues that the philosopher should be a "master of heartfelt contrast." His work is a good example of the recent philosophical return to philosophy's urban roots. Compare to Mumford, Lefebvre, Gavin, Conlon, and Kemmis.

"THE PHILOSOPHER AS MASTER OF HEARTFELT CONTRAST" (1999)

In the East and the West the philosopher has traditionally played an important role in the life of the city. Socrates in Athens and Confucius in the city-states of China practiced normative thinking in the most public way. The price they paid for this is also well known. The people of the city are not always happy to get the news that there are other, more desirable ways to conduct business. Nowadays, the philosopher's obligation to speak publicly has been exchanged for a much reduced role. No doubt it is safer to be but one more member of a university faculty, but the loss to the city is incalculable. What the philosopher can offer the city is threefold: a vision of the whole, measured public deliberation on values, and the capacity to speak truth to power for the sake of the poor and the vulnerable. Thus, the philosopher ought to offer the city a cosmology that outlines the contours of a fair and fitting city. The philosopher should also provide a public forum for the articulation of values within the city's continuing drama of emergent novelty. Lastly, the philosopher's heartmind ought to embrace the city's powerless and give voice to their concerns, for without them no community is complete. The city deserves a cosmology befitting its grandeur, a semiotics worthy of its values, and a praxis effective for all its citizens. The creation of such a vision would be a worthy way to put American philosophy back to work on important matters.

This study insists that there are always two dimensions at play in our thinking and feeling processes. There is at the forefront of our awareness a focus illuminating what is of immediate concern. But this foreground is given depth by the degree to which it connects with that which stays in the background and grants solidity and place to our present concerns. These contrasted dimensions of human experience find their most concretely interwoven expression in the subtle interactions of thought and feeling that mark city life at its best. [...] These urban dimensions form "the one thought" of urban cosmological thinking and "the many feelings" of their accompanying moods. And as expressed through the three signs of urban semiotics, they make up the warp and woof of city experience.

Now, the idea of contrast has been central to this study. It is among the categories used to describe the workings of the urban environment and is also synonymous with the concept of beauty. A contrast is a harmony that brings into a balanced relation aspects of a situation that normally would not hold together. In other words, a contrast is a unique act of creativity that enlarges the cityscape by widening what is included in its boundaries. Thus, a contrast is also directly related to the dimension of thirdness that is such a vital part of good city form. Finally, because of its special character, a contrast expresses both a feeling tone and an intellectual content. In sum, a contrast is the epitome of the cosmological, semiotic, and practical parts of this study.

The contemporary philosopher can best provide an important intellectual service to urban society by developing forms of normative thinking that stress the importance of contrast as an essential ingredient in contemporary culture. As a form of unity that brings together seemingly opposed aspects of experience, a contrast offers an important form of healing for a culture bedevilled by destructive forms of dualistic thinking. Its power to heal splits in our culture is grounded in the capacity to provide a vision wider than the reigning forms of orthodoxy. When this is appropriately carried out, the narrowness excluding important parts of experience is eliminated and alternate forms of culture become real options. What is more, precisely because the philosopher deals with only vague contrasts, intense community involvement is demanded as part of the task of finding specific solutions to particular problems. The philosopher is no divine being handing down universal edicts. Rather, what the philosopher can offer the civic process is width of vision that encourages alternative ways of looking at problems. And what is more, because the philosopher is also expected (at least in the tradition of speculative philosophy) to provide intellectually coherent and applicable ideas, the community can expect testable hypotheses, not empty generalities. Thus, the philosopher is part of the experimental process of developing better ways to live together. Paying strict attention to the feedback between theory

and practice ought to be a routine aspect of the philosopher's contributions to city life. The philosopher is neither an infallible guru nor a
substitute social scientist. The intellectual contribution that the philosopher can make to the contemporary city lies in the direction of providing
a wider understanding of what is possible within the real constraints of
the urban environment. In short, the philosopher ought to become a
master of contrast as a way of providing effective modes of thinking
about divisive issues.

But there is more to the philosopher's responsibility than abstract
intellectual effort. The contrast offered must also be "heartfelt." I employ this term (and I am aware of how sentimental the term may sound,
especially to cynical ears) in order to express the connection between
thought and feeling that has been so much a part of my argument. In
so doing I once again consciously place myself within the tradition of
American naturalism and pragmatism. Surely, when William James in-
veighed against vicious intellectualism, he was protesting against a form
of thinking that tore the heart out of human experience. And a great part
of Charles Peirce's labor to develop his semiotics of firstness, secondness,
and thirdness was given over to ensuring a central place for feelings
within philosophical reflection. Likewise, Dewey's insistence on the "had"
quality of experience was meant to remind us that feeling is a more
primary and concrete category than sensing and thinking. And there is
also Whitehead's doctrine of prehensions, a bold systematic effort to
refuse any ultimate distinction between thought and feeling. Heart and
mind go together within the spirit of American philosophy.

Questions for Review and Discussion

1. What does Grange think that the contemporary philosopher can
   offer the city?

2. What does Grange mean by saying that the philosopher is "the
   master of heartfelt contrast"?

3. Why is that quality of the philosopher important to the city?

4. What, in addition to intellectual effort, should the philosopher
   commit to the city?

James Conlon

James Conlon is Professor of Philosophy at Mount Mary College in Wisconsin. Conlon publishes and teaches on philosophical issues and their relationship to other disciplines and to the contemporary world. He has written about art, film, love, and cities. In this essay, Conlon argues that cities are the best type of places to do philosophy because cities act like "gadflies," shaking us out of our complacency and demanding that we engage in thoughtful questioning. Conlon defines cities as places that are fundamentally diverse, places that bring us into erotic relation with the Other. Following Plato, Conlon argues that such eros is the activity of philosophy. Conlon draws both on the image of Socrates as gadfly as well as on Plato's concept of eros. This essay explicitly links philosophy and the city and lends comparisons to Dewey, Lefebvre, Grange, and Gavin. See also Iris Marion Young, whom Conlon cites.

"CITIES AND THE PLACE OF PHILOSOPHY" (1999)

I want to argue the importance of urban places to philosophy. Being urban and being philosophical are significantly intertwined and the city is the surest place for philosophy to happen. This is so not just because philosophy, understood as the thoughtful questioning of conventional beliefs about human meaning, originated in the city, but because the dynamics of city life parallel and enable the life of philosophy. Admittedly, philosophy can, and sometimes does, happen outside the city. Admittedly, nature can, and sometimes does, offer the conceptual challenges necessary for great philosophy. But it is urban life that relentlessly raises the most disturbing questions. While the city is not the only place for philosophy, it is, I will argue, the place most supportive of it.

WHAT IS A CITY?

The obvious place to begin my argument is with a workable definition of a city. For most people, the city's defining element would likely have something to do with size. But if size were the only factor, some of history's most significant cities would not be labeled as such. By present standards, for example, the ancient Greek *polis* tended to be rather small. This is indicated by Aristotle's insistence that the citizenry of a *polis* not exceed a number that would allow for mutual recognition.[1] But the

---

1. Aristotle, *Politics*, trans. Ernest Barker (Oxford: Oxford University Press, 1995), p. 262 (1362b7–22).

Greek *polis* is so foundational to our understanding of what a city is, that any definition which excluded Athens or Sparta would be inherently flawed. The essence of the city must be found in something other than mere size.

The sociologist, Louis Wirth, acknowledges this in his commonly used definition of the city as "a relatively large, dense, and permanent settlement of socially heterogeneous individuals."[2] The value of Wirth's definition is that it understands the city more as a socio-cultural entity than a geographic one. Like the human being whom it mirrors, the city has a "body"—its physical size, shape and structure; but these geographical factors are not its defining essence, not its soul. The soul of a city lies in its heterogeneity.

A city is, fundamentally and essentially, diverse. Unlike a village, it is inhabited by people with radically different beliefs and values.[3] A city's size is a factor only because size usually affects the extent and manner of its heterogeneity. Contrary to Aristotle, at the heart of the city is not an encounter with the familiar, but a continual and inevitable encounter with the foreign.

Once the defining role of heterogeneity is understood, it becomes easier to see why the city has played such a pivotal role in human history. [. . .]

THE SIGNIFICANCE OF CITIES

In *The City in History*, Lewis Mumford has speculated that cities originated partly as vehicles for preserving and transmitting the accumulated accomplishments of a culture. As the knowledge, achievements and mythology of a people began to transcend the limits of individual memory, some method for storage became necessary. "The invention of such forms as the written record, the library, the archive, the school, and the university is one of the earliest and most characteristic achievements of the city."[4] But the city does not merely collect a culture's achievements; it also teaches them, passes them on to successive generations. Through its art and architecture, a city infuses the complexity of culture into the very bones of those who daily walk its streets. Living literally in the

---

2. Louis Wirth, "Urbanism as a Way of Life," in *Metropolis: Center and Symbol of Our Times*, ed. Philip Kasinitz (New York: New York University Press, 1995), 64.

3. I do not mean to imply that there are no differences in villages and no community in cities. However, Tönnies's *Gemeinschaft/Gesellschaft* distinction seems to me to be basically sound, even though it has often been simplistically applied.

4. Lewis Mumford, *The City in History* (San Diego: Harcourt Brace Jovanovich, 1961), 30.

shadow of the Parthenon, the Athenian learns the complex meaning of Athena in a way inaccessible to the village peasant.

But Mumford's vision of the good city, like Pericles' vision of Athens, was one in which inhabitants shared a common culture. Ideally, this common system of values was then collected and transmitted through the machinery of city life. However, the actual experience of cities, even ancient Athens, was not that they perfected the cultural homogeneity of village life, but that they forced homogeneity to interact with otherness, forced radical differences to share the same space.

In her revolutionary work, *The Economy of Cities*, Jane Jacobs hypothesizes that the first cities arose as trading points fortuitously located near prize goods and near routes that minimized geographical barriers.[5] For Jacobs, the primordial urban act, the city's founding myth, is an economic exchange with someone outside one's group, someone fundamentally other. Even if her thesis proves to be an inadequate historical explanation for the origin of cities, it still works to highlight something essential about them. Cities are places where the goods of foreigners, their food, clothing, gadgets and art, are made available for native experience. The city begins as a bazaar which, to native eyes, will inevitably be experienced as bizarre. Even when the original intent of a city's builders was to inculcate a specific value system into the populace, the economic nature of cities forced them to be forums for contrasting values. The growth and status of a city was intrinsically linked to the diversity of goods made available to its inhabitants.

Even today, the marvel of a great city, the rush and excitement of it, is the sheer multiplicity of things it contains. In a very real sense, great cities, "world" cities, contain the entire world, contain representations from every corner of space and time. Not only does the city *include* museums and libraries, it is itself a vast museum, a living library of faiths, tastes, styles and dreams packed densely together and available for experience in a reasonable amount of time.

As instrument for condensing and packaging the world's diversity, a city will obviously not be limited only to the world's "goods"; it will include as well the world's cruelties, perversions and deficiencies. In virtually every city there are places (Foucault calls them "heterotopias"[6]) which work to "suspect, neutralize, or invert" the established values of a society. Such places often prove the source for the frequent identification of the city with sin and crime in both the religious and popular imaginations.

---

5. Jane Jacobs, *The Economy of Cities* (New York: Vintage Books, 1969), 18–31.

6. Michel Foucault, "Of Other Spaces," in *Diacritics*, (Spring 1986), 24.

Eventually, it is even imagined that the city itself is the cause of corruption and that human beings would maintain their moral integrity if only they avoided the city and remained close to nature. Yet, even in the biblical myth, corruption originally happens in the garden. Cities do not create human degeneracy, they merely collect its varieties and market them. Just as city streets spread before their inhabitants a panoply of human achievements and refinements, so too is every conceivable perversion temptingly available there.

THE NATURE OF CITIES

Characterizing the city as a living museum correctly highlights its ability to condense the world and make it available for experience, but it is still an imperfect metaphor. The modern museum is a place one can choose to visit, a place where the world's artifacts and styles are neatly and conveniently categorized. The city is not at all like that; it often forces the world's diversity on its inhabitants—and in a random, chaotic flux. A mandated subway ride to work can include the haunting music of a Peruvian pipe band, the sexual preferences of a leathered couple, the stench of a homeless drunk, and the refinement of a perfectly tailored Armani suit. The rider cannot select experiences like channels on a television. The city has its own agenda and constantly insists that things beyond one's choice, unfamiliar things, be experienced and processed mentally. Collage is the inevitable urban art form because it is the inevitable structure of urban experience.

Admittedly, cities aren't the only places that have surprises. As Annie Dillard's meditations on Tinker Creek[7] prove so forcefully, even the most domesticated field can confront one with radical otherness. However, it is not a human, social otherness. A defining characteristic of village society is its homogeneity. This is not to stereotype the peasant as a rube or the village as a place devoid of difference. Genuine individuality of character is famously fostered by village life. However, a village is ordinarily a place where people know one another, know the happenings and histories of each other's lives and share the same general values. A village is ordinarily not a place of deep racial, religious or even occupational diversity. Thus, the structure and dynamics of rural life constantly affirm one's own values because they are mirrored in the faces and styles of whomever one meets. If a different value does present itself, for example, Hester Prynne's illegitimate pregnancy in Hawthorne's *Scarlet*

---

7. Annie Dillard, *Pilgrim at Tinker Creek* (New York: HarperCollins, 1974).

Letter, or—to use a more contemporary example—Teena Brandon's trans-sexual activities in Kimberly Pierce's film, "Boys Don't Cry" (1999), it is all-too-often marked as alien and denied the chance to occupy the same space with established members of the community. Thus, even its anomalies end up confirming the fundamental homogeneity of rural life.

The structure of city life works against such uniformity. This isn't to claim that city dwellers are inherently more virtuous, less xenophobic, than villagers. Sixteenth century Venice invented the ghetto in an effort to keep Jews on the fringes of city life and New York's recent efforts with the homeless demonstrate that cities still try to value-segregate their population. But the economic life of the city dictates otherwise. Shylock and Antonio are forced for confront each other in the bargaining space of the Rialto and, however different their private lives, the Park Avenue diva and the Bowery baglady face each other across the same space on the subway. The daily dynamics of city life, rather than providing affirmation of one's values, provide constant challenges to them instead. Different faces in the mirror keep one's mental life on edge and force it into accommodating and explaining such radical differences.

But the mental life on edge is the mental life awakened, the mental life at the beginnings of philosophy. It is precisely the forefronted anomaly that forces the mind to examine its rusty definitions and categories. The mind can rest comfortably in its conviction that all swans are white as long as it never sees a black swan. But once one is inescapably present, the habituated mind is jarred into rethinking its categories, is prodded, in other words, toward philosophy. Because the city condenses the boun-tiful confusion of reality into one place, if the world does contain any black swans, one will be passed sooner or later on a city street. Socrates claimed that the gods had sent him to Athens like a gadfly to a sleepy horse. His pestering questions provided the anomalies that awakened his listeners into philosophy. But the modern metropolis fulfills this same function; it is itself a gadfly, continuously pestering its inhabitants to include into their schema of reality foreign elements that they would often sooner forget. The city dweller, for example, does not have the luxury of choosing whether to think about the ethical issues of poverty; the poor cluster outside every grocery store and their pleas raise the same sort of questions Socrates did—and with the same annoying persistence.

This is not to claim, of course, that the city makes philosophy inevitable. City-dwellers themselves often find ingenious ways to evade the city, even while walking its streets (earphones, for example). But the flight from the city, in whatever form it happens to take, is often a disguised flight from philosophy, an effort to find some cave that will not pester one into thought.

But, some will argue, philosophy does not just need question-raising stimulation to carry on its life, it also needs undistracting and focused places in order to reflect on the questions raised. Is not nature the more "natural" place for such meditation? I do not see why. The city has as many nooks and crannies for quiet retreat as the country. To identify the city with noisy chaos and the country with peaceful calm is to grossly stereotype both places.

Likewise, it is mistaken to see the city as the antithesis of nature, as devoid of the important possibilities nature offers for reflection. Cities are obviously situated within nature and often must work closely with it, as do cities situated near water or mountain passes. Cities also make the variety of nature present in ways that nature herself never could, as in zoos and botanical gardens. And nature in the midst of the city, nature "framed," as it were, by the city, often takes on a focused intensity especially helpful to meditation, as does the lone tree in a cloistered courtyard, for example, or a flowering window box against a brick building façade. Assuming philosophical activity to be a dialectical rhythm of stimulation and reflection, cities effectively provide for both.

I have been arguing that the essence of the urban is that it condenses humanity's diverse cultural achievements into one place and makes them a part of everyday experience in such a way as to stimulate that most human of activities: thought, philosophy. Every great city has a specific, centralized space in which this essential urban dynamic is played out. This space takes a variety of physical forms. Sometimes it is geometrically located at the city's center; sometimes it is a square orientated around a crucial political or religious site. It might be carefully designed and officially designated, or evolve haphazardly over years of public use. It must be unrestricted space, space accessible to the entire population. It must also be a genuinely magnetic space, space which daily attracts the city's variety into it, not just for functional purposes, but to celebrate and savor the communality of city life. Its ancient examples are the Greek *agora* and the Roman forum. Contemporary examples would be Beijing's Tiananmen Square, New York's Central Park, Paris' Place de la Concorde and London's Trafalgar Square. Because such places are the symbolic hearts of cities, places where the essential urban dynamic is readily available for enjoyment and contemplation, they are a key to understanding the meaning of cities.

"*Agora*" simply means meeting place.[8] In early Greek cities the *agora* was the open air locus where major roads converged. Since it was used for civic meetings, it became synonymous with the place where public business

---

8. Spiro Kostof, *The City Assembled* (Boston: Little, Brown & Co., 1992), 57.

was discussed and decided. No town, however large, was considered a *"polis"* without an *agora*. By the time of Pericles (d. 429 BCE), the *agora* of Athens was a large square surrounded mostly by civic and religious buildings. It was a bustling city center where a multiplicity of activities was simultaneously available for participation and observation. [. . .]

PHILOSOPHY AND THE CITY

Philosophy has acquired the reputation of being ethereal and abstract, but if its paradigm is the Socratic dialogue, it was born amidst the bustle of the *agora*, born on the busiest corner of a great city. Socrates began his philosophical work by abandoning astronomy and turning his attention instead to the human diversity collected in the *agora*. To the condemned Socrates, Crito's offer of an escape from Athens meant escaping the sources of his own being, escaping philosophy itself.[9] Socrates could not imagine the dialectical intensity of philosophy without the urban intensity of the *agora*.

Although the *agora*, in its historical form, was a phenomenon peculiar to ancient Greek cities, some form of *agora* is essential to city life itself. Just as the city condenses the world, there must be a place (or, in large cities, several places) where the city is itself condensed, where its essential function as a meeting place for differences is savored and celebrated, where its life is, as it were, dramatized.

Scholars believe that dramatic theater originated in the *agora* and only later moved to ampitheaters constructed especially for it.[10] Sitting for a few hours on a bench in a modern *agora*—New York's Central Park, for example—is amazingly like attending a theatrical performance. The park becomes a stage on which the life of the city dramatizes itself and people are drawn to the park as both actors in, and audience for, this drama. The aesthetics of city theater, however, is not the unified action recommended in Aristotle's *Poetics*, but the found and fragmented unity of collage. Sitting on a park bench, one overhears pieces of passing conversation, accompanied always by the erratic rhythm of traffic. These aural pieces mix with unconnected visual vignettes: a Caribbean maid, for example, coaxing her white charges down a playground slide, a drug deal, an animated chess game, a woman quietly reading Baudelaire. These human vignettes are set against a sculptured skyline of tremendous power: "the majesty of piled-up stone, the spires pointing to heaven, the obelisks

---

9. Plato, "Crito" in *Five Dialogues*, trans. G. M. A. Grube (Indianapolis: Hackett Publishing Co., 1981), 42 (52b–53a).

10. Richard Sennett, *Flesh and Stone* (New York: W. W. Norton & Co., 1994), 57.

of industry spewing forth against the firmament their packets of smoke, the prodigious scaffolding of monuments under repair, . . . the tumultuous sky, charged with anger and rancor."[11] The overall effect of this multimedia collage is not numbing confusion but amazement that so many contrasting dramas, each with its own comic and tragic intricacy, are being played out on the same stage. Baudelaire rightly insists that this uniquely urban collage provides the same sublime awe, the same "spiritual intoxication" that the Romantics found in the experience of nature.[12]

But, some will argue, this urban collage perfectly illustrates the alienating cruelty of modern city life. Yes, there are personal dramas in the city, but they are all played out alone, anonymously isolated from community and the sustaining support that only it provides. Those raising this objection have as their implicit social ideal the kind of "co-presence of subjects" advocated in Martin Buber's *I & Thou*. It is an ideal of human society in which people cease to be alien or strange to one another, in which people achieve a thorough mutuality of understanding, a sympathy of shared lives and values. It is society envisioned as a village community.

Viewed from this ideal, the separate lives collected in Central Park on any given day are indeed a pitiable lot; their histories are unshared and their values isolated. Yet it is precisely this circumstance, this liberation from the necessity of mutual understanding and agreement, that makes the city a magnet for the new, the offbeat and the creative. There is something troubling about enthroning communal unity as the guiding model for all social experience. As Iris Young points out, "the ideal of community denies the ontological difference within and between subjects."[13] Communality is undoubtedly important and the city is adept at creating numerous communities of shared interest (gay communities, art communities, chess communities, etc.) that would be impossible in a rural setting. However, unity is only one side of human interaction; the other side is difference. If one person were really co-present to another, there would actually be no other left, only fusion. The energy of Central Park, or any alive city space, is that—to use Young's paradoxical phrase— it is "a place for the being together of strangers."[14] The last thing the

11. Charles Baudelaire quoted in Michelle Hannoosh, "Painters of Modern Life: Baudelaire and the Impressionists," in *Visions of the Modern City*, eds. William Sharp & Leonard Wallock (Baltimore: Johns Hopkins University Press, 1987), 176.

12. Ibid.

13. Iris Marion Young, "City Life and Difference" in *Metropolis: Center and Symbol of Our Times*, 256.

14. Ibid., 264.

occupants of Central Park would want is to get to know everybody there. They relish their anonymity and the freedom from pigeonholing that only anonymity provides. At the same time, however, they also relish "being together," seeing and being seen by other anonymous selves. The Park is not just a place where different people happen to be functionally collected like at an airport or a department store. People purposely go to a park to pursue their own individual projects, but to pursue them publicly, to publicly be their private selves.

There is a subtle dialectic between public and private being worked out in any active city space. Take, for example, a common urban pleasure like reading on a park bench or in a sidewalk cafe. Surely there are more comfortable, less distracting places to pursue the very private act of reading! But the reader in the park doesn't really want solitude, she[15] wants company—not in the sense of wishing she were conversing with friends instead of reading, but in the sense of wanting to pursue her own private ends in the company of others glad to be pursuing theirs. There is an undeniable bond in this, the quintessentially urban bond of sharing one's separateness with others, of together affirming the value of having radically different values, of having skateboarders and readers share a common space.

There is another aspect to the public/private dialectic that operates in urban space. The anonymity of the city, the fact that one is unknown to the vast majority of people encountered in a day, gives an excited edge to visual experience in the city, an edge akin to voyeurism and its psychological complement, exhibitionism. Reading in a city park or cafe mixes the pleasures of the text with the exhibitionist's pleasure of performing private acts in public. Strolling city streets has some of the thrill of a fashion runway, the ambiance of a parade. People move through the city knowing that their gait, their clothes, their every mannerism is being observed and interpreted; they know this because they themselves have sat in the same parks or cafes and gazed with the same contemplative delight, the delight of the urban voyeur. Only in the city are eyes granted such continuous opportunity for staring, for the sustained and intense observation of human behavior so basic to philosophy.

---

15. I am very aware that there are important gender differences in the way the city is experienced. A woman alone in a park or cafe, for example, has to worry about unwanted approaches in a way that a man doesn't. An excellent effort at understanding some of these differences is made by Elizabeth Wilson in her book *The Sphinx in the City: Urban Life, the Control of Disorder, and Women* (Berkeley: University of California Press, 1991). Important as these differences are, however, they do not invalidate the central point I am making about cities.

Nowhere is this visual dynamic better exemplified than in the behavior of lovers in the city. The intensity of romantic love, no matter where it arises, inevitably creates a private world of mystery and sensuous exploration. In the city, however, the sensuality which seems to be obliviously pursuing its own private course, is subtly affected by the gaze of others, by the excitement of displaying intimacy to objective eyes, of celebrating its mystery for strangers and making them complicit in its strangeness. Such a public display of erotic rites happens only amidst the anonymity of the city and the viewer attends to them with a mixture of reverence, embarrassment and philosophy.

CONCLUSION

It is not at all surprising or coincidental that lovers seek out and bask in the public privacy of urban places; as I have argued, urban places are, in their essential meaning, erotic places, places where the other is encountered, studied and enjoyed without any diminution of otherness. Roland Barthes saw this essential meaning of cities with perfect clarity:

> The city, essentially and semantically, is the place of our meeting with the *other*, and it is for this reason that the center is the gathering place in every city; . . . the city center is felt as the place of exchange of social activities and I would almost say erotic activities in the broad sense of that word. Better still, the city is always felt as the space where subversive forces, forces of rupture, ludic forces act and meet. Play is a subject very often emphasized in surveys on the center; . . . a center was always experienced semantically by the periphery as the privileged place where the other is and where we ourselves are other, as the play where we play the other.[16]

What city means in the human psyche, what it has meant in the cycle of history, why it continues to both attract and repel us, is that it is the surest place for encountering human difference, the most effective mechanism for meeting the other. Whatever is genuinely other unleashes subversive forces in us, forces that rupture our standard understandings and move us to try out, to "play" other understandings. Plato saw clearly that such dangerous and exciting play, such *eros*, is synonymous with the

---

16. Roland Barthes, "Semiology and the Urban," in *The City and the Sign*, eds. M. Gottdreiner & Alexandros Ph. Logapoulous (New York: Columbia University Press, 1986), 96.

activity of philosophy. This playful *eros* is found most surely and most intensely at the city's center. Why would the philosopher choose to be in any other place?

Questions for Review and Discussion

1. How does Conlon define cities? Or, what is their nature?

2. What does Conlon think distinguishes cities from rural villages?

3. What metaphors does Conlon use to describe and discuss cities?

4. How does Conlon understand the role of the philosopher in the city? Compare his view to those of Plato, Dewey, Gavin, Lefebvre, and Grange.

Susan Bickford

Susan Bickford is a contemporary American political theorist who teaches at the University of North Carolina. Her research and teaching focus on feminist political theory, political conflict and inequality, the practice of citizenship, and ancient Greek political thought. In this essay, Bickford analyzes the links between built environment, public life, and democratic politics, arguing that cities are being constructed in ways that adversely affect our concepts of politics and citizenship. The development of gated and other planned residential communities, urban gentrification, and new modes of surveillance remaps public/private space and boundaries. These trends serve to include some and exclude others from political participation and citizenship. Compare to Engels, Gavin, Foucault, Norberg-Schulz, and Mugerauer on the built environment of cities; to hooks on the concept of home; and to Young on city boundaries and democracy.

"CONSTRUCTING INEQUALITY: CITY SPACES AND THE ARCHITECTURE OF CITIZENSHIP" (2000)

This essay attempts to reconnect political theory to the study of cities by probing the link between built environment, public life, and democratic politics. By doing so, we can discern critical and troubling dynamics shaping contemporary democratic citizenship in this inegalitarian social context. [. . .]

For the purposes of this essay, the story begins in the suburbs. Suburbs are not a new phenomenon by any means, but suburban development blossomed after World War II. Over the years, many critics have condemned the suburbs for their sterility and uniformity, for their isolating and segregating effects on social life, and for the way they drain resources from the city. Contemporary developments in suburbs and "edge cities" continue and expand this trend. Perhaps the most publicized development is the rise of gated communities, residential developments that limit access to residents, their guests, and service people. Such enclaves have long been available for the very rich, but the significant current trend is that it is the middle class who is increasingly "forting up." [. . .]

The flip side of middle-class gated communities and CIDs [what Evan McKenzie calls "common interest developments"] are, of course, ghettoes—peopled not by "high resource choice makers" but by "low resource choice takers."[1] Like CID housing, ghettoes are not the result

---

1. For these categories, see Gregory Weiher, *The Fractured Metropolis: Political Fragmentation and Metropolitan Segregation* (Albany: State University of New York Press, 1991).

of "impersonal market forces" that respond to the desire of the races to live among "their own kind." Rather, survey work suggests that while African Americans would prefer to live in racially mixed areas, whites continue to have a very low tolerance for the residential presence of African Americans.[2] The construction of black ghettoes in the city and the continuation of residential segregation in the suburbs result partly from private racist attitudes and behaviors, but these behaviors have been and continue to be supported by institutional practices and policies. Examples range from the standards of risk and neighborhood stability that inform loan assessment to the limited enforcement authority of the 1968 Fair Housing Act.[3] [...]

"Gates" take a variety of forms, then: from an impenetrable wall to a simple mechanical arm, from barbed wire surrounding a housing project to red lines on a city map. Viewed from different angles, these gates have different social meanings. A gate that indicates safety and security to a resident of a middle-class development can communicate "danger—keep out" to residents of the poor neighborhood it borders. (A gate may have more than one meaning even for the same person; a tall wire fence may feel both protective and entrapping.) Most significantly, gates construct and manifest social relations—in this case, segregation.[4] I use *segregation* intentionally, for it seems to me to capture the relational quality of gates in a way that *exclusion* does not; these kinds of gates function not just to keep some people out, but to keep people on each side separate from one another—or, to put it paradoxically, to actively construct relations of separation.

The active quality of segregation is perhaps most clearly revealed when practiced in the mode of colonization. In older cities, condominiums are a common form of gentrification, the "conversion of economically marginal and working class areas to middle class residential use."[5] Those who buy in gentrified areas at least have an affection for and commitment to the city, but their experience of the city is often a strangely purified one. Gentrified areas are characterized by "boutique retailing, elite consumption, and upscale housing"; poor and working-class resi-

---

2. Douglas S. Massey and Nancy A. Denton, *American Apartheid: Segregation and the Making of the Underclass* (Cambridge, MA: Harvard University Press, 1993), 88–96.

3. Massey and Denton, *American Apartheid*.

4. See the examples in Peter Marcuse, "Walls of Fear and Walls of Support," in *Architecture of Fear*, ed. Nan Ellin (Princeton, NJ: Princeton Architectural Press, 1997).

5. Sharon Zukin, *Landscapes of Power* (Berkeley: University of California Press, 1991), 180.

dents are displaced as rents go up and low-income housing is destroyed or converted.[6]

The gentrification processes that purge neighborhoods and exacerbate housing problems also create incentives to keep the streets feeling safe for middle-class residents and clear of "disturbances" that might deter suburbanites and tourists from frequenting the city's cultural and commercial attractions. Safety, as Garreau says, is "the city-shaping category." Both old downtowns that have been "revitalized" and new edge cities display the qualities of increasingly policed versions of public space. Shopping malls are patrolled by private security forces, and some also have police substations in them.[7] The space in malls and renovated downtown shopping complexes is policed in part by asserting an unambiguous and singular function: consumption. The policing of function is a way of determining what kind of public is present. And those who fit security guards' stereotypes of nonconsumers or troublemakers (like black and Latino teenagers and elderly women of all races) are made to feel distinctly unwelcome.[8]

In the malls and on the streets, the presence of policing forces is enhanced through technological means: simple video camera surveillance, sophisticated communications systems, even helicopter fleets with fancy sensor equipment.[9] The built environment of urban space is designed to be amenable to this surveillance and to support its purpose of segregation. Flusty identifies a variety of "interdictory spaces," like space hidden

---

6. Neil Smith, "New City, New Frontier: The Lower East Side as Wild, Wild West," in Sorkin, *Variations on a Theme Park*. New York: Hill and Wang, 1992. Consequently, Smith points out, " 'the homeless' are more accurately described as 'the evicted,' since people don't simply fall out of the housing market—they are usually pushed." The big winners in all this are not the middle-class condo residents, but the real estate speculators (91, 82–86).

7. Joel Garreau, *Edge City: Life on the New Frontier* (New York: Doubleday, 1991), 48, 50; Davis, "Fortress Los Angeles: The Militarization of Urban Space," in Sorkin, ed. *Variations on a Theme Park*. "Mall cop" as a private occupation has achieved a level of visibility that political scientists can only envy; it is the occupation of the main character of a syndicated comic strip—*Drabble*. Drabble is a bumbling sort who rarely has to deal with anything more threatening than a fire in a trash can, which he puts out with chocolate milk.

8. On policing of function, see David Sibley, *Geographies of Exclusion* (New York: Routledge, 1995). Caniglia notes that the elderly have a special dilemma: "A woman talked about how they're careful to bring along the right number of bags on their trips downtown: enough to look as if they've been shopping, but not so many as to be branded bag ladies." Julie Caniglia, "Please Keep Off the Grass: Downtown Minneapolis," Minneapolis/St. Paul *City Pages*, May 20, 1992, 10–15, at 15.

9. Davis, "Fortress Los Angeles"; Steven Flusty, "Building Paranoia," in Ellin, *Architecture of Fear*.

by design, space visible but impossible to get to and from certain directions, space ostentatiously bristling with walls and gates. There is also "prickly" space, designed to be uncomfortable to occupy, particularly by the homeless. Its components include sprinkler systems, lack of protection from sun or shade, an absence of public toilets or water, "bag-lady proof" enclosures around restaurant dumpsters, and "bum-proof benches" on which it is impossible to lie down.[10]

THE PRIVATE AND THE PUBLIC

The constructions detailed in the previous section exhibit distinctly antipolitical impulses toward exclusion, control, security, sameness, and predictability—yet often under the guise of public space. One is tempted to say that what these phenomena share is that they are material and architectural constructions that obscure the presence of differences and inequality in the polity and create a tamed and prettified version of public space. But to put it that way is to inhabit the perspective that these practices take, and create, as normative. Who experiences it as tame? From whom is the presence of difference obscured? It is crucial to note that there is a distinct "public" in mind here and that these constructions embody its ascribed perspective and indeed are designed to obscure that the public has been reduced to a singular perspective.[11]

Let us analyze these practices from the perspectives of the multiple publics that coexist in our inegalitarian and diverse social order.[12] Building these spaces is an attempt to root out from the lived experience of the privileged both multiplicity and its attendant uncontrollability. The practices affect other "publics" differently, and they also operate to animate and entrench particular relations between publics, to shape citizens' experiences of one another. Specifically, these environments function to establish and secure relations of threat. If the consuming white middle-class public comes to feel at risk in the presence of those who do not

10. Flusty, "Building Paranoia"; Davis, "Fortress Los Angeles"; Caniglia, "Please Keep Off the Grass."

11. As theorists of race and gender have noted, this is a familiar technique of systems of oppression: to obscure the partiality of certain perspectives and treat them as universal (i.e., gender or race neutral). See, for example, Carole Pateman, *The Sexual Contract* (Stanford, CA: Stanford University Press, 1988); Elizabeth V. Spelman, *Inessential Woman* (Boston: Beacon, 1988).

12. See Nancy Fraser, "Rethinking the Public Sphere," in *Habermas and the Public Sphere*, ed. Craig Calhoun (Cambridge: Massachusetts Institute of Technology Press, 1992) on the importance of theorizing the public sphere in terms of multiple publics.

look or act like them, then purifying public space of risk for them means increasing danger, discomfort, or outright exclusion for those typed as alien or unknown. Renovated center city shopping complexes designed to feel safe to middle-class white suburbanites[13] are often perilous for others—African Americans who risk being accused of shoplifting or otherwise hassled by security guards, homeless people who suffer the same suspicions and are driven off benches and out of public toilets. The presence of the police, in either public or private manifestations, signals safety for some and danger for others.[14]

To the extent that they are successful, these purging techniques operate to screen and partition in a fairly thorough way some citizens from others. Often, then, the primary experience of "others" is through media stereotypes. The meaning and experience of "being in public" changes quite significantly in such a context. We are no longer moving with and negotiating around diverse strangers in a shared material world, but rather within a certain kind of bounded space that determines who and what we perceive. And who we "happen" to see regularly as we move through the world has an influence on who we think of as citizens and who we think to engage with as citizens—in other words, whose perspectives must be taken into account when making political decisions. Thus, we endanger the possibility of democratic politics when we settle in these enclosures, particularly when we become so accustomed to the walls that we forget they are there, for then we begin to imagine that "the world" consists only of those inside our gates.

This "forgetting" is of course only possible for the privileged; it is not as though minority groups can ever block out the dominant culture.[15] And those without socioeconomic resources have much less power to

---

13. I am not ignoring the existence of a black middle class, but rather accepting the well-documented phenomenon that even ostensible middle-class and professional status does not protect African Americans from racist assumptions. For example, Cornel West, *Race Matters* (New York: Vintage, 1994); Patricia J. Williams, *The Alchemy of Race and Rights* (Cambridge, MA: Harvard University Press, 1991).

14. Teenagers occupy an odd space in this dynamic of purging: at once dependable sources of revenue and potential disruptions, both residents of private developments and possible vandals, belonging neither on the children's playground nor in a bar. (Garreau, *Edge City*, 50–51; Edward J. Blakely, and Mary Gail Snyder, "Divided We Fall: Gated and Walled Communities in the United States," in Ellin, *Architecture of Fear*, 92–93; Sibley, *Geographies of Exclusion*, 34–35). That very unpredictability often makes their presence—especially in groups—feel threatening to adults.

15. Indeed, they often become sophisticated ethnographers of that culture; see Patricia Hill Collins, *Black Feminist Thought* (New York: Routledge, 1991), ch. 1; bell hooks, *Black Looks: Race and Representation* (Boston: South End, 1992), ch. 11.

build up the world in a way that secures feelings of safety and much less protection from threatening others. The freedom and security of some people is increasingly encroached upon as others attempt to secure it for themselves. But the shared danger is this: what we all risk losing in building up the worldly artifice in this way is the possibility of a democratic public realm, one that depends on the presence of a multiplicity of perceiving and perceived others. When citizens (on either side of the gates) are daily and thoroughly separated from those who are "different" from them (in terms of race or class, homelessness or joblessness), it requires an inhuman amount of imagination to have a genuinely democratic public.[16]

The issue of policed and segregated public space may seem separable from the issue of controlled residential space. While the character of public space is clearly a matter for public concern, is the character of residential choices—however much we may disapprove of another's choice—a private matter? Infringing on the right to choose where and among whom one lives would seem, in the American cultural context anyway, an unbearable imposition on privacy and freedom. To examine the issue of residential choice as a private matter is to consider two dimensions of "privacy-related liberty"—as a right to limit access and exclude others and as a right to decisional autonomy.[17] But such privacy claims must be scrutinized in light of their public meaning and effects. As feminists have argued, power is exercised in the very demarcation of public and private, and it is also reflected in the different senses of public and private realms that different groups have. The putatively private realm of the home often affords less privacy to women than to men, and increasingly, privacy is "a virtual commodity purchased by the middle class and the well-to-do," one not available to the economically disadvantaged, those in public institutions, and the homeless.[18] And the sense

---

16. bell hooks's memory of growing up in a poor neighborhood shows the mutual relations of threat that segregation constructs: "Black folks associated whiteness with the terrible, the terrifying, the terrorizing. White people were regarded as terrorists, especially those who dared to enter the segregated space of blackness" (*Black Looks*, 170).

17. The articulation of the two dimensions of privacy and the concept of "privacy-related liberty" are Allen's. Anita L. Allen, "Privacy at Home: The Twofold Problem," in *Revisioning the Political*, ed. Nancy J. Hirschmann and Christine Di Stefano (Boulder, CO: Westview, 1996). For other samples of feminist arguments about public and private, see Martha A. Ackelsberg and Mary Lyndon Shanley, "Privacy, Publicity, and Power: A Feminist Rethinking of the Public-Private Distinction," in *Revisioning the Political*, ed. Nancy J. Hirschmann and Christine Di Stefano (Boulder, CO: Westview, 1996); Carole Pateman, *The Disorder of Women: Democracy, Feminism, and Political Theory* (Stanford, CA: Stanford University Press, 1989); and Catherine A. MacKinnon, *Toward a Feminist Theory of the State* (Cambridge, MA: Harvard University Press, 1989).

18. Allen, "Privacy at Home," 197–198.

of the domestic realm as private has historically not been true for African Americans, not only as a result of the practices of slavery but because of the prevalence of black women's employment as domestics, where "the home" was the public place of employment.[19]

[. . .] As Weiher puts it, the *residential* space "is precisely the context in which people are least able to tolerate diversity."[20] In thinking about how boundaries shape consciousness and action, Weiher asks how suburban populations come to be homogeneous in terms of race and class. One part of the answer is overt exclusionary practices (e.g., on the part of real estate agents) and the lack of provision of housing and services (e.g., public transportation) for lower-income people. But what operates to "recruit" certain kinds of settlers (to use Weiher's language)— why do very similar kinds of people move into certain suburbs? Weiher locates the answer in the placement of political boundaries, which serve as primary sources of information in communicating distinct place identities. Such boundaries are precise and authoritative markings that are much more salient for location decisions than are more informally distinguished neighborhoods. The most significant political boundaries for would-be residents are those of the municipality and the school district. When these boundaries coincide—that is, when a school district and a town have identical boundaries, as in many suburbs—there is more likely to be an extremely homogeneous population.[21] When a school district overlaps different municipalities, or when a municipality includes more than one school district, the area is more heterogeneous—place identity is less distinct, and a variety of people are "recruited."[22]

---

19. Collins, *Black Feminist Thought*, ch. 3. Collins further notes a sense in which being "in private" meant being within the black community, and "public" was the realm in which one was among white people.

20. Gregory Weiher, *The Fractured Metropolis: Political Fragmentation and Metropolitan Segregation* (Albany, NY: State University of New York Press, 1991), 36; see also Andrew Hacker, *Two Nations*, rev. ed. (New York: Ballantine, 1995), 40–43.

21. Weiher, *The Fractured Metropolis*, ch. 2, 4. I use *homogeneous* and *heterogeneous* here in terms of race and class. Weiher prefers *eccentric*—people in a suburb may differ in a variety of ways but are eccentric (compared to the population at large) with respect to a particular characteristic.

22. Weiher, *The Fractured Metropolis*, ch. 5. Weiher notes that there are two patterns in areas with overlapping boundaries: sometimes the area as a whole is more heterogeneous, sometimes there are still black and white regions within the larger area (50–60, 146–147). So people of different races still may not live on the same street, but at least the financial resources of the community are shared, and with "strangers" who have an equal say in decision making about those resources.

Rather than possessing a singular distinct identity, then, urban and suburban spaces should be fuzzy and multilayered; Weiher's work suggests that cross-cutting political boundaries can help to foster this heterogeneity and complexity. "Overlapping" is important in other ways as well. Jane Jacobs has long argued for mixed-use space as central to city life, rather than segregating residential and commercial spaces from one another or creating "border vacuums." As Young says bluntly, the separation of functions makes city life "more boring, meaningless, and dangerous."[23] (And single-function space, as noted earlier, makes it possible to police and segregate publics more thoroughly.) Overlapping helps to form "complex, open borders"; it is with these "overlays of difference" that the "power of simultaneous perception is aroused."[24]

Let us reconsider from this perspective the "common interest developments" so dominant in the real estate market now. Their developers attempt to create a distinct (though not particularly deep) place identity; they may not be quite as authoritative as political boundaries, but they are much less fuzzy and permeable than older neighborhoods. CIDs and gated communities purposely design "border vacuums" to ensure seclusion and control. The analysis above would suggest that such development should be constrained—for the sake of democratic public life.

Certainly this would mean infringing on some people's ability to choose to live in a privately, precisely controlled environment. But when some people's pursuit of a purified notion of privacy has significant impact on others and on the public realm, it is surely a matter of concern for a democratic public.[25] What this means is that there is only so much privacy and privacy-related liberty that citizens can claim. It does not mean that privacy is not a legitimate and meaningful good [. . .] But, as Honig says, the need for spaces of nurturance and withdrawal "does not settle the question of how we ought to conceive of them." She offers the possibility of a "resignification" of home that does not rest on purging conflict and difference, while acknowledging that such a resignification does "admit and embrace a vulnerability that may *look like* homelessness"

23. Jacobs, *The Death and Life of Great American Cities* (New York: Vintage, 1961), ch. 8, 12, 14; Iris Marion Young, *Justice and the Politics of Difference* (Princeton, NJ: Princeton University Press, 1990), 246.

24. Richard Sennett, *The Conscience of the Eye: The Design and Social Life of Cities* (New York: Knopf, 1990), 202, 165–168.

25. Bowles and Gintis argue more forcefully that any "socially consequential use of power"—one that "substantially affects the lives of others"—should be a matter for democratic decision making rather than private choice. Samuel Bowles and Herbert Gintis, *Democracy and Capitalism* (New York: Basic Books, 1986), ch. 3.

from certain perspectives. Pursuing this possibility thus "depends on the ability to resist the forces that imbue us with an often overwhelming desire to go home."[26]

I am suggesting that both this resistance and this desire are tightly linked to the options that political institutions allow, encourage, or prevent. From this perspective, more can be done than asking individuals to resist culturally encouraged and institutionally supported choices; making change on the institutional level is a way to alter the context in which desires are formed and pursued and decisions made. I do not claim that this approach neatly resolves the complex problems that cultural and economic inequality pose for a democratic polity. But I do propose it, rather urgently, as a terrain of inquiry for political theorists in which many normative and pragmatic questions remain to be probed.[27] [. . .]

Questions for Review and Discussion

1. According to Bickford, why is public space important?

2. Why is Bickford critical of gated communities?

3. How can the built environment of cities cause a loss of public life/democracy?

4. Why is Bickford skeptical about arguments that say gated communities and CIDs are simply the outcome of private choices?

5. What does Bickford think we can do to correct the problems she outlines?

6. What are possible objections to Bickford's proposed solutions? How does Bickford address those objections?

---

26. Bonnie Honig, "Difference, Dilemmas," in *Democracy and Difference*, ed. Seyla Benhabib (Princeton, NJ: Princeton University Press, 1996), 269, 271.

27. Not the least of which (an anonymous reviewer points out) is how to adjudicate between the claims made for the democratic potential of both centralization and decentralization. Are there other institutional conditions or contextual features that need to be considered in conjunction with degree of centralization?

Eduardo Mendieta

Eduardo Mendieta is a philosophy professor and director of the Latin American and Caribbean Studies program at the State University of New York at Stony Brook. Mendieta serves as editor or associate editor on several important journals including *City*. His own writing covers Habermas, Apel, and the Frankfurt School as well as Latin American philosophy and theology and contemporary issues on race and social justice. He recently published a book on globalization as well as a range of articles on cities, space, war, and prisons.

The selected reading is a short excerpt from a complex article that provides an assessment of the city in the age of globalization and argues that we must view such cities "from below," that is, from the perspectives of those who are most oppressed, if we are to meet the challenges that the global city faces. In this excerpt, Mendieta engages the methodology of phenomenology to provide us with an understanding of how globalization is first and foremost a process of urbanization. Compare to Plato, Weber, and Mumford on the emergence and transformation of cities, and to West, Young, and hooks on contemporary urban identity and social justice.

"A PHENOMENOLOGY OF THE GLOBAL CITY" (2000)

[. . . A]ny phenomenology of globalization must also begin with what I take to be an equally momentous transformation of human societies, and this has to do with the mega-urbanization of the world. We can say that for most of its history, most of humanity has been rural. Cities developed as appendages to large agricultural areas. Cities were functional principles of rural areas. Eventually this relationship reversed, but only after the city ceased to be a communication node for agricultural exchange. Cities started to acquire their independence when they could produce their own commodities, namely knowledge and political power. This only began to happen after the Renaissance when major cities were not just ports but also centres of learning, culture and political power (Hall, 1998). This trend, however, only takes off when industrialization allows cities to become their own productive centres, even if they still remain tied to rural centres. The reversal of the relationship between rural and urban areas, however, began to shift in the 1950s; during these years already 30% of all humanity lived in cities. The United Nations projects that by the year 2005, 50% of humanity will live in cities. Here we must pause, and reflect that this means that a substantive part of humanity will still

219

remain rural, and that most of those 'farmers' and 'peasants' will be in so-called Third World countries. Nonetheless, as Eric Hobsbawn remarked in his work *The Age of Extremes,* the "most dramatic and far-reaching social change of the second half of the [the twentieth century] is the death of the peasantry" (Hobsbawn, 1994, p. 289). The other side of this reversal of the relationship between city and country is that most megacities will be in what is called the Third World. By the third millennium the 10 most populated metropolises of the World will be neither in Europe nor in the USA.

These trends can be attributed to a variety of factors. The most important factor in the elimination of the rural is the industrialization of agriculture, a process that reached its zenith with the so-called "green revolution" of the 1950s and 1960s. Under the industrialization of agriculture we must understand not just the introduction of better tools, but the homogenization of agricultural production, by which I mean the introduction on a global scale of the mono-cultivo (Shiva, 1993). We must also include here the elimination of self-subsistent forms of farming through the elimination of self-renewing biodiverse eco-systems. One of the most effective ways, however, in which the city has imposed itself over the countryside is through the projection of images that destabilized the sense of tradition and cultural continuity so fundamental to the rhythms of the countryside. Through television, radio and now the internet, the city assaults the fabric of the countryside. Tradition is undermined by the promises and riches projected by the tube of plenty, the cornucopia of other possibilities: the television, and its world of info-tainment (see Bauman's wonderful discussion of how, under the globalization of entertainment, the Benthamian Panopticon turns into the MacWorld/Infotainment Synopticon [1998a, pp. 53–54]).

Indeed, one of the most characteristic aspects of globalization is what is called the decreasing importance of the local, the state, the national. We therefore need to speak with Jürgen Habermas and Paul Kennedy of a post-national constellation in which sovereign nation-states as territorially localized have become less important, less in control of their own spatiality (Kennedy, 1993; Habermas, 2001). But what is forgotten is that there is a simultaneous process of localization in which place acquires a new significance, certain spaces of course (Featherstone, 1995). The city is the site at which the forces of the local and the global meet: the site where the forces of transnational, finance capital, and the local labour markets and national infrastructures enter into conflict and contestation over the city. As Saskia Sassen writes:

The city has indeed emerged as a site for new claims: by
global capital which uses the city as an 'organizational commodity,' but also by disadvantaged sectors of the urban population, which in large cities are frequently as internationalized
a presence as is capital. The denationalizing of urban space
and the formation of new claims by transnational actors and
involving contestation, raise the question—whose city is it?
(Sassen, 1998, p. xx)

The city, in fact, has become the crossroad for new denationalizing
politics in which global actors, capitals and moving peoples enter into
conflict across a transnational urban system. Habermas has noted with
acuity that one of the characteristics of the 18th and 19th centuries was
their pronounced fears of the "mass," the crowd" (Habermas, 2001, p.
39). Such fears were summarized in the title of the prescient work by
Ortega y Gasset, *The Revolt of the Masses* (1985). As was noted already,
the 18th and the 19th centuries signalled the reversal of the relationship
between countryside and city. This reversal meant the rapid urbanization
and demographic explosion in cities which accompany the rapid industrialization of certain metropolises of the West: London, Berlin, New
York, Chicago, Newark, Mexico City, Porto Alegre; and the non-West:
New Dehli, Tokyo, Beijing, Cairo, etc. Urbanization and Industrialization gave rise to the spectre of the irascible, insatiable, uncontrollable
mass that would raze everything in its path. Three classical responses
emerged: Sorel, and the celebration of the creative power of anarchical
and explosive unorganized mass mobilization; the Marxist-Leninist, and
the attempt to domesticate and train the creative and transformative
power of social unrest through the development of a party machinery
that would guide the ire and discontent of gathered masses of unem-
ployed and employed workers; and the conservative and reactionary response of an Edmund Burke, but which is also echoed in the works of
philosophers like Heidegger, which disdained and vilified the common
folk, the mass, in a simple term: *Das Man*. The crowd, the mass, is
consumed and distracted by prattle, and curiosity, as it wallows in the
miasma of inauthenticity and cowardness (Fritsche, 1999).

Today such attitudes seem not just foreign, but also unrealistic.
Most of our experience is determined by a continuous mingling with
crowds, and large, undifferentiated masses of people. We get on the
road, and we are confronted with traffic jams, we get on the subway, and
people accost and touch us from all directions. We live in continuous
friction with the stranger, the other. May we suggest that the "Other"

has become such an important point of departure for philosophical reflection precisely because we exist in such a continuous propinquity with it? Indeed, the Other is no longer simply a phantasmagorical presence, projected and barely discernible beyond the boundaries of the ecumene, the polis and the frontiers of the nation-state. At the same time, the discourse about the "other," what is called the politics of alterity, marks a shift from the negative discourse of anxiety and fear epitomized in the term "anomie" so well diagnosed by Durkheim, Simmel and Freud, and so aptly described by Christopher Lasch (1979), to the positive discourse of solidarity, inclusion, acceptance, tolerance, citizenship and justice, so well diagnosed and described by Zymunt Bauman (1998b), Ulrich Beck (1997), Anthony Giddens (1990) and Jürgen Habermas (2001).

Are there any morals to be extracted from this profound transformation in the way humanity in general understands itself? For the longest period of the history of humankind, groups remained both sheltered from and inured to otherness by the solidity and stability of their traditions and their worlds. Cultures remained fairly segregated maps of the world in which the foreign, strange and unknown was relegated beyond the boundaries of the controllable, and surveyable. To this extent, 'otherness' was legislated over by religion, the state, nature and even history, namely those centres of gravity of culture and images of the world. In an age in which all traditions are under constant revision, and human temporality converges with the age of the world itself, then 'otherness' appears before us as naked, unmediated otherness: we are all others before each other. In other words, neither our sense of identity, nor the sense of difference of the other are given a priori, they are always discovered, constituted and dismantled in the very processes of encounter. The other was always constituted for us by extrinsic forces. Now, the other is constituted in the very process of our identity formation, but in a contingent fashion.

We make others as we make ourselves. This reflection links up with some insights that Enrique Dussel has had with respect to the relationship between the emergence of cities and the development of the first codes of ethics: the Hammurabi Code, and the Book N of the Egyptian Book of the Dead (Dussel, 1998). Such codes arose precisely because individuals were thrown into the proximity of each other, and were thus confronted with each other's vulnerability and injurability. The injunction to take care of the poor, the indigent, the orphan, the widow, the invalid, could only arise out of the urban experience of the contiguity with the injurable flesh of the stranger. Today, the experience of the indigent other is of the immigrant, the exiled, the refugee, who build their enclaves in the shadows of the glamorous city of transnational capital (King, 1990; Sassen, 1999). For this reason, the other and the immigrant are interchangeable, but this also raises the issue of the new global city as a space for the representation and formation of post-colonial identities. Geo-cities are spaces for the reconfiguration of image, the imagination and the imaginary, as Arjun Appadurai argued (1996). In this sense, the centrality of the urban experience for humanity means that otherness is not going to be a mere metaphysical, or even phenomenological category and concern. Under the reign of the city: *Otherness has become quotidian and practical.*

BIBLIOGRAPHY

Appadurai, A. (1996) *Modernity at Large: Cultural Dimensions of Globalization.* Minneapolis: University of Minnesota Press.
Bauman, Z. (1998a) *Globalization: The Human Consequences.* New York: Columbia University Press.
Bauman, Z. (1998b) 'Postmodern religion?,' in P. Heelas (ed.) *Religion, Modernity and Postmodernity.* Cambridge: Blackwell.
Beck, U. (1997) *Was ist Globalisierung?* Frankfurt am Main: Suhrkamp.
Dussel, E. (1998) *Ética de la Liberación en la edad de globalización y de la exclusión* Madrid: Editorial Trotta.
Featherstone, M. (1995) *Undoing Culture: Globalization, Postmodernism and Identity.* London: Sage Publications.
Fritsche, J. (1999) *Historical Destiny and National Socialism in Heidegger's Being and Time.* Berkeley and Los Angeles: University of California Press.
Giddens, A. (1990) *The Consequences of Modernity.* Cambridge: Polity Press.
Habermas, J. (2001) *The Postnational Constellation: Political Essays.* Cambridge, MA: MIT Press.
Hall, Sir Peter (1998) *Cities in Civilization.* New York: Pantheon Books.
Hobsbawn, E. (1994) *The Age of Extremes.* New York: Pantheon Books.
Kennedy, P. (1993) *Preparing for the Twenty-first Century.* New York: Random House.
King, A.D. (1990) *Urbanism, Colonialism, and the World Economy: Cultural and Spatial Foundations of the World Urban System.* London: Routledge.
Lasch, C. (1979) *The Culture of Narcissism: American Life in an Age of Diminishing Expectations.* New York: Warner Books.
Ortega y Gasset, J. (1985) *The Revolt of the Masses.* Notre Dame: University of Notre Dame Press.
Sassen, S. (1998) *Globalization and Its Discontents: Selected Essays.* New York: New Press.

Sassen, S. (1999) *Guests and Aliens*. New York: New Press.
Shiva, V. (1993) *Monocultures of the Mind: Perspectives on Biodiversity and Biotechnology*. London and New York: Zed Books.

Questions for Review and Discussion

1. According to Mendieta, why is it important to reflect on cities if we are to understand globalization?

2. Summarize Mendieta's account of how cities have transformed over time.

3. How has the relationship between cities and rural areas changed over time?

4. What was the dominant fear during the urban industrial age of the eighteenth and nineteenth centuries? What were the classical responses to that fear?

5. What does Mendieta mean when he says: "Otherness has become quotidian and practical"?

Gail Weiss

Gail Weiss is a contemporary American philosopher who works in the areas of phenomenology and feminist theory. She teaches at George Washington University in Washington, DC. In this essay, Weiss explores "new possibilities for stylizing urban flesh" so that we better understand the relationship between bodies and cities as well as the role philosophy plays in that understanding. Weiss builds on the work of feminists and critical race theorists who challenge the city/nature as well as city/home and unity/difference dichotomies. In the selection excerpted here from her essay "Urban Flesh," Weiss discusses the attack on the World Trade Center and how it reminds us of our embodied emplacement in cities. She argues that phenomenological reflection on urban flesh helps us better understand the fragility of urban dwelling as well as "the privileges and responsibilities that accompany it." Social justice demands that we be attentive to the "differentiations of incarnate existence" and acknowledge and confront our limitations. Compare to Heidegger, Norberg-Schulz, Mendieta, and Mugerauer in terms of phenomenological approaches to the city; to Young, West, Bickford, and Gooding-Williams on issues of difference, urban identity, and social justice; and to Grosz on the relationship between bodies and cities.

"URBAN FLESH: THE FRAGILITY OF DWELLING" (2005)

Through a critical appropriation of Maurice Merleau-Ponty's conception of flesh, Luce Irigaray stresses those aspects of the flesh Merleau-Ponty merely hints at when he suggests that the flesh "brings a style of being wherever there is a fragment of being," namely, the differentiations of the flesh, how the flesh of one cannot be exchanged for the flesh of another. [. . .] Merleau-Ponty's provocative understanding of how the flesh stylizes being suggests an ongoing process of differentiation that cannot be reduced to sameness. And yet, insofar as it stylizes, the flesh also unifies, weaving together disparate gestures, movements, bodies, and situations into a dynamic fabric of meaning that must be continually reworked, made and unmade.

The city is itself an excellent example of such a richly textured fabric of meaning. We need only look to the checkered racist and sexist histories of so many American cities to recognize both the fragility as well as the strength of the ties that collectively produce the varied stylizations (liberatory as well as oppressive) of urban flesh. By emphasizing the corporeal connections and disconnections that differentiate what I

225

am calling urban flesh, this essay seeks to support the work of contemporary feminist theorists, critical race theorists, disability theorists and others who refuse the reductive violence of the binary logic that would have us privilege unity over difference or difference over unity. Such a position should not be construed as an escape from the violence of limitation, however, for this latter is encountered outside of as well as within binary systems.

[. . .] The very expression "urban flesh" invokes the specter of that which allegedly escapes the urban, namely, nature or natural flesh. To speak of urban flesh, then, requires that we come to terms in some way with the role that nature and the concept of the natural play in circumscribing the possibilities and limits of urban existence.[1] Just as it is no longer fashionable to embrace a Cartesian mind/body dualism, the nature/city divide is also held by many theorists to be passé, an artificial distinction that has traditionally taken the form of reifying the "purity" of nature in contrast to the "polluting" features of urban life.[2,3] Moreover, just as the gendered connotations of the mind/body distinction have been rendered visible by feminist theorists, so too has the nature/urban distinction been recognized as gendered; even more obviously it is racialized.[4] As a result of the important critical analyses provided by

---

1. Similarly, as Toni Morrison has powerfully shown in *Playing in the Dark: Whiteness and the Literary Imagination*, one cannot invoke whiteness without either implicitly or explicitly contrasting it with blackness. Moreover, as Frantz Fanon has also demonstrated in *Black Skin White Masks*, the more phantasmatically blackness is conceived, the more mythically entrenched the status of whiteness becomes.

2. Steven Vogel offers an extended critical discussion of this traditional binary approach in *Against Nature: The Concept of Nature in Critical Theory*. He advocates a social constructionist view of nature whereby nature is itself an ongoing product of cultural interpretation.

3. See Mary Douglas's *Purity and Danger: An Analysis of Concepts of Pollution and Taboo* for one of the most influential accounts of the significance of the cultural distinction between purity and pollution.

4. There are many excellent resources to turn to for a discussion of the gendered dimensions of nature and culture, though less work has been done on how the city is gendered. Elizabeth Grosz's work is a notable exception in this regard. See "Bodies-Cities" in *Space, Time, and Perversion: Essays on the Politics of Bodies* and *Architecture from the Outside: Essays on Virtual and Real Space*. Sherry Ortner's classic essay, "Is Male to Female as Nature is to Culture?" in *Making Gender: The Politics and Erotics of Culture* offers one of the best-known feminist accounts of the engendering of nature and culture respectively as feminine and masculine. Carol Bigwood's *Earth Muse: Feminist, Nature, and Art* offers a specifically phenomenological analysis that supports Ortner's critique of the phallogocentric identification of nature with an idealized feminine "earth mother" and culture with an idealized masculine master of techné.

feminist theorists, race theorists, and others, romantic invocations of the purity and peacefulness of nature versus the pollution and violence of urban existence appear naïve at best and run the danger of supporting sexist, racist, and classist political agendas. Exploring Merleau-Ponty's emphasis on the necessary violence of incarnate existence, the violence of the flesh, helps us to arrive at an understanding of urban flesh that does not accept the conventional nature/culture, pure/polluting, feminine/masculine binaries. [. . .]

While hard and fast distinctions between the world of nature and the urban world have often been challenged, the challenges themselves have taken different forms depending on the individual, social, historical, and ideological commitments of the theorists themselves. Eco-feminists such as Carol Bigwood advocate that we embrace and celebrate our primordial relationship to a "world-earth-home" that restores nature (and the feminine) to its rightful primacy as the very foundation of our world. Others, such as critical theorist Steven Vogel, argue that there is no such thing as nature insofar as the latter is romantically conceived of as a "pure" domain independent of the city and culture. Both Bigwood and Vogel seek the elimination of arbitrary distinctions between nature and culture, however they approach this project through opposite paths: Bigwood by reminding us that nature is everywhere, even in the heart of the city and Vogel that nature is nowhere: it is culture that is ubiquitous and which has posited nature as its alter ego and legitimizing origin. Whether nature is indeed "everywhere" or "nowhere," it is clear that it functions as an overdetermined, regulative ideal in our very thoughts about culture more generally and urban existence more particularly.

The inescapability of nature and the crucial role it plays in establishing our sense of place is also explored by Edward Casey in *Getting Back into Place: Toward a Renewed Understanding of the Place-World* (Indiana University Press 1993). [. . .] Reinforcing Heidegger's discussion in "The Origin of the Work of Art" of the earth which sustains and supports the world, concealing its active, constitutive presence in the process, Casey affirms that in our relations with cities, nature is always present, yet rarely registered as such. Rather than remaining within the confines of the Heideggerian tension between a self-concealing

---

Although urban analyses often concentrate on the racial and class implications of what Ruth Frankenberg has called a "racial social geography" in *White Women Race Matters: The Social Construction of Whiteness*, less work has been done on how nature is itself racialized. For an excellent and disturbing account of the consequences of failing to acknowledge the racism inherent in our understandings of "urban flesh" see Robert Gooding-Williams, ed., *Reading Rodney King Reading Urban Uprising* (New York: Routledge Press, 1993).

earth and a self-revealing world, Casey, in a Merleau-Pontian vein, turns his attention to the lived body which is the very site of this tension, that which grounds our own sense of "emplacement" within the world. For if, as Merleau-Ponty suggests in the *Phenomenology of Perception*, the body is itself a horizon for all possible and actual experience, it is imperative that we arrive at a better understanding of how our own bodies are themselves situated, or "emplaced" within the world in which we dwell.

The terrorist attacks on the World Trade Center towers in New York City on September 11, 2001 offer one of the most vivid recent examples of the powerful role the city plays in our very sense of our own corporeality. [. . .] In Edmund Husserl's language, the destruction of the World Trade Center towers has disrupted the "natural attitude," the "taken-for-granted" perspective toward our bodily surroundings that Americans have had the luxury of holding on to in a country that escaped the severe physical devastation Europe and Asia suffered in World Wars I and II and other wars of this past century.[5] Indeed, the seeming permanence of a city's buildings, and of the city itself has been materially and symbolically significant in anchoring its citizens' own sense of security and stability throughout history. For those countries that have been continually ravaged by war and by natural disasters, for those who have been displaced and who have no homes to (re)turn to, including those whose corporeal existence has always been marked by a sense of impermanence, the previous complacency many United States citizens experienced in relation to our own emplacement in the world must truly be incomprehensible. Indeed, ever since the famous fall of Troy, there have been warnings that the city, and therefore its inhabitants, is not as impregnable as it may seem.

If, as Casey suggests, bodies, cities, and nature cannot be understood apart from one another, it should not be surprising that the violent attacks on two of the U.S.'s most symbolically charged sites (i.e., the World Trade Center and the Pentagon) in two of our most symbolically charged American cities (New York City and Washington, D.C.), was registered by many as a violent attack on their corporeality, that is, on their bodily sense of well-being-in-the-world. While the horrific violence of these attacks should not be forgotten, there is also the danger that focusing too heavily on their exceptional character and buying into official

---

5. Indeed, to Iraqis and many others today, it is the willingness of the current U.S. government to endorse the displacement of others in order to ensure its own secure emplacement in the world that helps to fuel charges of U.S. imperialism.

U.S. propagandistic rhetoric that all we have to do is stamp out terrorism in order to live without fear of violence in the future, will lead us right back into a dangerous natural attitude, namely the belief that dwelling can be accomplished in peace, without violence. [...]

Even if it is possible (if only theoretically) to live nonviolently in a historical period in which the rule of law applies to and is acquiesced to by one and all, Merleau-Ponty implies that living in an epoch when life is volatile and the torn fabric of human relations must continually be mended presents more possibilities for social and political transformation. However, with this mending comes violence; the activity of reconstruction, whether this takes the form of rebuilding the environment after a period of destruction, or whether it involves repairing fragmented relationships between one individual or even one nation and another, produces violent changes that can serve the cause of liberation as readily as that of oppression. [...]

Our forms of labor, and our ways of loving, living, and dying, undoubtedly reveal much more than the state of a particular society. They reveal also our ongoing corporeal relations with everyone and everything that comprises our situation. This includes the inanimate as well as the animate; indeed, the visceral responses of so many Americans and non-Americans to the attacks on the World Trade Center Towers and the Pentagon poignantly illustrate that our relations with the inanimate can be just as powerful, just as violent, and just as disturbing as our relations with our fellow human beings. The material destruction of our world, whether this occurs deliberately or spontaneously, forces us to contend with the specific, but usually invisible ways in which our surrounding environment actively shapes the intercorporeal interactions that help to construct our own sense of bodily agency. And, as beings in and of the world, our sense of bodily agency provides the parameters that delimit the very nature of our emplacement within the world, that is, our ability to dwell within it. [...]

Questions for Review and Discussion

1. Why does Weiss argue that we should reflect on our bodily (corporeal) experiences?

2. Why does Weiss claim that the terrorist attacks on the World Trade Towers offer an important example of the role the city plays in our experience of ourselves as embodied being? Can you think of other examples?

3. Why might *philosophical* reflection on these experiences be important?

4. Why is dwelling important? Why is it important to become aware of the fragility of dwelling?

5. How do cities make dwelling possible? How do cities thwart dwelling?

PART II

Philosophy Matters, City Matters:
Cases for Discussion

What Is a City?

What is a city? What is its nature? What is the connection between human civilization and cities? When these questions are answered merely descriptively, the answers are not properly philosophical, for the philosopher's task demands moving beyond social scientific description to making normative claims about what cities *should* be like. In fact, philosophers offer critical insights into the ways we describe cities, showing that such descriptions are often not as value free as they claim to be. Philosophers therefore connect the question of the definition of a city to arguments about urban values and ideals.

Cities may never live up to those ideals, but normative definitions of the city provide us with two important things: a) a guidepost when cities face challenges and need assistance in responding, and b) a standard by which we can critically measure whether cities are at their best. The essay by Friedrich Engels provides us with an example of the latter; working from claims about social justice in the city, he offers a critique of the development of nineteenth-century industrial cities such as Manchester, England. Robert Ginsberg's essay describes the challenge that the Japanese city of Hiroshima faced after its annihilation during World War II when it was destroyed by atomic bombs. Citizens of Hiroshima had to rethink their city from the beginning—what did they want it to be?

Philosophers from Part I that are most useful when thinking about the question of the nature and definition of the city are **Plato, Augustine, Machiavelli, More, Weber, Mumford, Grange, Grosz, Conlon,** and **Mendieta,** although you may well find insights from other essays, too.

PHILOSOPHY MATTERS: FRIEDRICH ENGELS.
"THE FAILURE OF THE CITY FOR 19TH CENTURY
BRITISH WORKING CLASS"

Introduction

Friedrich Engels (1820–1895) was the son of a wealthy German Jewish merchant. Sent to England to explore family business prospects there, Engels focused more on the living and working conditions of the workers. Heavily influenced by Hegel (and then later Marx, with whom he collaborated on many works, including *The Communist Manifesto*), Engels took philosophy to the streets, exploring the alleys of Manchester to reveal the horrible ways in which the working class was treated, ways that usually remained invisible to the businessmen who exploited them. This reading forms part of Engels's first critical study entitled *The Conditions of the Working Class in England in 1844*.

"The Failure of the City for 19th Century British Working Class"

A town, such as London, where a man may wander for hours together without reaching the beginning of the end, without meeting the slightest hint which could lead to the inference that there is open country within reach, is a strange thing. This colossal centralisation, this heaping together of two and a half millions of human beings at one point, has multiplied the power of this two and a half millions a hundredfold; has raised London to the commercial capital of the world, created the giant docks and assembled the thousand vessels that continually cover the Thames. I know nothing more imposing than the view which the Thames offers during the ascent from the sea to London Bridge. The masses of buildings, the wharves on both sides, especially from Woolwich upwards, the countless ships along both shores, crowding ever closer and closer together, until, at last, only a narrow passage remains in the middle of the river, a passage through which hundreds of steamers shoot by one another; all this is so vast, so impressive, that a man cannot collect himself, but is lost in the marvel of England's greatness before he sets foot upon English soil.

But the sacrifices which all this has cost become apparent later. After roaming the streets of the capital a day or two, making headway with difficulty through the human turmoil and the endless lines of vehicles, after visiting the slums of the metropolis, one realizes for the first time that these Londoners have been forced to sacrifice the best qualities of their human nature, to bring to pass all the marvels of civilization which crowd their city; that a hundred powers which slumbered within them have remained inactive, have been suppressed in order that a few might be developed more fully and multiply through union with those of others. The very turmoil of the streets has something repulsive, something against which human nature rebels. The hundreds of thousands of all classes and ranks crowding past each other, are they not all human beings with the same qualities and powers, and with the same interest in being happy? And have they not, in the end, to seek happiness in the same way, by the same means? And still they crowd by one another as though they had nothing in common, nothing to do with one another, and their only agreement is the tacit one, that each keep to his own side of the pavement, so as not to delay the opposing streams of the crowd, while it occurs to no man to honor another with so much as a glance. The brutal indifference, the unfeeling isolation of each in his private interest becomes the more repellant and offensive, the more these individuals are crowded together, within a limited space. And, however much one may be aware that this isolation of the individual, this narrow self-seeking is the fundamental principle of our society everywhere, it is nowhere so shamelessly barefaced, so self-conscious as just here in the crowding of the great city. The dissolution of mankind into monads, of which each one has a separate principle, the world of atoms, is here carried out to its utmost extreme.

Hence it comes, too, that the social war, the war of each against all, is here openly declared. [. . .], people regard each other only as useful objects; each exploits the other, and the end of it all is, that the stronger treads the weaker under foot, and that the powerful few, the capitalists, seize everything for themselves, while to the weak many, the poor, scarcely a bare existence remains.

What is true of London, is true of Manchester, Birmingham, Leeds, is true of all great towns. Everywhere barbarous indifference, hard egotism on one hand, and nameless misery on the other, everywhere social warfare, every man's house in a state of siege, everywhere reciprocal plundering under the protection of the law, and all so shameless, so openly avowed that one shrinks before the consequences of our social state as they manifest themselves here undisguised, and can only wonder that the whole crazy fabric still hangs together.

Since capital, the direct or indirect control of the means of subsistence and production, is the weapon with which this social warfare is carried on, it is clear that all the disadvantages of such a state must fall upon the poor. For him no man has the slightest concern. Cast into the whirlpool, he must struggle through as well as he can. If he is so happy as to find work, i.e., if the bourgeoisie does him the favor to enrich itself by means of him, wages await him which scarcely suffice to keep body and soul together; if he can get no work he may steal, if he is not afraid of the police, or starve, in which case the police will take care that he does so in a quiet and inoffensive manner. During my residence in England, at least twenty or thirty persons have died of simple starvation under the most revolting circumstances, and a jury has rarely been found possessed of the courage to speak the plain truth in the matter. Let the testimony of the witnesses be never so clear and unequivocal, the bourgeoisie, from which the jury is selected, always finds some backdoor through which to escape the frightful verdict, death from starvation. The bourgeoisie dare not speak the truth in these cases, for it would speak its own condemnation. But indirectly, far more than directly, many have died of starvation, where long continued want of proper nourishment has called forth fatal illness, when it has produced such debility that causes which might otherwise have remained inoperative, brought on severe illness and death. The English working-men call this "social murder," and accuse our whole society of perpetrating this crime perpetually. Are they wrong?

[. . .] Meanwhile, let us proceed to a more detailed investigation of the position, in which the social war has placed the non-possessing class. Let us see what pay for his work society does give the working-man in the form of dwelling, clothing, food, what sort of subsistence it grants those who contribute most to the maintenance of society; and, first, let us consider the dwellings.

Every great city has one or more slums, where the working-class is crowded together. True, poverty often dwells in hidden alleys close to the palaces of the rich; but, in general, a separate territory has been assigned to it, where, removed from the sight of the happier classes, it may struggle along as it can. These slums are pretty equally arranged in all the great towns of England, the worst houses in the worst quarters of the towns; usually one- or two-storied cottages in long rows, perhaps with cellars used as dwellings, almost always irregularly built. These houses of three or four rooms and a kitchen form, throughout England, some parts of London excepted, the general dwellings of the working-class. The streets are generally unpaved, rough, dirty, filled with vegetable and animal refuse, without sewers or gutters, but supplied with foul, stagnant pools instead. Moreover, ventilation is impeded by the bad, confused method of building of the whole quarter, and since many human beings here live crowded into a small space, the atmosphere that prevails in these working-men's quarters may readily be imagined. Further, the streets serve as drying grounds in fine weather; lines are stretched across from house to house, and hung with wet clothing. [. . .]

I am far from asserting that all London working-people live in such want as the foregoing three families. I know very well that ten are somewhat better off, where one is so totally trodden under foot by society; but I assert that thousands of industrious and worthy people—far worthier and more to be respected than all the rich of London—do find themselves in a condition unworthy of human beings; and that every proletarian, everyone, without exception, is exposed to a similar fate without any fault of his own and in spite of every possible effort.

But in spite of all this, they who have some kind of a shelter are fortunate, fortunate in comparison with the utterly homeless. [. . .] because Manchester is the classic type of a modern manufacturing town, and because I know it as intimately as my own native town, more intimately than most of its residents know it, we shall make a longer stay here. [. . .] The whole assemblage of buildings is commonly called Manchester, and contains about four hundred thousand inhabitants, rather more than less. The town itself is peculiarly built, so that a person may live in it for years, and go in and out daily without coming into contact with a working-people's quarter or even with workers, that is, so long as he confines himself to his business or to pleasure walks. This arises chiefly from the fact, that by unconscious tacit agreement, as well as with outspoken conscious determination, the working-people's quarters are sharply separated from the sections of the city reserved for the middle-class; or, if this does not succeed, they are concealed with the cloak of charity. Manchester contains, at its heart, a rather extended commercial district, perhaps half a mile long and about as broad, and consisting almost wholly of offices and warehouses. Nearly the whole district is abandoned by dwellers, and is lonely and deserted at night; only watchmen and policemen traverse its narrow lanes with their dark lanterns. This district is cut through by certain main thoroughfares upon which the vast traffic concentrates, and in which the ground level is lined with brilliant shops. In these streets the upper floors are occupied, here and there, and there is a good deal of life upon them until late at night. With the exception of this commercial district, all Manchester proper, all Salford and Hulme, a great part of Pendleton and Chorlton, two-thirds of Ardwick, and single stretches of Cheetham Hill and Broughton are all unmixed working-people's quarters, stretching like a girdle, averaging a mile and a half in breadth, around the commercial district. Outside, beyond this girdle, lives the upper and middle bourgeoisie, the middle bourgeoisie in regularly laid out streets in the vicinity of the working quarters, especially in Chorlton and the lower lying portions of Cheetham Hill; the upper bourgeoisie in remoter villas with gardens in Chorlton and Ardwick, or on the breezy heights of Cheetham Hill, Broughton, and Pendleton, in free, wholesome country air, in fine, comfortable homes, passed once every half or quarter hour by omnibuses going into the city. And the finest part of the arrangement is this, that the members of this money aristocracy can take the shortest road through the middle of all the laboring districts to their places of business, without ever seeing that they are in the midst of the grimy misery that lurks to the right and the left. For the thoroughfares leading from the Exchange in all directions out of the city are lined, on both sides, with an almost unbroken series of shops, and are so kept in the hands of the middle and lower bourgeoisie, which, out of self-interest, cares for a decent and cleanly external appearance and *can* care for it. True, these shops bear some relation to the districts which lie behind them, and are more elegant in the commercial and residential quarters than when they hide grimy working-men's dwellings; but they suffice to conceal from the eyes of the wealthy men and women of strong stomachs and weak nerves the misery and grime which form the complement of their wealth. [. . .]

I know very well that this hypocritical plan is more or less common to all great cities; I know, too, that the retail dealers are forced by the nature of their business to take possession of the great highways; I know that there are more good buildings than bad ones upon such streets everywhere, and that the value of land is greater near them than in remoter districts; but at the same time I have never seen so systematic a shutting out of the working-class from the thoroughfares, so tender a concealment of everything which might affront the eye and the nerves of the bourgeoisie, as in Manchester. And yet, in other respects, Manchester is less built according to a plan, after official regulations, is more an outgrowth of accident, than any other city; and when I consider in this connection the eager assurances of the middle-class, that the working-class is doing famously, I cannot help feeling that the liberal manufacturers, the "Big Wigs" of Manchester, are not so innocent after all, in the matter of this sensitive method of construction. [. . .]

To sum up briefly the facts thus far cited. The great towns are chiefly inhabited by working-people, since in the best case there is one bourgeois for two workers, often for three, here and there for four; these workers have no property whatsoever of their own, and live wholly upon wages, which usually go from hand to mouth. Society, composed wholly of atoms, does not trouble itself about them; leaves them to care for themselves and their families, yet supplies them no means of doing this in an efficient and permanent manner. Every working-man, even the best, is therefore constantly exposed to loss of work and food, that is to death by starvation, and many perish in this way. The dwellings of the workers are everywhere badly planned, badly built, and kept in the worst condition, badly ventilated, damp, and unwholesome. The inhabitants are confined to the smallest possible space, and at least one family usually sleeps in each room. The interior arrangement of the dwellings is poverty-stricken in various degrees, down to the utter absence of even the most necessary furniture. The clothing of the workers, too, is generally scanty, and that of great multitudes is in rags. The food is, in general, bad; often almost unfit for use, and in many cases, at least at times, insufficient in quantity, so that, in extreme cases, death by starvation results. Thus the working-class of the great cities offers a graduated scale of conditions in life, in the best cases a temporarily endurable existence for hard work and good wages, good and endurable, that is, from the worker's standpoint; in the worst cases, bitter want, reaching even homelessness and death by starvation. The average is much nearer the worst case than the best. And this series does not fall into fixed classes, so that one can say, this fraction of the working-class is well off, has always been so, and remains so. If that is the case here and there, if single branches of work have in general an advantage over others, yet the condition of the workers in each branch is subject to such great fluctuations that a single working-man may be so placed as to pass through the whole range from comparative comfort to the extremest need, even to death by starvation, while almost every English working-man can tell a tale of marked changes of fortune.

Questions for Review and Discussion

1. What conditions does Engels observe in nineteenth-century British industrial cities such as Manchester? What are his major critical points?

2. Engels offers a critique of Manchester. What normative ideal of the city does Engels seem to hold as the basis of that critique? How might he describe the function, purpose, and character of a city? What might his ideal city look like?

3. Compare and contrast the descriptions of the city and city life offered by Engels and Conlon. Do Engels's observations challenge Conlon's argument? Did the nineteenth-century city of Manchester encourage philosophy?

4. Do the horrors of Manchester justify Jefferson's anti-urban philosophy? Explain.

5. Whose interests does the city of Manchester serve? Do citizens have a responsibility to try to make change? If so, which citizens?

6. Engels discusses the ways in which Manchester hides the situation of its working class from the bourgeoisie. Do cities still engage
   in such practices? If so, cite examples from your own experiences
   in cities.

CITY MATTERS: ROBERT GINSBERG. "AESTHETICS IN
HIROSHIMA: THE ARCHITECTURE OF REMEMBRANCE"

Introduction

Robert Ginsberg is Professor Emeritus of Philosophy and Comparative Literature at Pennsylvania State Delaware County Commonwealth
College. With specialties in value inquiry, social and political philosophy, and aesthetics, Ginsberg is well qualified to offer his reflections
on Hiroshima's efforts to rebuild after the atomic bomb destroyed most
of the city. But the question was not just of rebuilding but also remembering. How do we think about cities that have been destroyed? What
is worth preserving? How do the memories of a city's past affect its
present and its future? When a city has to rebuild, it is also presented
with the opportunity to reflect on its identity. What does the city want
to be? What ideals does it want to project? These questions are not
only practical but but philosophical issues.

"Aesthetics in Hiroshima: The Architecture of Remembrance"

Architecture is subsumed by aestheticians under the fine arts, even as a
master art, though the suspicion is felt that because buildings serve
human functions they may not even be works of art. But a philosophical
approach to architecture might reveal both aesthetic features of human
functions and the meaning of our activities.

This chapter is offered, then, as an explorative case study in linking
architecture and aesthetics, war and peace, philosophy and life. The case
selected is Hiroshima.

An aesthetic study of structures in Hiroshima might initially strike
you as an obscenity, for deeper concerns must address this place where
more human suffering may have unexpectedly occurred at one moment
than in all previous history. The 200,000 lives that were extinguished or
permanently injured here on 6 August 1945 eclipse the usual concerns
of aesthetics devoted to imagination, creativity, harmony, beauty, and joy.
The destruction of Hiroshima was unimaginably terrible.

But therein lies the challenge to those who would take the deep
measure of what happened in Hiroshima. The terrifying, as Aristotle
demonstrated in his *Poetics*, calls forth the greatest aesthetic powers. At
Hiroshima we need to visualize, to feel, to be moved, to resound, and
to be drawn beyond ourselves. Documentation and information is abun-
dantly available in the Peace Museum and the Peace Center, two highly
efficient modern buildings in the city's Peace Park. But we also need the

non-informational by way of evocative form that can seize upon our affective presence.

Four aesthetic problems are posed by Hiroshima. Number one is how to make the visitor a feeling participant in the event, a vicarious sufferer of the destruction, not just a curious observer of the aftermath. The second aesthetic problem is for those who live in Hiroshima: to find the form that may draw their hearts together in awesome commemoration of the victims. The first task is to crystallize horror, whereas the second is to purify piety. The third aesthetic challenge of Hiroshima is how to make a positive formal gesture that affirms humanity as joyous and loving. Hiroshima is not a fixed moment of Hell; it is a lively ongoing city of a million inhabitants pursuing fulfillment. And the fourth challenge is to find a formal link to the rich cultural past of the city, which, however, was almost totally destroyed.

These four aesthetic tasks have been accomplished in Hiroshima by means of striking variations in three-dimensional curvilinear forms and related crowning spaces. The forms and spaces speak to us and to each other. A dialogue of the imagination takes place in Hiroshima. In analyzing and relating the forms and spaces we follow the path of aesthetics, but at heart we are exploring what it means to live in the first city to be atom-bombed. These geometrical forms are also forms of human response, caring, and assertion.

1. The best-known building in Hiroshima is a ruin: the Dome. Indeed, it is the city's emblem: the identifier that partakes of the identity. The building, which was a chamber of commerce, was directly under the burst of the atom bomb.

"The ruins shall be preserved forever" explains a plaque near the protective ironwork fence. No other ruins of the blast have been preserved in Hiroshima. Because of a cultural preference for rebuilding, it is difficult to find ruins in Japan. Hiroshima today strikes any visitor as in no way ruined. It is a city of uncanny newness. Nothing is broken.[1]

Except the Dome. [...]

What undeniably assists our participation in the event of destruction is the presence of the ruin. The ruin is not simply a marker; it is a survivor. The ruin speaks silently to its visitors: "I was here, and I am here, and I will be here forever." The ruin refuses to be forgotten, to be torn down, or to be replaced. What happened won't go away. It adheres

---

1. See my "Report from Hiroshima," *The Acorn: A Gandhian Review*, 2:2 (September 1987), pp. 13, 14, 18. For a moving presentation in word and image of experiencing Hiroshima see Betty Jean Lifton and Eikoh Hosoe, *A Place Called Hiroshima* (Tokyo: Kodansha International Ltd., 1985).

to the stones. Even when all the living survivors (*Hibakusha*) have died out, the ruin will retain the impact of the blast it experienced. The ruin preserves the uniquely destructive event beyond the flow of time that washes everything away. "This too shall pass" may be said of all the modern department stores, apartment buildings, and sports facilities in Hiroshima, but Hiroshima refuses to have it said of this building. [. . .]

Two levels of experience occur at the Dome. First we feel the horror, thanks to the presence of the ruin. But then we are thankful for the ruin. We recognize, upon reflection, the deliberate act which has saved this site for us to experience. And we approve. In the act of preservation is something of value not only for those who were inciner-ated or maimed in Hiroshima, but also for all those who will come here. We admire those who preserved the brokenness of the building: a sin-gular act of will asserted in the face of enormous destruction.

We dwell upon the contrast between its brokenness and its appar-ently sound features, such as the girders of the dome. Those girders soar with unscathed elegance above the suffering of the site to meet in the sky. A beautiful form, emerging from the horror, has been offered to us as a work of architecture. Our hearts are filled with mixed feelings: admiration and regret, horror and beauty, alienation and at-homeness.

2. The Cenotaph in the Peace Park has a much different task: to commemorate those who lost their lives. Dignity, simplicity, tranquility are the desiderata for such a memorial. It must express respect for the dead, give comfort to the mourning individual, yet allow for massive public ceremony. The solution is a clean geometrical shape. It has no figuration or ornament, no specificity or allusion. Thus, it does better than the unfortunate allegorical figure of commemoration, "Peace," in Nagasaki, and better than other monuments in the Hiroshima Peace Park which are cluttered with messages, stories, and offerings. The Ceno-taph resists being personalized and particularized; it elevates the visitor by a cool abstractness.

The cement Cenotaph is saddle-shaped with two open ends. The lips of the openings move upward with grace, while the back of the saddle crouches protectively. Both shelter and release are materialized. In front and on both sides are extensive terraces to accommodate seated or standing visitors to public ceremonies. In 1987 I was one of 55,000 such participants at the events marking the anniversary.

Behind the Cenotaph is a reflecting pond out of which rises a large abstract open-handed form bearing an eternal flame, supposedly lit from the fires of the bomb blast. The pond keeps the sightline clear. The flame surrounded by water suggests the burning city amid its three rivers. The flame holder suggests the Buddhist image of a blossoming lotus that arises from waste. And what waste was made here. The fire that destroyed so many lives is tamed and sustained as their eternal memorial.

The Cenotaph sits in a bed of white gravel. A railing is provided in front for prayer and flower offerings, but the Cenotaph itself is unadorned and untouchable. It is just the right scale for an individual to approach, make obeisance, and harbor a prayer. The pure form of the Cenotaph is comforting and uplifting.

Yet the Cenotaph is not quite experienced as a beautiful form in itself. It is transparent as form. We do not so much notice it as see through it. It does house a commemorative stone in the shape of an altar. Dedicated to the souls of the dead, it assures them with these words, "For we shall not repeat the evil."[2] Addressed to those of the past, the utterance is made on behalf of whoever is present and in the name of the future. A deeply troubling act. This is not simply a fitting commemoration; it is an infinite commitment. The stone covers the list of names of those who have died due to the blast. New names are still being added. The parabolic curve of the lip of the monument springs out with expanding arms into the earth yet curves above the stone as a roof upon this place and moment.

What we see through the Cenotaph as transparent form is the Dome. The geometrical dome of the great ruin fits under the curve of the Cenotaph as we read the binding text. Curve cradles curve. The peaceful sky seen through the open dome of the ruin is contrasted movingly with darting flames of the commemorative fire framed by the saddle arch. That arch with ease composes a universe of air, fire, water, and earth, of past, present, and future, of dead and living and not yet born, of multitudes and individuals. The Cenotaph's artistry is in being non-artistic; it makes evident without effort a reverberating grasp of deep reality, a reality in which we stand. Architecture of the heart.

The Dome, which formalized terror, is used by the Cenotaph to dedicate commitment. The messages inscribed on both engage in dialogue: a ruin to be kept forever and a vow that such destruction will recur never. Architecture that speaks. We are in the dialogue. The prevention of atom-bombing must be by an act of will. We make that vow silently in the presence of those who died by atom-bombing. That act of will to prevent is linked visually, morally, yea ontologically, with the act

---

2. An alternative translation is, "The mistake will not be repeated." Cf. the study by John K. Roth, "Shall We Repeat the Evil?: Reflections on the Threat of Nuclear War in the 1980s," *Philosophical Essays on the Ideas of a Good Society*, eds. Yeager Hudson and Creighton Peden, "Social Philosophy Today," vol. 1 (Lewiston, N.Y.: The Edwin Mellen Press, 1988), pp. 277–286.

of preserving the event of being atom-bombed. The eternal presence of atom-bombing is concomitant to the commitment to prevent atom-bombing. Such a willing toward the future is the consolation offered those who died here. They may rest in peace only if we stop the bombing.

The alignment of Dome and Cenotaph contribute the backbone to the Peace Park. The Peace Museum, elevated on pylons, only partially closes the vista at one end. It also encourages the sightliness extending toward the Cenotaph and Dome. Other monuments are located throughout the park, offering everyone something to respond to. And other geometrical shapes here are noteworthy: The elongated dome for the Children's Monument, opened by three supporting legs as if about to take flight with the wind. The dome for the Peace Bell, also open and standing on four legs, as if a section cut from a bubble or parachute and tied to mooring columns. And a green mound, an omphalos or womb of the earth, in which are interred the ashes of tens of thousands of unidentified human beings. The Park is alive with forms.

3. But let us look elsewhere in the city for relief from such horrendous worldly cares. The Museum of Art is a welcome island of beauty and peace. The collection, housed in the main circular pavilion, is largely of the French Impressionists and related works.[3] A half dozen or so galleries, each windowless and with a single entrance from the central room, afford a gently protected space for a leisurely *tête-à-tête* with works of heart-warming beauty. The museum is a pure joy. At the center of the round pavilion is a Venus statue by, as I recall, Maillol. The superb female form is like a great beautiful flower placed under the dome. Yes, dome. The joys of creativity and human affirmation in the Art Museum of Hiroshima are organized as counter-statement to the human destructivity experienced in the Dome.

We approach the pavilion as something precious: an inner sanctum. Its strange dome is sensed as a shelter, but it is protected by a surrounding wall. We enter the wall. An excellent tea shop and other facilities occupy the wall. The pavilion is the center of a compound. At leisure we contemplate its shape. It is like a muffin, or a large hut, or a tended . . . pavilion. Only when inside this structure do we appreciate its form which contributes so substantially to our enjoyment of the art. This is what might be called a "user-friendly" building, although we are not using the museum but living more fully thanks to it. It harbors something of the best within us. We cannot miss the gesture of placing Love under this agreeable form of dome.

---

3. See the illustrated catalogue in Japanese and English, *Hiroshima Museum of Art* (1985).

The statue is raised above eye level on a pedestal so that it reigns in space. The galleries circle it as we move around it in our visit to them. Concentric circles in the flooring of the pavilion oblige us to step down if we would approach the statue, which has the effect of lifting it further. The sweeping purified dome, topped by a glazed cupola admitting light, contributes a celestial dynamism to the space emanating from the statue. Love, beauty, and humanity well up with divine joyfulness: we are at the pivot point of the universe.

The art works in Hiroshima are more beautiful because they are in Hiroshima. This museum maximizes their existence as human joys. This would be a good art museum anywhere in the world. Though upon entering the museum we tend to forget that we are in Hiroshima, or even in Japan, the statue under the dome lovingly reminds us before we leave that this selection and arrangement is an achievement of Hiroshima. The museum addresses what it is to live in a city that had been destroyed by an atom bomb but which insists on its worth as civilized community. "Here in Hiroshima," the museum says to us, "we know the value of beauty and love." The theme of the museum is formally proclaimed to be "Caritas et Pax." [. . .]

Although the Cenotaph speaks visibly to the Dome, the dialogue of the museum with the Dome is invisible. It is entirely imaginary. The Cenotaph, the Dome, and all the rest of Hiroshima is shut out of view. Our view is entirely of art. Nothing intervenes. No distractions. No destruction. But the Dome flutters like a ghost in our heart as we stand under the pavilion's dome. The shock of remembrance. We cannot shake off the image of the Dome once we have seen it and as long as we are in Hiroshima. [. . .]

Having left the Dome behind, we nonetheless bring the Dome into the museum with us, or else we find it there, after all—after all that wonderful art and heartfelt pleasure. The remarkable achievement of the architecture is to have set the stage for this happening, while avoiding outright reference. Without allusion the connection happens.

4. The geometrical experience of Hiroshima encourages the visitor to detect the other variations upon the central and symbolic forms. We re-see the city, organizing our encounters with it so that things relate to one another and the continuation of life makes sense. The eye of the visitor yearns to make connections as if we need to redeem life in Hiroshima as well as our own life. Hiroshima is a great field for discovering value. We are form-seeking creatures as well as creators of form. We need to greet and order experience formally. Thus, a visit to the celebrated public garden, Shukkei-en, is likely to arrest us before another geometrical form as its dynamic center: the arched Chinese stepped bridge.

We can approach the bridge from either end and climb up the steps to cross it—an amusing activity. But the visually organizing power of the bridge comes in viewing it from its side. Seen this way it is the graceful curved culmination of the great pond. It is manifestly a human construction that harmoniously takes center stage among natural forms. Its bright stone color is a welcome contribution to the greens and blues. It rewards us with two arches. The outer one, upon which people may pass, is a noble rising, while the inner one, through which the water runs, is a gentler, smaller, entrance. The bridge is a crossing in two directions. The transitory is its eternal business.

The Chinese bridge is a triumph of Hiroshima's past. It not only has endured but it suggests the imperturbable continuity of human existence in the garden of life. Here, out of doors, away from the bustle of the metropolis, we find ourselves drawn to the reassuring beauty of the bridge's shape. It is an alternative to the Dome, which we have forgotten. Yet a fading photographic plaque in the park shows the gardens after the bomb blast: while the vegetation is destroyed the bridge retains its shape. So we are reminded that this corner of Eden is also in Hiroshima. The past that has been saved is more valuable because it has escaped total destruction. Everything valuable in the existence of a city may be destroyed at any moment; hence, we ought to cherish now what there is and what it means to us. Who we may become and the joys of a heritage are bridged. Architecture as connector.

Shukkei-en is more than a leisurely break from the city-life of Hiroshima. Thanks to the curvature of its bridge, it is a disclosure of life as worthwhile, even in Hiroshima. Whereas the Cenotaph and the museum were constructed after the bomb and address, either explicitly or implicitly, the geometry of the Dome that survived, the bridge is an unchanged older structure not designed to allude to these other forms. We re-discover the bridge as cultural treasure in the context of the forms of this city. We are the avid connector, the imagination that ties forms together, the architect of meaningful experience. We re-make the bridge.

The order in which we have visited the four works dictates itself, as "stations of evocation."[4]

Footbridge, museum pavilion, official cenotaph, and preserved ruin: four types of architecture. Four distinct forms of service to humanity. But four forms that play off one another and play upon our feeling and imagination. How shortchanged we would have been to have visited only one or two. How many more remain to be known? What if I missed

---

4. I owe the phrase to Roberta Kevelson and am grateful for her response to these reflections.

the decisive structure, the culminating form?[5] Forms have life; life has forms. Each architectural presence is not limited to site but makes itself felt throughout an entire city, as the Colosseum in Rome, the Parthenon in Athens, the Empire State Building in New York, the Capitol in Washington. Architecture as a shaping force in civilized life. We take its forms with us as we walk through the terrain. It sends us forth with formative impulse. We do not easily clear our sensibility of works of architecture as we do with paintings, in order to meet each work on its own terms. Works of architecture work upon their environment, converting surroundings into force fields. Form travels through the very ground in which the buildings are rooted or through the air in which they raise their heads. We too touch that ground and breathe that air. Just as architecture has this special presence in its site that is lacked by mobile objects of art, so we experiencers of architecture have a special presence with it that lacks in our dealings with other arts.

Our presence may have little consciously to do with architecture as an art. In Hiroshima we were visiting the garden for its horticulture and landscaping, the museum for its art works, the Cenotaph for its commemorative value, and the Dome for its historical significance. In other words, we went to these structures because of their functions rather than their aesthetic identity. To have thought at the outset that the Dome could have aesthetic identity might have been repulsive. But once we get there things change. Forms arise and are detected. Images arise in us and are applied. Discovery and imagination work hand in hand. What is experienced is aesthetic, and we are present in the architectural.

Our presence, filled with the burdens and expectations of our life, is the indispensable partnership we bring to architecture. Only by making the trip can we find how the work works upon our experience and how our experience works upon the work. A guilt trip, it may be said, is what I have been recording under the guise of a critical exploration. What of the Japanese responsibility for mass killings in China, Korea, and elsewhere? What of the American justification for dropping the atom bomb on Hiroshima in order to rapidly end the Second World War and save the lives of perhaps a million American troops? What of the Japanese manipulation of the Peace Park and of Hiroshima, the "Peace City," in order to make the Japanese out as the innocent victims of the Second World War? Excellent points. These considerations might well override our experiences in Hiroshima. Our political and moral commitments may

---

5. "Sightseeing Attractions in City Center," reprinted from brochure, "Welcome to Hiroshima: City of International Peace and Culture" (Hiroshima City Tourist Association, ca. 1986).

close us to the workings of the architecture. Could you have such experiences as I have recounted even while assigning guilt to the Japanese for World War II, while arguing for justification of the American atom-bombing, or while criticizing the Japanese for the self-righteous packaging of their role in the war and the bombing? Would the power of suffering and power of forms still work upon you, and would you be ready to commit yourself morally and politically to the messages of the monuments, those inscribed and those unspoken? Go and see.

Questions for Review and Discussion

1. What are the four aesthetic problems posed by Hiroshima?

2. What are the four forms of architecture that Ginsberg focuses on? What meaning does each convey?

3. Why does Ginsberg argue that it was important to preserve the ruins of the dome? What meaning does it convey about the city?

4. Taken together, what does Ginsberg think that the four architectural forms reveal to us about the nature and identity of Hiroshima?

5. Why is it important to remember cities? Compare and contrast Hiroshima's remembering to Pericles' efforts.

6. New York City is facing similar challenges as officials and citizens debate about rebuilding at ground zero after 9/11. What might New York learn from the case of Hiroshima?

7. Ginsberg argues that Hiroshima has rebuilt successfully, that is, it has rebuilt in a way that remembers and preserves the past while at the same time projecting a strong sense of identity for the present and future. Do you agree? Think about other philosophers who discuss the identity of cities (e.g., Weber, Simmel, Mumford, Grange, Conlon). How might they evaluate the case of Hiroshima?

Exercises for discussion on philosophyandthecity.org: Rebuilding NYC after 9/11; reflecting on the metaphors we use to define cities.

SECTION B

Citizenship

Although today we usually equate citizenship with membership in, or recognition by, a national state, the term "citizen" has its origins in the city (and thus shares the same root word). In his book *The Good City and the Good Life*, Daniel Kemmis argues that, in the age of globalization, the city is enjoying a renewed level of importance. He argues that we can revitalize the concept of citizenship through reflection on our experiences of city life and should let the ancient Greek thinkers such as Pericles, Plato, and Aristotle who originally defined ideals of citizenship in Western civilization be our guides in this process. But ancient Athenians—even those like Pericles who lived during the golden age of the Athenian democracy—lived with a concept of citizenship that limited citizen rights to a minority of persons. Only male landowners of Athenian descent born on Athenian soil qualified for citizenship. Women, children, slaves, and foreign-born residents were excluded.

Thus some thinkers question Kemmis and others who invoke ancient Athenian ideals of citizenship. Is it possible to draw from Greek thought while still developing a more inclusive understanding of citizenship? Why might a more inclusive concept of citizenship be desirable? Is citizenship a right or a privilege? Should citizens have responsibilities as well as rights? If so, what are they? These are the questions with which philosophers from classical Greece to the present day continue to grapple.

Philosophers from Part I who are especially useful when thinking about citizenship include: **Pericles, Aristotle, Hobbes, Rousseau, Addams, West, Young,** and **Bickford.**

251

PHILOSOPHY MATTERS: ROBERT GOODING-WILLIAMS.
"CITIZENSHIP AND RACIAL IDEOLOGY" (1993)

Introduction

Robert Gooding-Williams is the Ralph and Mary Otis Isham Professor of Political Science and the College at the University of Chicago. This essay comes from a volume that Gooding-Williams edited on the aftermath of the Rodney King uprising entitled *Reading Rodney King Reading Urban Uprising.*

On March 3, 1991, a black man named Rodney King was pulled over by police and brutally beaten. The beating was caught on videotape, and the police officers were tried for violating Mr. King's civil rights. Defense attorneys effectively neutralized the damaging video evidence against the accused police officers by playing on racial imagery, and four of the officers were acquitted. Immediately following news of their acquittal in May 1992, uprisings broke out in several major U.S. cities, but the focal point was South Central Los Angeles. Gooding-Williams demonstrates the value of a philosophical analysis of the media representations of urban "riots" by blacks following the Rodney King verdict. He argues that both liberal and conservative commentators failed to understand the uprisings as acts of protest because they failed to see the blacks as citizens.

"Citizenship and Racial Ideology"

Channel surfing in Berkeley during the L.A. uprising, I noticed that two views dominated the television representation of the "rioters." Call the first of these "the conservative view," and the second "the liberal view." In essence, the conservative view saw the "rioters" more or less as the defense attorneys had encouraged the Simi Valley jury to see Rodney King. Thought to be primarily black (before evidence of substantial Hispanic involvement in the uprising had come to light), the people in the street were seen as embodying an uncivilized chaos that needed to be stamped out in order to restore law and order. According to this view, the "rioting" had nothing to do with the King verdict, and would be better seen as expressing a repressed opportunism just waiting for an excuse to flout the law.[1] The liberal view was a bit more complex, as it

---

1. For more on this point, see Mark Shubb's "Race, Lies, and Videotape: The L.A. Upheaval and the Media" (especially the section entitled "Thugs, Hooligans and Savages"), *Extra* 5 (July/August 1992): 8–11.

emphasized the social causes of the "riots"—joblessness, poverty, and, in general, socioeconomic need—but like the conservative view, it suggested that the burning of Los Angeles had little to do with what happened to Rodney King.

By dissociating the uprising from the King verdict, both liberals and conservatives were refusing to see in it an expression of moral indignation.[2] Though "rioters" in the streets were readily cast as bearers of chaos, or as agents of need and deprivation, their actions simply could not be seen as involving the view that the injustice suffered by Rodney King was symbolic of a larger social injustice. While "looters" could be construed as acting from need, they could not be construed as implicitly characterizing that need as stemming from a repressive social and political order, one aspect of whose repressiveness the trial videotape seemed explicitly to have exposed, and against which they would now strike a blow.

To be sure, there is no point in romanticizing the uprising, or in losing sight of the fact that, like all complex social events, it was causally overdetermined. The motives bringing people to the streets were, no doubt, numerous. But it strains credulity to deny, as many conservative and liberal pundits immediately wanted to do, that the uprising in Los Angeles was not for many an act of political protest. The incapacity of television newscasters to see it that way points largely, I think, to their and many white Americans' general failure to regard black people, even those who have not engaged in "riotous" behavior, as fellow citizens; what they cannot admit, in other words, is that the speech and/or action of a black person might be thoughtfully entertained as making a statement about issues which concern us all as members of the same political community. Blacks can be cast as lawless opportunists, as unfortunate victims, or in any number of other roles, but rarely as persons with a reasonable point of view about their and white Americans' shared circumstances. If blacks are needy, then their neediness needs to be managed and contained; that blacks' interpretations of their and other Americans' needs might be taken seriously seems to be beyond the pale of intelligibility. Even when the media permit some respected "black leader" to speak, one worries that most white Americans will dismiss his or her voice, and that they will see the media as pandering to "special interests."

Racial ideology in contemporary America works relentlessly to exclude blacks from many white Americans' conceptions of who their fellow citizens are. The antiblack sentiment reported in a recent *New York*

---

2. Appearing on *Crossfire*, William Allen of the United States Civil Rights Commission was the only person I heard dispute the liberal-conservative consensus.

Times article about the Greenwood section of Chicago begins to tell the story. Putting succinctly all he claims to know about black Americans, 23-year-old William Knepper says that "they came from Africa, and they can get away with a lot of stuff because they're black, they're a minority." Peggy O'Connor, a waitress and the wife of a police officer, is a bit more blunt: "I don't want to be too close to them. I think they've been whining too long, and I'm sick of it."[3] As it turns out, the image of the whining black recurs frequently among white Americans, as according to a poll CNN reported on the weekend of the L.A. uprising, 46% of the whites queried agreed that blacks "[a]re always whining about racism."[4] For many whites, then, black speech is not the speech of fellow citizens, but the always-complaining speech of spoiled children. Casting blacks in the infantilizing role of whiners from Africa, the racial ideology of these white folk works against the possibility of recognizing blacks as partners in a broadly conceived social and political enterprise.[5]

Read as sociopolitical allegory, the remarks and thoughts of Knepper, O'Connor, and many others can be said to envision America as a white nation that has got itself beset by a bunch of whimpering interlopers who get away with too much. DuBois's words and the Amherst College effigy protest exemplify discursive strategies for demythifying and resisting this vision. Other discursive strategies are possible as well. Absent demythification and resistance, we should anticipate endless echoes of Fanon's leitmotif:

---

3. *New York Times*, 21 June 1992.

4. The poll was taken on 30 April 1992 by the firm of Yankelovich Clancy Shulman, located in Westport, Connecticut.

5. Television media's tendency to use images of black bodies to represent people on welfare contributes substantially to the view that black people, *in general*, are clients but not citizens of the larger political community. Note also Gertrude Ezorsky's observation that "15 to 19 percent of whites would not vote for a qualified black candidate nominated by their own party either for governor or president. According to Linda Williams, senior research associate at the Joint Center for Policy Studies, their 1986 poll showed that 'the higher the office, the more whites there were who would admit that they would never vote for a black.'" See Gertrude Ezorsky, *Racism and Justice: The Case for Affirmative Action* (Ithaca, NY: Cornell University Press, 1991), 13.

For an insightful discussion of the ways in which the failure of whites to recognize blacks as fellow citizens has (mis)shaped contemporary policy debates about race in America, see Adolph Reed and Julian Bond, "Equality: Why We Can't Wait," *The Nation* 20 (December 1991): 736. For a provocative *philosophical* discussion of the issues of recognition, membership, and citizenship which I have raised here, see Michael Walzer, *Spheres of Justice* (New York: Basic Books, 1983), 31–63.

Look at the nigger! . . . Mama, a Negro! . . . Hell, he's getting mad. . . . Take no notice, sir, he does not know that you are as civilized as we. . . ."

My body was given back to me sprawled out, distorted, recolored, clad in mourning in that white winter day. The Negro is an animal, the Negro is bad, the Negro is mean, the Negro is ugly; look, a nigger. . . ."[6]

Questions for Review and Discussion

1. Even though African Americans are legally citizens, Gooding-Williams claims that they are not recognized as such. What would such recognition entail?

2. Why is citizenship recognition important?

3. Compare and contrast Gooding-Williams's views with those of Addams and West.

4. Might some of the philosophical concepts of citizenship contribute to perceptions that blacks and other marginalized groups are not citizens? How so?

5. How can philosophical understandings of citizenship that we have studied help us develop a more inclusive concept?

---

6. Frantz Fanon, *Black Skin, White Masks* (New York: The Grove Press, 1967), 113.

CITY MATTERS: DANIEL KEMMIS.
"TAXPAYERS VS. CITIZENS" (1995)

Introduction

Daniel Kemmis is the former mayor of Missoula, Montana, and now director of the University of Montana's Center for the Rocky Mountain West and a board member of several nonprofit organizations that focus on public policy, democracy, and place. This case study comes from his book *The Good City and the Good Life*. In it he describes a situation that he confronted while he was mayor of Missoula, although it is a phenomenon that happens in most American cities.

"Taxpayers vs. Citizens"

The Missoula Area Conferencing System was an early version of a computer network that served, among other functions, as a kind of town hall where a variety of citizens, elected officials, and local government employees exchanged news and views about a broad range of issues. The exchanges were informal and open, often educational, and occasionally heated.

One day, shortly after the city's semiannual tax statements appeared in mailboxes throughout Missoula, one of the network's participants entered an inquiry into the system concerning the increase in her taxes. This very polite request triggered a passionate response from a fellow named Jerry. I have since learned that computer bulletin boards often evoke fully uninhibited, blindly passionate entries, and that this kind of response has earned the title "flaming." Jerry was flaming, which is to say that, like many others who address themselves to public issues, he was literally beside himself. Here is the unedited text of Jerry's message:

> you are not alone in your frustrations with the city. all thay
> want is more tax money so thay can do less. thay can't take care
> of what thay have now what can we look forward to when thay
> inlarge the city, more potholes, more taxes. thay (the people in
> power of the city, these are not the taxpayers) will vote in a rase
> for themselfs when the #$%& is about to hit the fan.

The lack of literary refinement in Jerry's treatise is purely incidental; in fact, one of the strengths of this electronic forum is that many people who would not otherwise feel comfortable about putting their political sentiments in writing are for some reason less inhibited in this medium. The system then in use in Missoula also carried with it a nicely leveling effect, in that it offered only the crudest of editing tools, so that participants were always sending out plenty of misspelled words. Still, there is something remarkable about Jerry's consistent misspelling of "they." His rendering it as "thay" captures as the correct spelling never could the forbidding otherness which Jerry, like so many others, perceive as the essence of the political system.

"Thay" in their self-seeking perfidy are to blame for it all. And to whom are "thay" contrasted? Why, to "the taxpayers," of course. Now to Jerry's credit, let it be understood that he speaks for vast segments of the populace, both in his inadvertently eloquent rendering of the overwhelming otherness of "thay" and in his naming of all those whom "thay" victimize as "the taxpayers." But it is time that we looked this hard reality in the face: the growing magnitude of the numbers for whom Jerry speaks so plainly is proof that all our smug pride in our "democratic" form of government is an increasingly untenable delusion.

People who customarily refer to themselves as taxpayers are not even remotely related to democratic citizens. Yet this is precisely the word that now regularly holds the place which in a true democracy would be occupied by "citizens." Taxpayers bear a dual relationship to government, neither half of which has anything at all to do with democracy. Taxpayers pay tribute to the government, and they receive services from it. So does every subject of a totalitarian regime. What taxpayers do not do, and what people who call themselves taxpayers have long since stopped even imagining themselves doing, is governing. In a democracy, by the very meaning of the word, the people govern—they create among themselves the conditions of their lives. But in our political culture, "thay" govern, victimizing "the taxpayers" and delivering a uniformly unsatisfactory level of services, not only because of their incredible ineptitude, but because, as Jerry and so many others are darkly convinced, "thay" are draining "the taxpayers" tribute into their own pockets.

Given the ever worsening dysfunction in the political system at the federal and often at the state level, this sullen attitude is in a large sense entirely justified. Increasingly we seem to be governed at all the "important" levels, where we have learned to judge democracy, by governments that appear to be bought and sold by special interests through PAC contributions, gridlocked by unbending partisanship, unable to solve any major problems, adept only at creating vast new pockets of indebtedness. In the face of such a gigantic failure of democracy, the language that Jerry applies to all politics is not in the least surprising. But perhaps nothing in this scene tells us more about the decline of democratic culture than the lack of any lived, human connection to the concept or practice of citizenship.

It would never have occurred to Jerry to use the word "citizen" instead of "taxpayer." In this he is fully representative of our prevailing political culture. If we do use the word "citizen," it is almost certain either to be part of the phrase "concerned citizen" (as if citizenship were essentially a form of anxiety) or part of the hopelessly confused phrase "private citizen"—the civic equivalent of dry water. Standing by itself, which it rarely does, the word "citizen" evokes all the weariness and unhappiness we associate with public life, so that most of us would not readily, let alone enthusiastically, call ourselves "citizens." But this is only a confirmation of the fact that this word and indeed all of public speech and public life have been so thinned and diluted that we cannot connect them with anything truly vibrant and sustaining.

It would do no good at all simply to insist that we start calling ourselves "citizens" instead of "taxpayers," unless citizenship was already being experienced as something important, worthwhile, and humanly satisfying. People do in fact have an experience of citizenship which is often satisfying, but it does not go by the name of citizenship and is therefore not understood as a political experience, let alone as having any potential to revitalize democracy.

The place to begin, then, is with the experience of citizenship rather than with the word.

Questions for Review and Discussion

1. What, according to Kemmis, are the main differences between citizens and taxpayers?

2. Why does Kemmis think it is problematic that many people call themselves taxpayers rather than citizens?

3. Why does Kemmis argue that it is insufficient simply to shift terminology? What has to happen if persons are really to become citizens rather than taxpayers?

4. Would Pericles and Aristotle understand the distinction between a taxpayer and a citizen? Explain.

5. Which philosophers would agree with Kemmis's conception of citizenship? Which might disagree?

6. Do you think that it would be helpful if more people understood themselves as citizens rather than taxpayers? Why or why not?

Exercises on philosophyandthecity.org: Institute for Citizenship (UK) and National Civic League (U.S.); "Live and Let Live" (the case of Laramie, WY).

Urban Identity and Diversity

At least since the turn of the twentieth century, cities often have been identified in terms of diversity—both the diversity of the activities available and the diversity of their residents and visitors. Cities particularly are identified in this way when contrasted with rural areas. Although some identify the diversity of the city as a good thing, others view diversity as the greatest challenge (or even threat) to city life.

Despite the fact that cities boast diverse populations, not all people feel equally included. Some groups face discrimination and are excluded from at least some aspects of city life. Often people feel that their own identity is threatened when they are expected to fit into existing norms or expectations. Such issues raise the age-old philosophical question of the one and the many—how can we recognize diverse persons and contributions while at the same time seeing the city as some sort of unified entity?

Do urban dwellers have different characteristics from those of rural dwellers? If so, what are they? How does our understanding of diversity, especially racial diversity, play a role in thinking about urban identity? Should we value the diversity of the city? Philosophers have addressed these questions since ancient Athens and continue to do so today.

Philosophers from Part I who are especially useful when thinking about urban identity and diversity include: **Aristotle, More, Rousseau, Simmel, Jefferson, Addams, Gavin, West, hooks, Young, Conlon, Mendieta,** and **Weiss.**

PHILOSOPHY MATTERS: LEE FRANCIS.
"WE, THE PEOPLE: YOUNG AMERICAN INDIANS
RECLAIMING THEIR IDENTITY" (2003)

Introduction

Lee Francis, a member of the Laguna Pueblo and a resident of Albuquerque, New Mexico, has published widely and directs the Wordcraft Circle of Native Writers and Storytellers. Although Native American philosophy is only starting to be recognized by "mainstream" philosophers for its valuable wisdom and contribution to the Anglo-European philosophical canon, Francis tells us how urban Indians have drawn on Native American philosophical understandings of story to preserve and sustain their sense of identity as Urban Indians.

Because of both formal and informal United States' policies, most American Indians have been relocated twice: first, from their original lands (which included their own cities now buried beneath ones built by European settlers) to reservations, and second, from reservations to contemporary cities. The majority of American Indians now live in cities. Disconnected from their nations, tribes, and families, many have created new identities by bonding with other dislocated Indians and creating an "urban Indian" identity. Yet this identity is fragile, as Urban Indians face racism and poverty in the city as well as occasional rejection from Native Americans who have remained on reservations. In this essay, Lee Francis argues that Native American philosophy and identity is based on storytelling, and that such is particularly crucial for Urban Indians if they are to retain a positive sense of identity and resist assimilation. The Native American understanding of identity challenges contemporary European concepts that focus on the individual rather than "the People."

"We, the People: Young American Indians Reclaiming Their Identity"

For the People, whether urban- or reservation-born, it's really about story. The ancients among the People understood that all of creation— seen and unseen—tells story. In the long-ago time, from birth to earth, the People learned about their harmonious place in the order of all creation by listening to and telling story. Their identity was inextricably interwoven in the stories they were told. For Native People, story was and continues to be essential to an individual's identity construction and development.

Most young urban American Indians live in a world very different from the long-ago past. They face many challenges. Drug use, alcohol abuse, and violence are a regular part of their lives. Living with a single parent is not unusual either. After school they come home to an empty place because their parent is working. At school their classmates mock them if they say they are American Indian. They rarely fit in because they know they are somehow different from the others. Their identity as an American Indian becomes blurred. They do not know the history of Native American Indian people. They do not know the stories.

No one tells them that a couple of centuries ago, our non-Native relatives came across the great waters to the land of the People. As more and more immigrated from their original homelands, the People told stories to their non-Native relations. They told stories about all of creation. About being connected. Related. They told stories about walking in harmony and balance and what the consequences are when that doesn't occur. Stories were told about protecting and caring for the earth long before there was an Environmental Protection Agency. In the stories, the People revealed their identities to their non-Native relations.

As the People died by the millions from massacres and the disease brought by their non-Native relations, fewer and fewer stories were told. The task of telling story fell to the few remaining elders. The stories changed. The elders told story about smallpox and greed. They told story about rape and murder. About the massacres of Native men, women, and children. They also told story about generosity, caring, and community. The elders among the People told story after story. Yet, the influence of their non-Native relations was evident as the creation and migration stories began to subtly change. They began to include the beliefs, values, and attitudes of their Christian non-Native relations. For example, honoring and celebrating the importance of women in Native societies was discouraged. And the stories began to emphasize men having control over women. Men never controlled women prior to the arrival of our non-Native relations. Each had their own important tasks to ensure that their community was completely functional.

Then came the boarding school experiment. Indigenous children were abducted and taken thousands of miles from their home place. The purpose of the boarding school was to indoctrinate or brainwash the children. Telling story in their own languages was forbidden. Those who disobeyed were held in solitary confinement in small prisonlike cells for weeks or even months. In the boarding schools they were told different stories. These stories were about selfishness, getting ahead, isolation, and "rugged individualism." Some returned to the reservation. Even so, the stories emphasizing the values, attitudes, and beliefs of the People told in community settings since the beginning of time were slowly lost.

Later, many of the People were forcibly relocated or migrated to towns and cities. The majority of stories urban Native youth heard and learned were those told on the stage, and later on radio shows and in movies. Today stories are seen on television, videos, and DVDs. No longer are the stories about community. Instead, urban Native youth hear and see stories that focus on me instead of we. Little wonder, then, about the dysfunction among Native youth both on and off the reservation in today's world.

To reclaim their identity, American Indian urban youth need to learn the stories of the People. They need to learn, remember, and tell the ancient origin and migration stories, the stories that focus on Native values, attitudes, and beliefs. And they need to tell new stories about growing up and living urban lives. These new stories need to incorporate the wisdom of the People about the land and relatedness to all of creation. To tell new urban stories requires learning about the People who first inhabited the land in the urban area where they now live. Once these stories are learned, it is important to tell stories about those People. They need to tell stories of their accomplishments and tragedies. What they believed and experienced. Link those stories with those of the People from whom urban Native youth are descended. In this Internet age there is no excuse for not knowing. It is in the stories, old and new, where urban Native youth will be able to reclaim their Native identity. They will be able to know their harmonious place in the order of all creation. [. . .]

Working with urban Native students who take my classes is always a challenge. Whether I am teaching Native American Philosophy, Life and Thought, Spirit of Place, or Contemporary and Traditional Native Storytelling, the sad reality is that a majority of urban Native students do not have a clue about the trials, tribulations, joys, and hopes of the People. Few know about the treaties between the United States government and those from whom they are descended. Within weeks, however, they begin to remember the stories they were told as children. Stories their grandparents, elders, aunties, and uncles told them suddenly come into their conscious mind. They remember stories about generosity. Community. Caring for others.

The urban Native students in the class tell story about their lives. How they just knew that something they did or did not do was right or not. On further reflection, they remember "something my dad said when I was little" or "my grandma used to say . . ." A Native student in my Contemporary and Traditional Native Storytelling course wrote:

I have always listened to the stories whispered to me by the trees, by the flowers with their sleepy heads drowsing in the sun, by the wind as it journeys from one part of the planet to another. I have seen the beat of the butterfly's wings and heard the story of the hurricane it would someday cause.

I have also wondered for most of my life what people who do not have stories in their heads do have in there. If they are not listening to the stories that are constantly being told, what are they hearing? Is anything going on inside their heads? Is it like the snowy screen of a station that is off the air? Is it the sound of static on AM radio? Is it just a blue screen?

I also have to wonder if they hear the stories that are passed on from blood to blood. When we told our origin stories, I told not only what I had experienced in my lifetime but what my mother and father experienced with my conception and my birth. Though I was just an un-united egg and sperm at the time, I know inside me the joy and love my parents felt at my making. I have listened to that story for my entire life.

The student ended her paper talking about her son.

Here, then, I have told another story of understanding and loss. Those who have not seen their children grow up urban will not understand my sorrow of what he has lost due to the choices that I made. They will not understand that I still hope within me that someday I will be able to show him these things [about life]. (Stormy Stogner, Critical Analysis Paper #1, 9 September 2002).

In instance after instance, urban Native students complete the semester filled with a new sense of purpose about their harmonious place in the order of all creation. They have a renewed sense of their identity. I don't have to, nor have I ever had to, force urban Native students to remember. They do that all by themselves. I don't have to harangue them about the evils of alcohol, drugs, and violence. They remember the ancient stories. They remember the stories of the past and tell them. And they interweave the lessons in stories of the past as they begin to tell story about the present and the future. In the process of remembering and telling, they discover their core identity.

Urban American Indian youth need to understand that one's identity is not about me, me, me, me. It's about we, the People.

Questions for Review and Discussion

1. How does story connect Native Americans to one another?

2. How does story connect Native Americans to their sense of home/place?

3. Why might Urban Indians have an even greater need to learn and tell their story than their rural counterparts?

4. Compare the concept of "identity" for which Francis argues, one grounded in a concept of "We, the People," to other philosophical concepts of identity developed in this text.

5. Compare and contrast hooks's understanding of homeplace with that of Francis. How are these views similar or different to the understanding of "dwelling" developed by Heidegger, Norberg-Schulz, and Weiss?

CITY MATTERS: GERALDINE PRATT.
"DOMESTIC WORKERS, GENTRIFICATION AND
DIVERSITY IN VANCOUVER" (1998)

Introduction

Geraldine Pratt is a feminist urban geographer at the University of British Columbia in Vancouver, Canada. Pratt's work focuses on issues of democracy and place, the gendering of urban spaces, and the distribution of domestic work. This case appears in her longer article, "Grids of Difference: Place and Identify Formation," in which she explores the complexity of urban identify formation. In this excerpt, Pratt tells the story of yuppie urban pioneers in Vancouver, Canada, who love their new, diverse neighborhood, but who look outside the neighborhood for childcare. The case raises questions about privilege and how it affects people's experience of, and commitment to, urban diversity. The study also highlights the fact that persons hold "multiple and sometimes contradictory subject positions" (Pratt, 26); identities are not static.

"Domestic Workers, Gentrification and Diversity in Vancouver"

The ways in which border crossings can maintain old identity classifications and grids of difference, as well as privilege, are also apparent in an interview that I carried out in the summer of 1995 with parents who employ domestic workers. In writing about just one interview, I sketch the outlines of their childcare history and then "let the tape run" at length in order to unravel some of the complexities that emerge in thinking about identities and places.

This couple lives in a gentrifying inner-city neighborhood, adjacent both to Vancouver's "skid row" and "Chinatown," and home to a good number of Chinese and Vietnamese residents. The couple with whom I spoke were white professionals who owned a home in the area. That identities are crafted from fragmented and often contradictory subject positions was evident from the remarks made by the woman (Teresa), who seemed less comfortable living in her multicultural neighborhood when her children's childcare was involved. They had taken their first child to a day-care center outside the neighborhood, close to Teresa's workplace, until he was 18 months old. Because of a bureaucratic mishap, their child lost his day-care space at this age. This is the point at which the real dilemmas of living in a multicultural neighborhood began to be debated in the household. Teresa first looked into a family day-care arrangement in her neighborhood, run by an Italian woman in her home.

She tapped into her multicultural networks to check this out: "I have a friend who is Italian so I asked: 'How does this woman check out?,' wanting as much collateral as possible. 'Can I trust this person with my child?' " The woman was recommended highly, which meant that Teresa "just felt worse after being there": "I went to visit on a very bright sunny snowy morning. The TV was on. The curtains were drawn. There were about six kids all sort of bouncing off each other, in a very bold way." She rejected the day-care arrangement because "the sort of sensory deprivation put me off." She felt that she had exhausted her networks and "advertising was the very last thing that we wanted to do," so her husband (Tom) started to inquire through his networks. Eventually, a friend knew of a "fellow" worker who might want the job: "That's how we met up with the other woman. . . . She brought her own [8-month-old] child to be here. And that situation lasted for about a year and half [until their next child was born]. And it was a very very good situation."

TERESA: It was great. She came over the first time and she was younger than I had imagined this person should be. But she was mature. Early twenties. Really confident. And energetic and had lots of experience.

TOM: And she and [her daughter] had lovely manners.

TERESA: Both really gentle.

TOM: With her own child and with [their son].

As the discussion about this caregiver progressed, it became clear to me that a norm of similarity was very important to Teresa.

TERESA: We had sort of agreed at the beginning about discipline, and sort of philosophy.

G.P.: How did you agree?

TERESA: I had taken the Parent Effectiveness Training course. I'll show you the book later. But it's very clear about giving kids choices. And preserving self esteem. Let them experience competencies. So I sort of talked to her about the highlights that were important to me in this book. And our philosophy was in common. Just sort of . . . I don't know . . . comfortable with each other. And her spirituality was similar. And all that stuff. And she was pretty well vegetarian. I'm not vegetarian. That's not really important to me. But she had good food choices. She wasn't going to fill the kids up with candy, and chips and pop and stuff, which I could see happening with other baby-sitters. And so that part was important to me as well.

When their second child was born, they had to rearrange childcare.

TERESA: One option that keeps coming up from living in this area, which has a lot of Chinese and Vietnamese people, was that many people have the old Chinese grandmother looking after their kids. The woman across the park who is Caucasian and both her kids have had this older Chinese lady looking after them. . . . But I felt really like I didn't want to do that because I didn't want to have anyone here who I couldn't communicate with.

TOM: I did want it. But we didn't agree.

G.P.: Because you weren't worried so much about . . . ?

TOM: No, I felt it would have been a great situation. But it wouldn't have been a great situation if Teresa was worried. So I couldn't pursue it. But I thought that would be great.

G.P.: Because of the language?

TOM: Yes. And being able to stay in the home. And there is a network in the park of grandmothers and kids.

TERESA: The downside is that, while learning Cantonese would be great and learning about another culture, but what I also observe is that the old ladies don't have a lot of energy for stimulating the kids. So on rainy days they are all kind of in front of the television, and behavior is dealt with by either yelling or bribing with candies. So it didn't meet my kind of standards.

G.P.: [Directed toward Tom] So you kind of liked the connectedness of the neighborhood?

TOM: That's one of the reasons why we live here. The neighborhood has a great sense of community. That for me would have just been another way of living that way. But if Teresa wasn't going to be comfortable with it, it wouldn't have worked.

G.P.: And there is a different balance [between you]. Because they are different priorities.

TERESA: Yes.

TOM: Mmmm.

So it becomes evident, in listening to Teresa speak, that although she feels comfortable living in the neighborhood herself, she is less comfortable with cultural differences when it affects her children's care. Eventually, after hiring a Filipina nanny to care for their children in their home, two spaces became available at their son's original day-care center. They accepted those spots, even though this arrangement cost roughly $300 more a month and required car transport. (Tom in particular expressed a commitment to a carless lifestyle and mentioned the sacrifices in this regard that went along with their childcare choice.) It is also interesting to note that a number of middle-class parents in the area transport their children out of the neighborhood for childcare. Teresa estimated that eight children within a two block radius of their home go to their sons' day-care center, a migration precipitated by their enthusiasm for it (As Tom put it, "I think it's just a question of, a sort of snowballing thing"). There is a day-care center in the neighborhood, but it is on Hastings Street (skid row) "and no one wants to use it because it is part of the Hastings traffic" (Teresa). The Hastings Street day-care center undoubtedly is used by some parents in the area (or it would be closed) but seemingly not by middle-class parents in their neighborhood.

There are several aspects of this interview that point to the complexities of theorizing the links between identity formation and place. First, Teresa appears to be divided in relation to her neighborhood—we see the fragmentation of identity in play—and, second, the multicultural neighborhood eventually works for her (and evidently a good number of other white middle-class families) because she is able to cross outside of it in one part of her life (her role as a mother). Her privilege allows her to do this, and being able to do so allows her to enact middle-class child-rearing standards. Further, by taking their children out of the neighborhood, these families possibly reproduce a new generation of social and cultural boundaries among children in the neighborhood. But, third, this interview demonstrates how a geographical boundary can sustain an openness to cultural difference. Tom's acceptance of cultural difference is very much tied to a sense of neighborhood. He embraces the Chinese grandmother option because it is a way of living as part of the community. Further, he was exploring an exchange with a Mandarin-speaking neighbor, offering English instruction in exchange for Mandarin instruction for his children. Tom was much less receptive to the idea of hiring a Filipina caregiver, not because of her cultural identity, but because she was coming from outside their local networks: "I felt less um . . . When we hired [the Filipina caregiver] the whole process of deciding whether to have someone to come in somehow wasn't comfortable. I felt. . . . It's complicated. I felt like we would be passing over our children to some other person who we had no idea about at all. Even with the references, there was part of me saying it didn't feel quite right. . . . I wasn't going to block it, but when the decision was made to put them in [day care], I felt much better."

Questions for Review and Discussion

1. What do Teresa and Tom value about their multicultural neighborhood?

2. Why do Teresa and Tom ultimately decide to place their children in daycare outside their immediate neighborhood?

3. In what ways does Teresa embrace the value of urban cultural diversity? Are there ways in which it seems threatening to her?

4. In what ways do Teresa and Tom have race and/or class privileges? How do they exercise that privilege?

5. Think about philosophers who define the city in terms of diversity (e.g., Simmel, Conlon, Young, Mendieta). Can they provide insights into this case? Or does the case challenge some of their ideas? Explain.

6. How might bell hooks respond to this case?

Additional exercise available on philosophyandthecity.org: city walking tour—mapping boundary lines, both formal and informal; questionnaire that students can use when exploring an urban neighborhood that raises questions about boundaries, diversity, and privilege.

SECTION D

The Built Environment
(Planning and Architecture)

Philosophical reflection on ideals of how cities should be planned and built extend at least as far back as Aristotle's *Politics*, and philosophers such as Machiavelli also reflected on site selection and other aspects of what we now call "the built environment." St. Thomas More spent a good deal of time thinking about the physical plan for his utopia. However, the built environment of the city did not become a dominant contemporary philosophical interest until 1961 when urban neighborhood activist Jane Jacobs published her now classic *The Life and Death of Great American Cities*. Although Jacobs was not formally trained as either a philosopher or an urban planner, her book shook both worlds, as she criticized the scientization of urban planning and the failure of modern architects and planners to take real lives into consideration. Heidegger's reflections on the environment eventually served as a powerful resource for philosophers interested in responding to Jacobs cry that cities were becoming meaningless as homes were destroyed in the name of urban renewal.

In the last decade, environmental concerns such as sprawl, the placement of environmental hazards, and general questions about urban sustainability have also entered into the discourse about the built environment.

Philosophers from Part I who are especially useful when thinking about the built environment include **Aristotle, Machiavelli, More, Benjamin, Lefebvre, Gavin, Habermas, Norberg-Schulz, West, hooks,** and **Bickford**.

PHILOSOPHY MATTERS: ROBERT MUGERAUER.
"DESIGN ON BEHALF OF PLACE" (1994)

Introduction

Robert Mugerauer is a former dean of the College of Architecture and Urban Design at the University of Washington and is currently Professor of Urban Design and Planning there. A philosopher by training who brings a Heideggerian phenomenological approach to the study of urban architecture and planning, Mugerauer has published widely on the philosophy of architecture and urban planning. This reading comes from his pathbreaking work, *Interpretations on Behalf of Place.*

In this excerpt from the final chapter of that book, Mugerauer demonstrates how philosophical questions can assist in the process of urban planning and design. He specifically connects philosophical questions about the nature of the self and of community to the built environment. He demonstrates how Heideggerian concepts, particularly the importance of "dwelling," can inform good urban design. He then provides us with an example of good planning. The example he discusses is a public housing project in Kreuzberg, a predominantly Turkish neighborhood in Berlin, Germany.

"Design on Behalf of Place"

QUESTIONS FACING DESIGN ON BEHALF OF PLACE

Design partially begins in reflection, perhaps in what Martin Buber calls the realistic imagination.[1] We can begin to articulate what the city designed as a place, or a site for becoming a home, would be like by focusing on *the questions* which follow from our human nature and serial dislocations, from the essence of the modern and technological epochs and the possibility of an orginary alternative. Persisting in questioning does not imply that designers, planners, and architects are not already working on these issues, as we will see. Many are. The point is to resist facilely passing over the fundamental issues. Only after focally sustaining them as questions would a review of the current responses be appropriate—as part of the next step.

To remain in the question, how can we delineate the city as a site for a healthy belonging to and release of the old, as a part of our being

---

1. On Buber and the "realistic imagination," see Martin Buber, *Between Man and Man* (New York: Macmillan, 1972) and my "Buildings, Imagination, and Reality," forthcoming in ACSA *Proceedings*.

responsibly open to new phases of growth and the possibility of a new home? Think of the self's stages in vital, normal development. For each stage of life, a city would have to be designed with homes which would provide for the needed basic stasis—unified rest—and also places where one could experience the new, unsettling, and strange without its destroying the self with chaos or inassimilable shock. The environment would include or provide physical stimulation, intellectual challenge, emotional range, and cultural diversity. Traditionally, neighborhoods and streets, markets and busy downtowns, parks and playgrounds, schools and libraries, taverns and beauty parlors, fairgrounds and sports stadiums have been the sites where experiences occurred. What will the new forms be?[2]

It is apparent that design questions developing from a concern for the growth of the self quickly involve the growth of many selves in plural relationships, that is, in community and perhaps in a coherent, yet heterogeneous society. Hence, a crucial question for design for cultural life: how would we attempt to nurture both concretely enriching differences and also a generally intelligible social identity? This is the issue of the truly particular and the still shared, an issue of many distinctive places which yet make one place.

Surely all this is not simply a matter of grand boulevards and a merely visual schematic with details left to laissez-faire. We do not need "the city beautiful" with ward bosses just a block off the main streets.[3] Nor is it a matter of lavish attention to individual but isolated buildings which are the result of the romantic cult where the architect appears as modern artist and the buildings as autonomous art objects or commodities.[4] Grandiose designs and atomic buildings will not do. Neither, however, will modern and technological planning of logistical systems which lack the power to establish place and fail to provide existential satisfaction. Of course, both modern and technological design and planning have responses to these issues—responses which still need to be taken seriously.

---

2. Ray Oldenburg, *The Great Good Place: Cafes, Coffee Shops, Bookstores, Bars, Hair Salons, and Other Hangouts at the Heart of a Community* (New York: Marlowe & Company, 1989); Jane Jacobs, *The Death and Life of Great American Cities* (New York: Vintage Books, 1961); William Whyte, *Social Life in Small Urban Spaces* (Washington, DC: The Conservation Foundation, 1980); Oscar Handlin, *The Uprooted* (Boston: Little, Brown, and Co., 1973).

3. See Mario Manieri-Elia, "Toward an 'Imperial City': Daniel H. Burnham and the City Beautiful Movement," in Manfredo Tafuri et al., *The American City: From the Civil War to the New Deal* (Cambridge, Mass.: MIT Press, 1973), section on the laissez-faire city, 1ff.

4. See, for example, Jusuch Koh, "Survival Kits For Architects through Cultural Changes into the Post Industrial Age: An American Perspective," in *Proceedings* (EDRA 16, New York: July, 1985).

The shortcomings of modernity and the technological recall the deeper historical displacement of modern culture. How would we design a city that realistically deals with the industrial and technological epochs, and yet provides possibilities beyond what currently dominates? We know that displacement involves the destruction of traditional patterns and stability, as found in the heritage of a common landscape.[5] Even leaving open the issue of whether that is avoidable or undesirable in the end, we can more modestly say that in today's homelessness people are displaced who need not be. For a variety of reasons, chiefly economic, according to those who appear to know or even champion the process, people are moved from their homes, families, and neighborhoods when they would choose not to be. We must design so residents are not displaced from the fragile physical, emotional, and intellectual-spiritual situations which nourish them. We need to try to provide for those who already have been displaced or are lost and who likely never will be replaced anywhere.

At the same time, people naturally like to move, to change. How would we design the city, and make available its housing, work, and culture, so that people can move in and begin a new life? While we want to design for coherence and stability rather than chaos, we also need openness and variety so as not to become fossilized and sterile, as happens when cultures and "places" become too closed in on themselves, too homogeneous or absolute, rejecting anyone new as an "outsider."[6]

Or, consider the *crucial transition* from the industrial to the technological era, a transformation beyond the full understanding and influence of individuals, or even whole societies, in which occur major shifts in perception, experience, and interpretation. Currently, large numbers of people are beginning to find themselves discarded as obsolete. Once part of the dynamic of the modern industrial era, now they cannot even live out their lives as producing subjects and socially compliant objects controlled by those who command capital. Increasingly, neither skilled workers nor laborers are part of the technological system of transformation of credit, energy, information, and services. Caught between eras, they have the ambivalent prospects either of finding another role as modern subjects-producers (by changing from the steel industry to housing construction

---

5. See J. B. Jackson, *Discovering the Vernacular Landscape* (New Haven: Yale University Press, 1984) and *The Necessity for Ruins* (Amherst: University of Massachusetts Press, 1980); John R. Stilgoe, *Common Landscape of America: 1580 to 1845* (New Haven: Yale University Press, 1982).

6. Scholarship shows that such closure and "stability," though certainly real, has not prevailed to the extent that the stereotype would have it. See Oscar Handlin's analytical and concluding remarks on the peasant village, *The Uprooted* (Boston: Little, Brown and Company, 1973), 308ff.; Max Beloff, "The Uprooted," *Encounter I* (December 1954): 78ff.

or to crafting toys for tourists) or of being themselves transformed into part of the human resources of the technological era.[7]

How could we design cities so that people, buildings, and the entire city itself might endure the reigning phase of displacement and be able to move from the latest dislocation to becoming at home again? An answer is vital to individuals and to our cities, lest the latter become ghosttowns as countless sites have over time.

Instead of thinking of one city as an industrial city (a once upon a time place, now just a space to leave) and another city as a technological city (just now trying to become a place, a space to come to and transform), *what if we thought of and designed each city to be the place which is simultaneously the scene of displacement (the industrial city) and the site of a possible recovery of place (if such can be done in a technological city), or, if not, as a city of the next, originary mode.* Because the requisite designs would help us leave the one dimension behind and, at the same time, provide a means to enter the new dimension, they could be the occasion for a genuine homecoming—leaving and returning to the same place, but with its meaning somehow transformed.[8]

Planning and carrying out the integrated, self-contained transition from the industrially defined self and city is not a matter of cranking out new and attractive service modules or high-tech office parks and amenities for young professionals. It will require thinking down beneath the surface phenomena into the inner essence of technology and its components. If the technological generates the modular because the modular is the homogeneously interchangeable, that is, place independent and always in stock, how should design be related to the modular?

Should design embrace and exploit the modular since all else is fruitless nostalgia? Or, should design proceed as a form of mole warfare, in the time-honored manner of colonizing or converting sterile and hostile environments into livable cubbyholes—designed by subversion and occupation?[9] Or should the modular be ignored or actively resisted, in an attempt to begin an entirely new mode of dwelling? In any case, design would have to become a path-finding which will let technology be technological, yet in a way which keeps us human, perhaps in an originary manner as Heidegger suggests and as was considered in the previous chapters.

---

7. On the transformations of people in the technological systems, see Manuel Castells, *The Spatial Question.*

8. This is the lesson of Hölderlin's experience and poetry. See Heidegger's famous interpretation of Hölderlin's elegy "Homecoming": "Remembrance of the Poet," translated by Douglas Scott, in Werner Brock, editor, *Existence and Being* (Chicago: Henry Regnery, 1967).

9. See Michael Thompson's paper on occupation of space in inner London, "Your Place or Mine?," delivered at IAPS 8, Berlin, July 1984.

To shift to a still larger context, we have seen that the individual self and community, in order to become fully themselves, need placement in relation to the containing natural and spiritual realms. The design issues are as profound as they are broad. How would we design in order to regain a sound relationship to the natural environment, to the rhythms of the heavens and earth? Could we learn again to harmonize with the seasons and the attendant cycles of birth, growth, and death of plants and animals by experiencing them in parks, or in yards and community gardens, or . . . ? Could we again become attuned to the sky, say at night, which now is almost totally absent from our focal experience, by somehow attending newly to the stars and moon and tides and nocturnal animal life? How could that be done with safety, in a real, dense city?

Or, what sorts of designs and buildings would aid those who seek to maintain an experience of the sacred, or those who strive to remain disposed to it, or those who find themselves better off without it? Buildings or open places; places for one, or a few, or for many; places evoking the past or somehow new, alternative sources of enrichment for our age? Would we use traditional building forms and materials or try to discover new ones?

Clearly, the possibility of our originary recovery of a profound communal, natural, and spiritual environment and life requires a new mode of architecture and planning as well as urban design. We can move to answer questions such as those just posed by reflecting on whether or how an originary beginning is underway in recent work. Figures as diverse as Louis Kahn, Alvar Aalto, Aldo van Eyck, Charles Moore, and Christopher Alexander, and movements for design as community activity often are considered promising.[10] For example, Moore's figure of the

---

10. On the figures noted, see Heitz Renner et al., *Louis I. Kahn Complete Works, 1935–74*; M. Quantrill, *Alvar Aalto: A Critical Study* (New York: New Amsterdam, 1989); Herman Herzberger et al., *Aldo van Eyck* (Amsterdam: Stichting Wonen, 1982); Johnson, *Charles Moore: Buildings and Projects* (New York: Rizzoli, 1986); Christopher Alexander, *Pattern Language*. On the movement of community design, see Gary Coates, *Resettling America* (Andover, Mass.: Brick House, 1981), passim.

The figure most obviously missing from this list is Hassan Fathy. In earlier drafts, I had elaborated his contribution, but now do not include it because of the evidence that the projects do not finally work economically and politically and because of the vexing questions about the authenticity of his "invented" vernacular forms and artificial behavior patterns. There is no doubt, however, about his importance as an inspiration and explorer of what can be done. His groundbreaking efforts to incorporate historical and cultural interpretations of bioregions into the design process in projects for the rural community in Gournia on the upper Nile begin to work out the problems faced by an effort in today's technological world to rejuvenate traditional building techniques and materials, which, in turn, might establish a pattern of belonging to the local earth and climate, cultural and religious-cosmic forms. The question substantially is how to memorialize systems of value and also unfold future possibilities.

See Hassan Fathy, *Architecture for the Poor* (Chicago: University of Chicago Press, 1988) and *Natural Energy and Vernacular Architecture* (Chicago: University of Chicago Press, 1986); James Steele, *Hassan Fathy* (New York: St. Martin's Press, 1988).

building as a geode allows an unpretentious exterior and relationship to the surrounding buildings and landscape that is interesting and yet an interior that is as creative and amazing as the most eclectic American could demand. This strategy not only is a design solution, but is a social update of the perennial democratic dilemma of how to unify the many into the one.[11]

What design strategies would be harbingers of the beginning of a solution to the technological; what actually a deepening of the technological mode? We can not expect to find our way very far unless we can begin to sort out (1) which designs and modes of building are still modern or radically "post-most" modern and, hence, substantially disinterested assemblages,[12] and (2) which may be genuinely post-technological and on the verge of originary dwelling. The project is especially important because Western intellectuals have been proclaiming the end of the modern era and the beginning of the "new age" for more than a century. The twilight of the gods is past and the new dawn is perennially at hand. Apparently, we are stuck, caught in a place where we are not able to see clearly. [. . .]

DESIGN WITHOUT CULTURAL OR ENVIRONMENTAL DISPLACEMENT

As we have seen, individual life patterns and the need for place are bound together. But, local place can occur only within the context of specific, culturally developed bioregions. Finally, then, we need to consider some of the work of urban designers, community and regional planners, and architects already engaged with recovering and rebuilding our belonging to the appropriate human and natural realms.

The work in the Kreuzberg section of West Berlin, undertaken as part of the IBA (Internationale Bauausstellung in Berlin) and directed by Professor Hardt-Waltherr Hämer, is a well-known example of a large-scale effort to plan and implement urban design in a way that overcomes dreadful conditions, a long period of neglect, and the pressures of systematic, technological development. The project has kept the goal of fulfilling the spectrum of residents' needs without creating further estrangement. It is a wonderful case of, as Hämer calls it, "careful urban renewal" (an approach echoed by Roberta Graz's *The Living City*, which

---

11. See Charles Moore, Gerald Allen, Donlyn Lyndon, *The Place of Houses* (New York: Holt, Rinehart, and Winston, 1974).

12. As noted in chapter three of *Interpretation on Behalf of Place*, postmodern architecture needs to be deconstructed, since the postmodern is itself a deconstruction of tradition.

reports on small-scale projects that rejuvenate parts of the city's fabric and life).[13] Two aspects of the process are especially important.

First, the long-range planning and building have aimed to satisfy both the private needs of the residents and also their larger social needs. Naturally, special emphasis was placed on the individual dwelling places. In the general context of dilapidated nineteenth-century rent houses, unrepaired devastation remaining from World War II, extensive squatting in buildings by students and other tenants, and plans to clear away large corridors for a highway project, the need for decent places to live was crucial.

But, from the first, the goal was more than a certain amount of decent square footage with some access to public utilities—though even that would have been a massive accomplishment. In addition, it was insisted that the living spaces would really be places where people belonged and could live in a satisfactory set of relationships.

A central feature of planning and design was seeing the individual dwelling spaces in relation to their context, thereby enabling places to be established and cultivated. Kreuzberg had a chronic shortage of open space, which meant insufficient connection to both the natural world and the shared public sphere. One solution for enlarging access to both realms involved increasing public green space. Open green spaces provided fresh air, trees, grass, and plants and also a site for social life which was stimulated by the public atmosphere. As neighbors worked in their individual yards and in the communal areas of the courtyards, designing and maintaining them, they cultivated not only relationships to cycles of growth and life, but to each other.

Of course, emphasis on relation to earth and sky came through other avenues too, such as the intensive effort at ecological design and Green Architecture, of which, more shortly. In this regard, nature has done its share, as can be appreciated when experiencing how much more mature the landscape has become after only eight or nine years of growth. The change is especially dramatic in the interior courtyards of IBA housing. And there were other ways in which the fabric of social

---

13. H.-W. Hämer and Stan Krätke, "Urban Renewal without Displacement," *Architecture in Progress: Internationale Bauausstellung Berlin 1984*, edited by Frank Russell (New York: St. Martin's Press, 1983), 27–30 and H.-W. Hämer, "The Center City as a Place to Live," *Urban Design International 2*, no. 6 (Sept./Oct. 1981): 18–19; Dennis Domer, "Building among Builders in Berlin: The IBA," *Proceedings: 1984 Southwest Regional ACSA Meeting* (Austin: University of Texas Press, 1984), *International Building Exhibition Berlin 1987* (Tokyo: ATU Publishing Co., 1987). Hämer's idea of "careful urban renewal" is close to Roberta Graz's "urban husbandry," in *The Living City* (New York: Simon & Schuster, 1989).

relationships was encouraged, such as by reclaiming the streets for play and social use and by the participation of the residents in the planning and design process.

Hence, the second major aspect of the Kreuzberg project: constant participation of the residents in the planning and design process. The intention never was for the architect to do projects *for* the area, as was the plan of the grander, avant-garde Neubau portion of IBA. In Kreuzberg, the reverse occurred. The needs, fears, and hopes of those who lived there were transformed, often through sheer tenacity, into design by the architects, who took on a role of specially trained "articulators" and, one could say, advocates, of ways of life that wanted delineation in the forms of buildings, open spaces, and community patterns.

Questions for Review and Discussion

1. What philosophical questions does Mugerauer think are most important to the urban design and planning process?

2. What challenges do urban designers face in light of the displacement and estrangement from our environment that we face in our modern, technological age?

3. Why does Mugerauer think that the Kreuzberg public housing project is a good example of urban design?

4. How did the designs solve Kreuzberg's shortage of open space?

5. Why was it important for the Kreuzberg designers to involve the residents in the planning process?

6. In what ways is Mugerauer's analysis informed by the work of Heidegger and/or Norberg-Schulz?

7. Consider other philosophers who address aesthetic considerations (e.g., Benjamin, Gavin) and those who address concepts of place from nonphenomenological perspectives (e.g., hooks, Bickford). Would they agree or disagree with Mugerauer's analysis? What would they add or subtract from Mugerauer's recommendations for the future?

8. Visit a local public housing project or another residential neighborhood and analyze it, using Mugerauer's analysis as a model.

CITY MATTERS: HRH THE PRINCE OF WALES.
"TALL BUILDINGS" (2001)

Introduction

His Royal Highness, The Prince of Wales, is the immediate heir to the British royal throne. There is no formal constitutional role for the Prince of Wales, but the Prince has created a role for himself as public spokesperson for several issues that he has identified as important to Great Britain. The Prince has demonstrated deep interest and concern for the built environment, and is a frequent speaker on the topic. In 2005, he was awarded the Vincent Scully prize for his contributions to architecture by the National Building Museum in Washington, DC. He generally is quite critical of modernist architecture, preferring more traditional plans. Here the Prince of Wales weighs in on tall buildings, or skyscrapers. This speech was presented just three months after the destruction of the World Trade Towers on 9/11. Additional speeches on urban planning and architecture are available on the Prince's Web site: www.princeof wales.gov.uk/index.html.

'Tall Buildings,' Invensys Conference, QE2 Centre, London, 11th December, 2001

I suspect there are many people who remain profoundly uneasy about the current plans for their city and who often feel powerless to affect them in any way. Like me, I daresay, they may want to ask how the horrific events surrounding the World Trade Centre may affect the way we live and work in our cities, and the implications for the way we build in them? I rather doubt whether everything will go on as though nothing has changed, but neither, I am quite sure, will terrorism drive people away from urban centres.

Cities are extraordinarily resilient places, as we witnessed immediately after September 11th in New York City, and adversity, far from undermining civic confidence, can bring about a renewed and determined spirit of community and common endeavour.

Nor too, is it yet possible, I believe, to do more than speculate on the precise effects these events will have on the way future buildings are designed and constructed. After all, cities have endured, and absorbed, all manner of physical calamities throughout history and, in most cases, they have emerged stronger, with new ideas, techniques and technologies to help overcome their problems.

Here, in London, a rich Renaissance heritage of brick, stone and stucco buildings owes much to the outlawing of building with timber after the Great Fire of London in 1666. Necessity is truly the midwife of invention.

Similarly, I suspect that the destruction of the World Trade Centre is unlikely to mark the end of tall buildings in cities, although it may require rather more to be expected of them before new ones are constructed. Doubtless, the challenges of finding ever more sophisticated ways to evacuate people in the event of emergencies, or devising more resilient engineering, will become more dominant in the future architecture of skyscrapers.

However, I do believe, it has now become more important than ever to question how such buildings should be built in future, and most crucially, how they may be designed to create not just safe, but also truly civilised environments?

These questions relate not just to the matter of height, but of scale and context, and London offers an ideal backdrop to the issues at stake.

London's built form stands firmly in the tradition of most European cities, dominated by low to medium-rise buildings. The city's buildings and skyline are overwhelmingly the product of an era when neither technology, culture nor economics enabled the construction of very tall buildings.

This has left a remarkable array of buildings that, whether large, medium or small, have lent a coherence and human scale to the urban environments they compose. In almost all cases, they worked within a code—either explicit or implicit, that expected, encouraged and enabled harmonious streets and neighbourhoods. [. . .]

In my view, very tall buildings can undoubtedly threaten this sensitive balance. Indeed, they may very well wreck it.

Towers, of course, have long been very much a part of many historic city skylines (although at a considerably lower height than those being proposed today). But these Renaissance, Georgian and Victorian contributions to the skyline were usually as much associated with the notion of balance and hierarchy as the lower buildings around them.

This, of course, was because towers were almost entirely reserved for monuments with a special ecclesiastical or civic status. Yet the "skyscraper" in its modern form is something very different. Most obviously, it is a building whose function is utilitarian and commercial, rather than civic or sacred; a so-called "statement building" that is self-referential, and fulfilling no communal purpose whatsoever. [. . .]

These are giant buildings, with immense public visibility, but serving only a private, indeed, a privatised, purpose.

Now it has, of course, inevitably been suggested that holding this somewhat critical view amounts to little more than a nostalgic, and uniquely English, obsession with the past, and places too great an emphasis on the conservation of the historic city. [. . .]

To seek to protect historic views and vantage points, and oppose the planning of random new towers, is not, I believe, synonymous with supporting what some have rather disparagingly called a "museum city."

London is perhaps the most culturally and economically diverse city on the planet and the millions who flock here will, I imagine, continue to do so because of the cultural riches and historic architectural wonders that help it retain its unique vibrancy and attraction.

It is precisely this historic urbanity of a city built at a reasonable height, with dignity in its buildings and life in its streets, that continues to attract visitors in their millions. This isn't history as a museum; it is living history, and that's what needs to be protected.

The skyscraper or tower block has had a difficult history in the United Kingdom. One thinks of the gas explosion at the Ronan Point slab block in east London in 1968—an event that triggered a widely welcomed moratorium on the building of more residential towers, but, sadly, too late for the hundreds of thousands who were already trapped in their new flats. Or the Centre Point block at the end of Oxford Street, built entirely for speculative purposes, and unoccupied for years.

Such examples—and there are countless others—have given credence to the notion that these structures are alien; that in their very scale and their functionalist aesthetics they simply don't "fit" within the city and are doomed to long-term failure.

It is this sense of inappropriateness, rather than any nostalgic reverence for the past, that has caused so many people to feel offended by very tall buildings.

So, the fundamental problem facing those who plan and design tall buildings is only partly, I believe, to do with the simple matter of building height (problematic though this can be), but rather more to do with the difficulties faced in connecting these heights into the fabric of a city.

The essential value and virtue of a city is almost entirely defined in how successfully it is able to help people connect, whether for formal or informal exchange. This crucial function is defined and expressed in the networks of city streets, squares, parks and plazas, all of which require disciplined and well-articulated buildings to form and frame them.

This, of course, has been the basic building block of urbanism for all of recorded history, and in all cultures, until the 20th century, when this template for the traditional (or timeless) city, became challenged by new notions of urbanism, the most potent of which was the Modernist vision of a city of towers in a new parkland landscape—a city on stilts and steroids.

Its greatest polemicist and practitioner was Le Corbusier, who looked forward to the day when the entire city of Paris would be razed and rebuilt; when the—and I quote—"wretched pitched roofs are swept away, along with the casual cafes and places for recreation? that fungus which eats up the pavements of Paris!"

The consequences of making this vision a reality, as most now recognise, have been disastrous, producing the shattered urban wastelands that have desolated entire communities and disembowelled some of our greatest cities.

The human and economic costs of this catastrophic experimentation with industrialised building, and mechanistic planning, has been huge, and the consequences will remain for decades, even centuries to come.

Tall buildings will, by their very geometry and scale, always struggle to relate to the spaces that a city needs in order to work successfully. They cast long shadows; they darken streets and suck life from them; they tend to violate the sense of public space so vital to a living street, either by requiring a plaza to give them light, or by refusing to align with existing buildings, because of the difficulties of entering and servicing them without a large and cluttered forecourt.

They also create "hot spots" of pedestrian movement that are a major burden on nearby stations and pavements, and because their forms of architectural expression are towering pieces of sculpture, rather than a well-mannered contribution to the public realm, they seldom blend into either the streetscape or the skyline with good aesthetic manners.

"The city is a place where people learn to live with strangers" wrote the urbanist Richard Sennett. A place, in other words, where the values and virtues of sociability and exchange are learnt casually, intuitively, and for necessity as well as pleasure.

It is the very density and connectedness that the traditional city offers that makes such socialisation possible, and yet I fear that the tall, utilitarian building is ultimately alien to that purpose.

In geometric terms, it has more in common with an up-ended suburban cul-de-sac than with the creative networked urbanism of streets and squares.

Now it is true that there are some places where towers and streets have worked successfully together, and one thinks immediately of the example of Manhattan, with its uniform grid.

Yet Manhattan is, and will remain, unique in sheer scale and wealth, and its towers are, of course, far from the whole story of the city of New York.

Jane Jacobs' Greenwich Village with its tenements and brownstones, has been as much, or more, a part of Manhattan's liveability as the Trump Tower and the Rockefeller Centre.

It is interesting to think of the greatest, and most successful skyscrapers of Manhattan—like the Chrysler, Empire State and Woolworth Buildings. These astonishing achievements, built through the 1920s and 1930s, still obeyed many of the basic rules of the city, holding the street line and delighting the eye at street level with their craft embellishments.

Although they framed a new skyline with their pinnacles and spires, these were essentially elongated classical or gothic buildings, which did little damage to life at street level, and this is, I am convinced, why they are still so well loved and used today. Far more so, I hasten to say, than many of the glass perpendicular towers that replaced them, which snub the scale of the street, and stand in self-important isolation from the surrounding city.

The point I want to make is that I am not opposed to tall buildings purely because they are tall buildings. My concern is that they should be considered in their context; in other words, they should be put where they fit properly. [. . .]

So, if new towers are to be built, then it seems self-evident to me, that they should stand together to establish a new skyline, and not compete with or confuse what is currently there—as has already happened to a depressing and disastrous extent.

If clustered, then the virtue of height becomes something that can, in the hands of creative architects, be truly celebrated. This solution, so clearly the case in Manhattan or La Defence in Paris, requires locations where intrusion into historically protected views, either at height or at street level, can be avoided, and is, therefore, difficult to justify in places such as the City of London, where the pressure to build at height is often greatest.

Some have suggested that unless this pressure is released, by allowing new towers, then London's status as a financial capital will be endangered. I really do wonder. [. . . .]

I rather suspect that the enduring success of London's financial services economy has more to do with its legal environment, the tradition of honest dealing, the network of business connections, long-standing firms and an ethos of probity—what may be called "living traditions"—than with new glass towers.

This raises a further point too. The City of London is, without doubt, a hugely successful financial centre. But it is a social disaster! Only a handful of people live there; only the City churches and a few schools perpetuate the memory of its social life and culture; and the bleak towers, and many of the surrounding streets, stand deserted at night.

But just a few hundreds yards away, where low-level, smaller-scale buildings remain, people are flocking back. [. . .] The reasons aren't hard to fathom. These are places that have retained a genuinely urban architecture, built to a human scale and easily adapted to change.

Factories, workshops and warehouses become offices, loft apartments and shops. These are buildings that fit, that give something worthwhile to the streets and help them thrive; streets where the sunlight occasionally slants along the pavement and where the good manners, variety and craftsmanship of the facades are timeless.

People need to "fit" into the public realm and this is why we always used to cultivate manners, modesty, and gentleness. The same should be true of buildings, although I fear that so much of the Modernist aesthetic is based on the notion of "standing out" rather than "fitting in."

And what of the viability and sustainability of tall buildings? There can surely be no doubt that structural and security concerns will weigh heavily on those designing tall buildings in the future. [. . .]

Yet, I can't help but suspect that the price of meeting these new demands, whether in direct construction costs, or valuable space forgone for new servicing, will place a considerable strain on the economic rationale of the buildings themselves. [. . .]

The huge costs of construction, the loss of useable space through building set-backs, circulation and service space, the maintenance and management obligations, all place strains on the commercial viability of building high.

One wonders how some of the new security and structural concerns that are now being raised, may further call into question the economic case for high-rise?

A new sporting stadium that seats 80,000, requires, by law, every one of the 80,000 spectators to be able to find a place of safety within eight minutes. [. . .] Yet, for tall buildings, there is no similarly strict rule for escape—and, indeed, were there to be so, then one wonders how viable the buildings would remain.

Similar concerns about tensile strength in the event of a serious collapse will now, I suspect, have to be incorporated into future designs. [. . .]

There are further viability challenges too, especially in social and environmental terms. The rush-hour strains caused by large numbers of people arriving and leaving from these new buildings, can only cause more congestion for a public transport system that can barely cope with existing numbers; what hope will there be if new towers are further to increase the commuters that use the trains and tube?

There is no doubt that towers, because of their very structural demands, also rely on huge amounts of electricity to power their lifts, air conditioning and other infrastructure. You cannot usually open windows—so nature's own cooling system is shut down. Heat losses escalate as one builds higher, because neighbours can no longer help to keep you warm. Externally, conditions can deteriorate, because of shadow, wind shear or echo.

I'm afraid I remain somewhat sceptical of the claims that are now being made for overcoming these and other problems, as they are often based on new technologies that remain unproven and in some cases even untested. [...]

One of the fundamental principles of sustainable development, and I hope, of sustainable architecture, is the idea of building for change; the construction of buildings that can "learn" and adapt to new and unforeseen circumstances over time.

This is extremely difficult to achieve with very tall buildings, which are often constructed to meet the particular needs of financial institutions or individual global corporate organisations at a single point in time. As utilitarian buildings of great expense and inflexibility, they may be "fit for purpose," but that is almost always a very fixed "purpose" in a very changing world. [...]

If we are obliged, and there is no alternative, to having new tall buildings, at least here in the United Kingdom, then there could at least, surely, be some way of overcoming some of the difficulties I have mentioned.

Measures could include a clear policy on the location of new buildings, ideally in clusters away from any likely intrusion of important site lines or skylines. Other possibilities may include a requirement for buildings beyond a certain mass or height to be mixed in use, a home for a variety of businesses and residents as well, and capable of meeting differing needs over time.

Perhaps, too, any new towers should pay more attention to the base and the top of their structures.

At the base, new buildings should properly address the streetscape and help define a public realm that is truly public in form and function. Ground floors need to include shops, restaurants and other amenities that bring people into the building and help it integrate with the surrounding townscape. [...]

And at the top of these new structures, let's see genuine artistry that truly reaches the hearts and souls of those who look on, rather than the overblown phallic sculptures and depressingly predictable antennae that say more about an architectural ego than any kind of craftsmanship. [. . .]

At last, people are beginning to see that what I can only call "living traditions" can help create lasting sustainability and enjoyable social exchange. I fear, though, that unless these concerns are shared more openly, honestly and widely, and especially perhaps, beyond these shores, then we risk witnessing a rapidly urbanising world population plunged into solutions that have already failed in much of the developed world.

There are some truly terrifying predictions that billions will be living in high-rise towers within the next few decades, nearly all in the developing world, and unless those responsible choose to learn from recent experience, both good, but also bad, then the consequences for the longer term may haunt many generations to come.

Ladies and gentlemen, there are many, like myself, who are not experts like yourselves but who are inspired and incredulous at the skills and technologies you have come to master.

However, this mastery of technique is different from a responsibility in its stewardship, and it is here, I fear, that errors have been, and continue to be made; never more so than when clever technique and technological innovation masquerades as a philosophy that rejects tradition, the inherited wisdom of our forbears. . . .

It has taken thousands of years to achieve the sophistication to create living cities, but just two or three generations to destroy them.

Ladies and gentlemen, it is, I believe, only by striving to integrate the best of the past with the best of the new; by tradition once again being defined and practised as something living and not dead, that we can be offered the choices that a truly contemporary architecture demands.

Questions for Review and Discussion

1. Does the Prince believe that the tragedy of 9/11 suggests that we should not build more tall buildings? Why or why not?

2. What are the crucial questions that the Prince thinks must be addressed when considering architecture in urban environments?

3. What are the Prince's criticisms of tall buildings?

4. The Prince anticipates a possible criticism of his argument— what is it? How does he reply?

5. Evaluate the Prince's argument by drawing on other philosophers whom you have read.

Additional exercise available on philosophyandthecity.org: a link to
research on "nearby nature," where social scientists have found a
strong correlation between the presence of trees and other greenery
and people's sense of place; a link to a case on women and urban
sustainability; a link to the New Urban Congress's powerpoint on new
urbanism; a city walking tour exercise.

Social Justice and the Ethics of the City

In his *Republic*, Plato creates an imaginary city, a city in speech, so that Socrates and his interlocutors can examine the question of justice in the city. Cities bring large numbers of diverse persons together and require tremendous resources in terms of economic, political, and social capital. The concentration of large numbers of humans in one geographic area also places stress on natural resources. Cities also produce goods as well as social and political arrangements. Questions of justice concern both questions of distribution, that is, how resources and goods are allocated and used as well as questions of social and political equity, that is, how fair the social and political structures are. Although Plato and Aristotle differ on many points, both agreed that the social and political structure of a city needs to create harmony among the diverse parts of the city. But neither Plato nor Aristotle thought that harmony was best created by treating everyone in the same way; rather, they argued that each citizen had to contribute according to his role or function, and each would be rewarded accordingly. But today many would question whether treating different people differently is just, and whether doing such creates harmony. And how do we decide what differences matter?

Another major social justice issue that has arisen concerns how people relate to their natural environments. Natural resources are not distributed evenly. The poor are more likely to live with environmental hazards near their homes and often lack the resources to resist their placement in their neighborhoods. On the flipside, the poor often have less access to positive natural resources like neighborhood parks. In the cases that follow, Andrew Light argues that environmental philosophers should take cities seriously, and that philosophical assumptions affect how we treat cities and their residents. Friedrich Hayek makes a philosophical case against interference and regulation, arguing that we should let the market economy determine urban planning and housing issues.

Philosophers from Part I who are especially useful when thinking about social justice issues include: **Plato, Aristotle, More, Addams, Young, West, Bickford, Mendieta,** and **Weiss.**

PHILOSOPHY MATTERS: ANDREW LIGHT.
"ELEGY FOR A GARDEN" (2003)

Introduction

Andrew Light is a philosopher who works in the areas of environmental ethics, aesthetics, film theory, and public policy. Currently he teaches at the University of Washington, but he also holds fellowship positions at the Institute of Philosophy and Public Policy at the University of Lancaster (England) and at the Center for Sustainable Development in the School of Architecture at the University of Texas. He has placed himself in the vanguard of environmental ethicists who have taken up urban issues, and is unusual in the fact that he embraces cities as valuable environments that deserve philosophical reflection and treatment.

In this essay, Light argues that environmental ethicists have often worked from a false distinction between nature and city that causes them to ignore real environmental issues in our urban backyards. In this sense, the urban community organizers who built Esperanza Garden on Manhattan's Lower East Side have something to teach philosophers, for they treated their garden as a place of environmental activism, adopting tactics used by wilderness preservation activists. Light demonstrates, though, that philosophers can and should contribute to this fight for our cities.

"Elegy for a Garden"

On the morning of February 15, 2000, I watched as the New York City Police Department and a city construction company demolished Esperanza Garden (fully named, "El Jardin de la Esperanza," "The Garden of Hope"), a narrow lot at the corner of East 7th and Avenue C on the Lower East Side. Esperanza was established as a community garden by local resident Alicia Torres in this Puerto Rican neighborhood over twenty-two years ago. Thirty-one protestors were arrested following a prolonged direct action campaign to save the garden, once a part of the city's official Green Thumb program, which had encouraged the preservation and creation of some 600 gardens throughout the city.

Tellingly, the scene at the destruction of Esperanza, and the struggle put up to defend it, was highly reminiscent of the sites of conflict to defend old growth forests throughout the North American west. Recently known as the focal point of ongoing protests against Mayor Rudolph Giuliani's decision in the spring of 1999 to sell off community garden plots to developers (ostensibly to create low and middle-income housing), Esperanza, in its final stages, was a site to behold. Environmentalists, especially the group "More Gardens!," along with community activists, had constructed a giant coqui over the front entrance of the garden six months before, looking out over the front wall of the garden and protecting it from bulldozers. The coqui is a thumb-sized frog important in Puerto Rican mythology as the symbolic defender of the forest—in one story its loud croak scares off a demon threatening to destroy a rain forest. In this guise it became both a symbol for community pride and a focal point for environmentalist and pro-garden organizers in the city.

But the creators of this coqui had more than symbolic significance in mind. Activists had loaded the structure with civil disobedience equipment—bike locks, chains, and huge cement blocks to lock themselves into the structure and on the site should the need arise. A high tripod in the shape of a sunflower (the same sort used in forest "sit-ins" in Oregon and Idaho) was erected to house a lookout chair 26 feet above the ground where a defender could lock down. Even during the coldest parts of the winter, the garden housed a full time environmental encampment, with tents, a kitchen, and bonfire for those keeping a twenty-four hour vigil on the garden. Here, one could see a powerful connection between humans and nature. The garden served as a strong enough moral motivator to protect green space against short-term economic gain to inspire acts of self-sacrifice and civil disobedience.

To me, observing the arrests from a nearby corner, it was striking that the tactics used to protect the garden were reminiscent of similar struggles in the American wilderness that I had seen years previous when I had taught environmental ethics at the University of Montana. I finally felt that I understood a passage from Aldo Leopold, the 1940s godfather of much contemporary environmental thinking, which had eluded me before: "The weeds in a city lot convey the same lesson as the redwoods. . . . Perception . . . cannot be purchased with either learned degrees or dollars; it grows at home as well as abroad, and he who has a little may use it to as good advantage as he who has much." That day it seemed as if Leopold was right: the smallest city plot really could be as inspiring as the most treasured old growth.

But strangely, some of the contemporary heirs to Leopold, especially philosophers working on environmental issues, do not seem ready to take this message seriously even in light of experiences like those at Esperanza garden. An old standby of today's environmental ethics is that achievement of true environmental sustainability is to be found only in the creation of a non-human centered ("nonanthropocentric") ethic. Much of contemporary environmental ethics distinguishes itself from more traditional ethics by setting for itself the goal of articulation of the value of nature in terms independent of the human attribution of that value. Accordingly, environmental philosophers have spent the last thirty or so years pursuing various forms of nonanthropocentrism, including biocentrism and ecocentrism. Most, especially those in the wilderness rich areas of North America and Australia, have in common a unified belief that the inspiration for extending moral consideration beyond the boundaries of the human community will come from connection with those spaces unsullied by humans, especially wild areas, or at least vast tracks of otherwise protected land. Accordingly, the vast majority of environmental philosophers, and I believe, the majority of environmentalists, assume some kind of opposition between culture and nature, city and countryside, urbanity and wilderness.

For example, Holmes Rolston III, the dean of this burgeoning subfield of philosophy in the U.S., argues that the future of environmental responsibility lies in the creation of what he calls an "Earth-centered ethic." In a recent polemical essay, Rolston reasserts this claim by arguing that in contrast to previous centuries, where we worried primarily about destroying ourselves through inter-human conflict, the overriding cause for distress for the next century is that we will destroy the planet itself. "The challenge of the next millennium is to contain those [human] cultures within the carrying capacity of the larger community of life in our biosphere. (. . .) If we humans are true to our species epithet, 'the wise species' needs an Earth ethics, one that discovers a global sense of obligation to this whole inhabited planet." For Rolston, this ethic should not focus on the way that the Earth is valuable from an anthropocentric perspective, which may entail seeing it only as a resource, as a means to human ends. This is not to say however that there is no role for human value and experience in the creation of such an ethic. Rolston also argues that humans must actively become an integral part of a place as one necessary condition, or perhaps, even literally as a living foundation, for such an ethic.

While I appreciate Rolston's sentiments, and similar such views of some my other colleagues in environmental ethics, I think that to fully realize the goal of global environmental protection we need to seriously consider a different form of environmental thinking bound to a similar sense of responsibility, though one also grounded in humanly produced environments such as Esperanza garden. For all of Rolston's emphasis in this essay, and in most of his work on the importance of human attachment to place, it seems that only certain kinds of places count as acceptable spaces for forming moral bonds with nature. It turns out that the built world, for example, is not part of the "Earth" for Rolston, and so presumably will not play as vital a role in our new ethic of environmental responsibility. Says Rolston, "In finding our place in the built environment, we have tended to get displaced from our natural environment." When it comes to the sort of relationship we should have to a place, it is one that focuses on our connection to "biotic" communities, "tracks of nature," and Rolston's version of "natural kinds." To prevent ourselves from destroying the planet we must somehow reject, or at least reassess, the world we have made and instead embrace the fecund ground of our existence—the natural world, or at least, the realm of nature as Rolston envisions it can be separated from human culture.

Is this right? Is the correct context for environmental thinking to be found in connecting ourselves to nature in a deeper way and leaving behind our culture, or indeed in accepting this controversial distinction between nature and culture? In its most egregious forms (not Rolston's), such ethics require us to go native in a sometime romantic dream of the noble savage who was part of the world instead of apart from it. But is this the only option, and more prosaically, is it the most realistic option? Can we imagine a more harmonious world where we all re-embrace a "native" attachment to place? I don't think so. True, if our species is fortunate enough to survive it will come from recognizing our relationship with nature as residents of the natural world. But this sense of relationship need not only come from the wild places that Rolston loves.

Here in my home, New York City, I see an environment well worth engagement and deserving of responsibility. I don't mean just the "green space" of the city, such as the large urban parks, but also the "brown space" of the sidewalks, the buildings, and the myriad places in between. I see a landscape alive with multiple senses of value, multiple relations to place, obvious to anyone who has spent any time in it. This city is not just the background that urban inhabitants move through, it is the foreground of most everyday conversations. Live in a city that is alive as a place, where inhabitants actively conceive of having a sense of it as a place, and you will experience the phenomenon of the city as the object of most discussion. It is a character in everyday life akin to a member of one's extended family. Though no doubt often mistreated, it cannot be ignored. Perhaps though, we only see this connection most clearly when the urban environment is threatened. In the destruction of Esperanza, I re-experienced the importance of the city as a ground for strong environmental responsibilities.

The need for the elaborate civil disobedience precautions at the garden described above, came all too soon. Late on the night of February 14th a call went out from the local residents and environmentalists encamped at the garden for sympathizers to come to stay over and help defend Esperanza, after activists spotted tale-tell signs of heavy police activity scheduled for the next day. The timing was not coincidental. Lawyers for the New York State Attorney General's office were scheduled to

appear the next day before Justice Richard D. Huttner of the State Supreme Court in Brooklyn to seek an injunction against plans to demolish
the site. According to State Attorney General Eliot Spitzer, Esperanza, and
the other Green Thumb gardens, should be considered legally as parks,
which can only be sold after a state environmental review or act of the
Legislature. But by the time the hearing had finished in the early afternoon
of the 15th, as the city attorneys pointed out to Judge Huttner, the garden
had already been destroyed. For Esperanza at least, the argument between
the Mayor and the State Attorney General was moot.

Though the garden defenders' original plan was for only 12 people
to be arrested, many more people who answered the late night call volun-
teered for arrest as well. By 7:00 a.m. the crowd of protesters had grown
to 150. By 10:00 a.m. police began cutting protesters loose from their
locks, hacking away at the coqui with metal-cutting chain saws until one
last activist, entrenched within the right eye socket portal of the frog, was
left. In the mean-time, 50 or so chanting protestors supporting the resist-
ers from a nearby corner were cleared from the sidewalk and forcibly
moved by riot police across the street to an "official viewing area," conveniently out of view of the garden. By 11:45 the giant frog had been
replaced by a giant backhoe and the garden was leveled. Only a few
stragglers remained by noon, myself included, watching as construction
workers, still guarded by up to a hundred police, busily erected a plywood
fence to hide the further destruction from passers-by. While spirits ran high
that so many had turned out to protect the garden, most people appeared
plainly in shock to see the efforts of their long labors—for some months,
for many years—destroyed in an hour. One local resident put it bluntly:
"There is nothing to live for here if you don't have any green."

At the end of the day Mayor Giuliani held a press conference, again
restating his reasons for selling off the garden, focusing on the need for
more affordable housing in the city. Giuliani did not discuss the disregard he had shown for the judicial process by circumventing an imminent decision by a State magistrate and proceeding with the destruction
of Esperanza. He was quick however to lampoon the protestors: "If you
live in an unrealistic world then you can say everything should be a
community garden." The Mayor hoped to sell the property to a devel-
oper planning to build a 75 unit "80–20" apartment complex on the
site, with 80 percent of the apartments going at market rate (renting
monthly at approximately $1,500–$2,000 per bedroom) and 20 percent
going to low income families for a limited period of ten years. Apparently, somewhere in-between resisting the supposed desire to put gardens everywhere and instead create affordable housing, the Mayor
sacrificed Esperanza for dubious low-income housing gains.

One cannot help but think that more was lost here than simply a symbol of urban green space and community empowerment, attributions that even the most wilderness-oriented environmental ethicist would admit to this garden. For Alicia Torres and her family and neighbors who had worked for months in the late 1970s to clear the land that eventually became this garden, something much more important had been lost. Four generations worked the soil over the ensuing decades at Esperanza— the latest were Alicia's great grandchildren. The garden contained flowers, vegetables, and also medicinal plants used by local residents. This garden was not just a patch of green on a brown landscape or a clever bit of utopian protest art. It was a schoolhouse for this particular community where elders could teach the young something about their environmental traditions, their past, and also their aspirations for the future. The land, in this case, as has been true in so many other places, became the literal ground for intergenerational community and the sort of environmental responsibility which writers such as Rolston see as coming more from wilderness than tiny urban plots like this one. But the value of this garden was unique to this locale; it was tended by these residents because it was where it was and not somewhere else. It was worth the sacrifice of defending it because it was local, rather than remote. There was no "unrealistic" desire here to create gardens everywhere, as the Mayor contended, but to maintain this one in this particular place. If plans go forward to build on this site, then the unique set of environmental and social values embodied in this location cannot easily be replaced. The garden helped to make this community a site for local environmental responsibility even as it eventually came to stand for the larger environmental community's dream of a greener city.

Reflecting on the name, "Esperanza," one cannot help but feel that a small part of this city lost a source of its hope that day in February— the precious and ephemeral connection, which Rolston and other environmental ethicists seek, that sometimes arises between local residents and the land they inhabit and come to care for. Such connections are a necessary condition for long-term environmental sustainability even if they are made to such humanly produced landscapes. These small plots connect us to our everyday environment in a tangible, rather than abstract, way. The point is not that we can therefore disregard the wilderness, but more that we must pay serious attention to the power of all environments to draw us in as a partner worthy of protection.

Inhabited places are not opposed to those relatively less so through any natural order of things. It is only we who drive conceptual wedges in the world. A fully "environmental" ethic ought to include all environments, not for theoretical reasons, but because urban spaces like Esperanza can and do represent an important connection between humans and the natural world. To paraphrase, and possibly extend Leopold's intuitions, we will only have a complete environmental ethic when we turn our attention to the preservation of richly textured urban spaces as often as we do to old growth forests.

Questions for Review and Discussion

1. Why was Esperanza Garden important?

2. Mayor Giuliani argued that affordable housing was more important than the community garden. Here two justice principles seem to contradict one another. Drawing on philosophers you have read in this text (including Light), how do you think this conflict should be resolved?

3. Does Light think that the distinction between nature and civilization is a false one? Would other philosophers we have read agree or disagree? What advantages are there in refusing the distinction?

4. Given what Light argues, how might environmental philosophers contribute to the social justice of the city?

CITY MATTERS: FRIEDRICH HAYEK.
"HOUSING AND TOWN PLANNING" (1960)

Introduction

Friedrich August van Hayek (Austrian, 1899–1992) was an economist and political philosopher. He was a leading proponent of laissez-faire economics and enjoyed particular prominence in the 1940s. He held academic positions at the London School of Economics, the University of Chicago's Committee on Social Thought, and the University of Freiburg. His political philosophy works include *The Road to Serfdom* (1945) and *The Constitution of Liberty* (1960). Often labeled a "conservative," Hayek himself refused that label. Many contemporary libertarians hold Hayek in high esteem because he favored individual freedom over state control. He argued that all social and political arrangements should be guided by free market principles and was suspicious of collective activity.

Hayek argues against policy interventions intended to relieve poverty in cities (rent controls, government subsidized planning, etc.), claiming that such policies interfere with the liberties of property owners and often do not have the intended effects. Some philosophers would argue that Hayek's position is one that rejects rather than embraces social justice considerations in favor of individual rights.

From "Housing and Town Planning"

> If the government simultaneously abolished housing subsidies and cut working class taxation by an amount exactly equal to the subsidies the working classes would be no worse off financially; but they would then without any doubt prefer to spend the money in other ways than on housing, and would live in overcrowded and inadequately provided houses, some because they do not know the advantages of better housing, and others because they value these too lightly in comparison with other ways of spending their money. That is the case, and the only case for housing subsidies, and it is put here in its crudest form because the matter is so often discussed in left wing literature without facing reality.
>
> —W. A. Lewis[1]

---

1. *The Principles of Economic Planning* (London: 1949), p. 32.

1. Civilization as we know it is inseparable from urban life. Almost all that distinguishes civilized from primitive society is intimately connected with the large agglomerations of population that we call "cities," and when we speak of "urbanity," "civility," or "politeness," we refer to the manner of life in cities. Even most of the differences between the life of the present rural population and that of primitive people are due to what the cities provide. It is also the possibility of enjoying the products of the city in the country that in advanced civilizations often makes a leisured life in the country appear the ideal of a cultured life.

Yet the advantages of city life, particularly the enormous increases in productivity made possible by its industry, which equips a small part of the population remaining in the country to feed all the rest, are bought at great cost. City life is not only more productive than rural life; it is also much more costly. Only those whose productivity is much increased by life in the city will reap a net advantage over and above the extra cost of this kind of life. Both the costs and the kinds of amenities which come with city life are such that the minimum income at which a decent life is possible is much higher than in the country. Life at a level of poverty which is still bearable in the country not only is scarcely tolerable in the city but produces outward signs of squalor which are shocking to fellow men. Thus the city, which is the source of nearly all that gives civilization its value and which has provided the means for the pursuit of science and art as well as of material comfort, is at the same time responsible for the darkest blotches on this civilization.

Moreover, the costs involved in large numbers living in great density not only are very high but are also to a large extent communal, i.e., they do not necessarily or automatically fall on those who cause them but may have to be borne by all. In many respects, the close contiguity of city life invalidates the assumptions underlying any simple division of property rights. In such conditions it is true only to a limited extent that whatever an owner does with his property will affect only him and nobody else. What economists call the "neighborhood effects," i.e., the effects of what one does to one's property on that of others, assume major importance. The usefulness of almost any piece of property in a city will in fact depend in part on what one's immediate neighbors do and in part on the communal services without which effective use of the land by separate owners would be nearly impossible.

The general formulas of private property or freedom of contract do not therefore provide an immediate answer to the complex problems which city life raises. It is probably that, even if there had been no authority with coercive powers, the superior advantages of larger units would have led to the development of new legal institutions—some division of the right of control between the holders of a superior right to determine the character of a large district to be developed and the owners of inferior rights to the use of smaller units, who, within the framework determined by the former, would be free to decide on particular issues. In many respects the functions which the organized municipal corporations are learning to exercise correspond to those of such a superior owner.

It must be admitted that, until recently, economists gave regrettably little attention to the problems of the co-ordination of all the different aspects of city development.[2] Though some of them have been among the foremost critics of the evils of urban housing (some fifty years ago a satirical German weekly could suggest that an economist be defined as a man who went around measuring workmen's dwellings, saying they were too small!), so far as the important issues of urban life are concerned, they have long followed the example of Adam Smith, who explained in his lectures that the problem of cleanliness and security, "to wit, the proper method of carrying dirt from the streets, and the execution of justice, so far as it regards regulations for preventing crimes or the method of keeping a city guard, though useful, are too mean to be considered in a discourse of this kind.[3]

In view of this neglect by his profession of the study of a highly important subject, an economist perhaps ought not to complain that it is in a very unsatisfactory state. Development of opinion in this field has, in fact, been led almost exclusively by men concerned with the abolition of particular evils, and the central question of how the separate efforts are to be mutually adjusted has been much neglected. Yet the problem of how the effective utilization of the knowledge and skill of the individual owners is to be reconciled with keeping their actions within limits where they will not gain at somebody else's expense is here of peculiar importance. We must not overlook the fact that the market has, on the whole, guided the evolution of cities more successfully, though imperfectly, than is commonly realized and that most of the proposals to improve upon this, not by making it work better, but by superimposing a system of central direction, show little awareness of what such a system would have to accomplish, even to equal the market in effectiveness.

---

2. A valuable attempt to remedy this position has recently been made in R. Turvey, *Economics of Real Property* (London: 1957). Of earlier works the discussions of local taxation by E. Cannan, especially in his *Royal Commission on Local Taxation: Memoranda Chiefly Relating to the Classification and Incidence of Imperial and Local taxes* (London: H. M. Stationery Office, 1899; Cmd. 9528, pp. 160–75, are still among the most helpful on the crucial issues.

3. Adam Smith, *Lectures on Justice, Police, Revenue, and Arms* (delivered in 1763), ed. E. Cannan (Oxford, 1896), p. 154.

Indeed, when we look at the haphazard manner in which governments, with seemingly no clear conception of the forces that determined the development of cities, have generally dealt with these difficult problems, we wonder that the evils are not greater than they are. Many of the policies intended to combat particular evils have actually made them worse. And some of the more recent developments have created greater potentialities for a direct control by authority of the private life of the individual than may be seen in any other fields of policy. [. . .]

The greater earning power and other advantages that city life offers are to a considerable degree offset by its higher costs, which generally increase with the size of the city. Those whose productivity is greatly increased by working in the city will derive a net advantage, even though they have to pay much more for their limited dwelling space and may also have to pay for daily transportation over long distances. Others will gain a net advantage only if they do not have to spend money on travel or expensive quarters or if they do not mind living in crowded conditions so long as they have more to spend on other things. The old buildings which at most stages of the growth of a city will exist in its center, on land which is already in such great demand for other purposes that it is no longer profitable to build new dwellings on it, and which are no longer wanted by the better-off, will often provide for those of low productivity an opportunity to benefit from what the city offers at the price of very congested living. So long as they are prepared to live in them, to leave these old houses standing will often be the most profitable way of using the land. Thus, paradoxically, the poorest inhabitants of a city frequently live in districts where the value of the land is very high and the landlords draw very large incomes from what is likely to be the most dilapidated part of the city. In such a situation property of this sort continues to be available for housing only because the old buildings, with little spent on them for repair or maintenance, are occupied at great density. If they were not available or could not be used in this manner, the opportunities for increasing their earnings by more than the additional costs of living in the city would not exist for most of the people who live there.

The existence of such slums, which in a more or less aggravated form appear during the growth of most cities, raises two sets of problems which ought to be distinguished but are commonly confused. It is unquestionably true that the presence of such unsanitary quarters, with their generally squalid and often lawless conditions, may have a deleterious effect on the rest of the city and will force the city administration or the other inhabitants to bear costs which those who come to live in the slums do not take into account. Insofar as it is true that the slum dwellers find it to their advantage to live in the center of the city only because they do not pay for all the costs caused by their decision, there is a case for altering the situation by charging the slum properties with all these costs—with the probable result that they will disappear and be replaced by buildings for commercial or industrial purposes. This would clearly not assist the slum dwellers. The case for action here is not based on their interest; the problems are raised by "neighborhood effects" and belong to the questions of city planning, which we shall have to consider later.

Quite different from this are the arguments for slum clearance based on the presumed interests or needs of slum dwellers. These pose a genuine dilemma. It is often only because people live in crowded old buildings that they are able to derive some gain from the extra earning opportunities of the city. If we want to abolish the slums, we must choose one of two alternatives: we must either prevent these people from taking advantage of what to them is part of their opportunity, by removing the cheap but squalid dwellings from where their earning opportunities lie, and effectively squeeze them out of the cities by insisting on certain minimum standards for all town dwellings;[4] or we must provide them with better facilities at a price which does not cover costs and thus subsidize both their staying in the city and the movement into the city of more people of the same kind. This amounts to a stimulation of the growth of cities beyond the point where it is economically justifiable and to a deliberate creation of a class dependent on the community for the provision of what they are presumed to need. We can hardly expect this service to be provided for long without the authorities also claiming the right to decide who is and who is not to be allowed to move into a given city.

As happens in many fields, the policies pursued here aim at providing for a given number of people without taking into account the additional numbers that will have to be provided for as a result. It is true that a part of the slum population of most cities consists of old inhabitants who know only city life and who would be even less able to earn an adequate living in rural conditions. But the more acute problem is that raised by the influx of large numbers from poorer and still predominantly rural regions, to whom the cheap accommodation in the old and decaying buildings of the city offers a foothold on the ladder that may lead to greater prosperity. They find it to their advantage to move into the city in spite of the crowded and unsanitary conditions in which they have to live. Providing them with much better quarters at an equally low cost will attract a great many more. The solution of the problem would be either to let the economic deterrents act or to control directly the influx

---

4. This possibility has not infrequently been used in various parts of the world to drive out unpopular racial minorities.

of population; those who believe in liberty will regard the former as the lesser evil.

The housing problem is not an independent problem which can be solved in isolation: it is part of the general problem of poverty and can be solved only by a general rise in incomes. This solution, however, will be delayed if we subsidize people to move from where their productivity is still greater than the cost of living to places where it will be less, or if we prevent from moving those who believe that, by doing so, they can improve their prospects at the price of living in conditions which to us seem deplorable.

There is no space here to consider all the other municipal measures which, though designed to relieve the needs of a given population, really tend to subsidize the growth of giant cities beyond the economically justifiable point. Most of the policies concerning public utility rates which are immediately aimed at relieving congestion and furthering the growth of the outlying districts by providing services below costs only make matters worse in the long run. What has been said of current housing policies in England is equally true about most other countries: "We have drifted into a practice of encouraging financially, out of taxes collected from the whole nation, the maintenance of over-grown and over-concentrated urban fabrics and, in the case of large cities still growing, the continuance of fundamentally uneconomic growth."[5]

Questions for Review and Discussion

1. What does Hayek identify as the costs and benefits of city life?

2. Why does Hayek argue that centralized intervention into city planning is usually not a good idea?

3. What is Hayek's explanation for the existence of urban slums? Why does Hayek argue that housing subsidies will not actually improve slums?

4. Evaluate Hayek's analysis, drawing on other philosophers to assist you.

Additional exercise available on philosophyandthecity.org: the urban planning game, a game designed to help students think about planning issues in which they have to take a wide range of social justice issues into consideration.

---

5. Sir Frederick Osborn, "How Subsidies Distort Housing Development," *Lloyds B.R.*, April, 1955, p. 36.

Index

About the Author

Sharon M. Meagher, Ph.D., is Professor of Philosophy and Director of Women's Studies at The University of Scranton in Pennsylvania. She also has served as a director of an applied policy institute in Washington, DC, and as the founding president of an urban community development organization in Scranton, PA. Meagher was a founding member of the American Philosophical Association's Committee on Public Philosophy and has served on numerous boards and advisory groups. She has published on literature and ethics, community development, and feminist theory, and her previous publications include *Women and Children First: Feminism, Rhetoric, and Public Policy*, coedited with Patrice DiQuinzio, and also published by SUNY Press, and she is completing a monograph on philosophy and the city tentatively entitled *Philosophical Streetwalking: Grounding Philosophy and the City*. Readers may contact the editor through her website devoted to this anthology and her work on philosophy and the city: http://www.philosophyandthecity.org.